ALAMEIN

ABOUT THE AUTHOR

Philip Warner (1914-2000) enlisted in the Royal Corps of Signals after graduating from St Catharine's, Cambridge in 1939. He fought in Malaya and spent 1,100 days as 'a guest of the Emperor' in Changi, on the Railway of Death and in the mines of Japan, an experience he never discussed. A legendary figure to generations of cadets during his thirty years as a Senior Lecturer at the Royal Military Academy, Sandhurst, he will also be long remembered for his contribution of more than 2,000 obituaries of prominent army figures to *The Daily Telegraph*.

In addition he wrote fifty-four books on all aspects of military history, ranging from castles and battlefields in Britain, to biographies of prominent military figures (such as *Kitchener: The Man Behind The Legend*, *Field Marshal Earl Haig* and *Horrocks: The General Who Led from the Front*) to major histories of the SAS, the Special Boat Services and the Royal Corps of Signals.

The D-Day Landings was republished by Pen & Sword Books to mark the 60th Anniversary of this historic event and was adopted by *The Daily Telegraph* as its official commemorative book.

By the same author

Auchinleck: The Lonely Soldier
(republished by Pen & Sword, 2006)
Battle of France
Battle of Loos
Best of British Pluck
British Battlefields 1: The North
British Battlefields 2: The South
British Battlefields 3: The Midlands
British Battlefields 4: Scotland
Daily Telegraph Book of British Battlefields
British Cavalry
Castles in Britain *(illustrated edition)*
Civil Service
Crimean War
D-Day Landings
(republished by Pen & Sword, 2004)
Disputed Territories
Distant Battle
Famous Scottish Battles
Famous Welsh Battles
Field Marshal Earl Haig
Fields of War: Letters Home from the Crimea
The Great British Soldier
Growing Up in the First World War

A Guide to the Castles in the British Isles
Horrocks: The General Who Led from the
  Front   *(republished by Pen & Sword, 2005)*
Invasion Road
The Japanese Army of World War II
Kitchener: The Man Behind the Legend
The Medieval Castle in Peace & War
Panzer
Passchendaele   *(republished by Pen & Sword)*
Phantom   *(republished by Pen & Sword, 2005)*
Political Parties
Roman Roads

ALAMEIN

PHILIP WARNER

Pen & Sword
MILITARY

First published in Great Britain in 1979 by William Kimber & Co. Ltd
Reprinted in this format in 2007 by
PEN & SWORD MILITARY
an imprint of
Pen & Sword Books Ltd
47 Church Street
Barnsley
South Yorkshire
S70 2AS

ISBN 978 1 84413 623 8

A CIP catalogue record for this book is
available from the British Library.

Printed and bound in Great Britian
By Biddles

Pen & Sword Books Ltd incorporates the Imprints of
Pen & Sword Aviation, Pen & Sword Maritime, Pen & Sword Military,
Wharncliffe Local History, Pen & Sword Select,
Pen & Sword Military Classics and Leo Cooper.

For a complete list of Pen & Sword titles please contact:
PEN & SWORD BOOKS LIMITED
47 Church Street, Barnsley, South Yorkshire, S70 2AS, England
E-mail: enquiries@pen-and-sword.co.uk
Website: www.pen-and-sword.co.uk

Contents

List of Maps

List of Illustrations

Acknowledgements

This book was made possible by the *Daily Telegraph* which in April 1978 published a letter in which I requested survivors of the Alamein battles or their relations or friends to get in touch with me. Hundreds did so. I therefore wish to take this opportunity to thank the *Daily Telegraph* for making the book possible and all those very kind people who wrote or telephoned to give me material to include in the book.

Introduction

Before beginning this book I asked various people who had been born since 1945 what the word 'Alamein' meant to them. All said it was the name of a battle in *either the First* or Second World War and some knew that Rommel was concerned. However, nobody appreciated its significance. These were people with no particular interest in military history but they were intelligent and educated. It became clear to me that the battles of the First World War – Somme, Ypres, Passchendaele – are better known than those of the Second. Probably the fearful slaughter of the First World War battles, so aptly conveyed in BBC and part-work series, was something to catch anyone's attention. Of the Second World War, Dunkirk and the D-Day landings were apparently the only memorable occasions. This seems extraordinary as numerous television programmes and films have been made of events around the aerial Battle of Britain and the Italian campaign. The battles of the Far East, land, sea or air, have made no impact on the minds of people who are now in their twenties and thirties. Perhaps this is not surprising but it is regrettable that so much in the way of toil, endurance and dedication should be forgotten so completely.

Even among those who were alive during the Second World War the importance of Alamein is by now scarcely appreciated. Too much has happened since. There have been other battles and other wars : the world has changed, though not for the better. The Britain of today is vastly different in terms of resources and morale from the Britain which played a vital part in the world conflict in the 1940s. But the significance of Alamein should not be forgotten or underrated. It was one of the decisive battles of history, but like many other critical battles it was less famous because the defenders won than it would have been if they had lost.

For many who were old enough to fight in the Second World War – and the fighters include those who stoically endured the bombing, rockets and privations at home – Alamein was once a magic word. The Second World War had begun on 3rd September 1939 and the following years had seen several bitter defeats and no victories against the main adversary. The Battle of Britain in September 1940 had convinced the Germans that daylight air attacks on Britain were not feasible, but in spite of that battles in the air continued for many years. In fact, the achievement of the Battle of Britain was lessened by the fact of the German bombers coming over and pounding British cities night after night. Britain had been saved from invasion, but that fact was scarcely considered by people huddled in air-raid shelters. The victories against the Italians made little impact on the public for there was a widespread impression that the Italians were not wholehearted soldiers. Losses of shipping in the Atlantic were scarcely realised, although they were critical and through them Britain could have lost the war. Dunkirk, which followed devastating defeats in France, was mistakenly regarded as a victory. Of the Far East even less was known. The jungle, the monsoon rains, the insects and the diseases were almost incomprehensible to people living in a temperate zone. Small wonder that the men fighting in Burma regarded themselves as 'the forgotten army'.

Even when battles are known to the public there is often something missing. This is particularly true of battles of the Second World War. During 1914-18 there was little room for strategic or tactical manoeuvre. The main front was in France and there were few subtleties in the head-on slaughter of trench warfare. The other fronts, in Africa, in Russia, in the Middle East, caught public attention for a while and then were obliterated. Even the slaughter and heroism of Gallipoli were soon forgotten as the casualties mounted upon the Western Front. For nearly ten years after 1918 the public, even those who had fought, wanted to forget the war. Then suddenly there came a stream of individual stories. Erich Maria Remarque portrayed the German side of the war, Henri Barbusse gave the French,* Robert Graves (*Goodbye to All That*), Edmund Blunden (*Undertones of War*), Siegfried Sassoon (*Memoirs of an Infantry Officer*), gave the British. And there were others. Many of these writers were also poets and their descriptions were graphic and memorable. Thus the First World War, although a form of national suicide and mass extermination, became vividly individual through men's memoirs. The story of the soldier, his hardships, his miseries, his dedication and his triumphs came over clearly and vividly.

From the Second World War there has emerged little to compare with the First. In 1939 men went to war expecting to be killed within the first few hours or days after joining the colours. Expectation, based on the 1914-18 war and subsequent scientific discoveries, gave scant

---

* Written during the war.

confidence in survival. Yet in the event many people found the war, with its variety and flexibility, the most interesting and pleasurable period of their lives. Others, of course, had a different experience. Yet overall it is the study of the strategic and tactical which has been written up. The soldier's story has come to light less often. Yet the soldier in 1939-45, as in all previous wars, was the person who ultimately mattered. You can fight a war without generals, although not very well, but without soldiers you cannot fight a war at all.

In the Second World War it was realised – and most of the credit for this must go to Field Marshal Montgomery – that the soldier can only give of his best if he knows what is going on and why. Soldiers were therefore informed about strategy and tactics and war aims, and many other matters – such as social reform – in which they did not show great interest at the time. And meanwhile they fired their rounds, and drove their tanks and trucks and did those endless tasks every army needs performing. As they did so, they thought their thoughts. Those thoughts may not have been profound, nor their opinions and assessments accurate, but they were what was felt at the time. To some the enduring memory of the Second World War is sand and flies, to others insects and rain, to others the whine of a three-ton truck, to others a bellowing sergeant-major, to others the peculiar taste of wartime NAAFI tea.

Whatever the memory, particularly in battle, it is important to a full portrayal of the event. In the following pages there appear many different viewpoints, some from units which the civilian might not recognise as being important in battle at all. All were in danger at different times. An enemy bomber does not merely bomb a fashionable cavalry regiment; it is very happy to demolish a convoy of rations or ammunition trucks. The value to the war effort of some of the less glamorous activities is easily forgotten but is recalled sharply enough if vital supplies do not arrive. There are no safe areas on a battlefield and behind the lines can often be more hazardous than the front. Who would wish to drive a petrol tanker through enemy shellfire?

The recollections which follow in these pages may not seem of great importance but they are the material of history. We can only guess at what men thought at Hastings and Crecy and Agincourt and our picture of these battles is therefore far from complete. We can know – if we seek it before it is too late – what men thought at Dunkirk, Alamein, Crete, at Anzio or at Arnhem. That way our picture of a battle, though not complete, is at least first-hand.

PART ONE

I

Why the Alamein battles were fought

The Second World War alternated between periods of inactivity and periods of violent action. The first month, from 3rd September 1939, saw violent action in Poland and some British losses at sea. Within a few weeks Poland was defeated and dismembered, the battle of the Atlantic continued and the Royal Air Force dropped leaflets over Germany. The Germans were pleased at their success in Poland and undismayed by the warnings in the RAF leaflets. So placid did it all seem that the Americans nicknamed the period 'the Phoney War' or 'the Great Bore War'. It was not of course boring for those on the look-out for submarines, and it was far from boring for those under training. For those administering evacuation schemes or rationing goods or generally interfering in the lives of others – as many petty officials appeared to be doing for no good reason – it may well have been a very interesting and purposeful period.

In May 1940 the situation changed dramatically. On 9th May Germans were reported to be in Norway and Denmark. At 5.30 am on 10th May Germany invaded Holland, Belgium and Luxembourg. There was an important change of leadership in Britain as Neville Chamberlain resigned and Winston Churchill took over the post of Prime Minister. However, it would need more than political changes to stop the flood of German tanks and well-trained infantry. Rotterdam was 'blitzed' by German bombers on 14th May, with an estimated loss of 40,000 civilians dead. The Dutch army surrendered after receiving heavy casualties. The Germans, with relentless air power and apparently unlimited numbers of tanks, stormed on and overwhelmed Belgium and France. On 14th June German troops entered Paris.

The news of these disasters was so appalling that British people could hardly believe it. Each day seemed to bring yet another humiliation. Mussolini had declared war on 10th June, calculating that all was over but for sharing out the spoils. Little he knew. On 1st July the Germans occupied the Channel Islands and though these were farther away than Calais it seemed almost more menacing as they were British territory. The only bright spot in the general gloom was the fact that 338,226 troops (of whom 120,000 were French) had been evacuated in what was known as the miracle of Dunkirk. So well publicised was this event that many people began to believe that evacuating the remnants of a beaten army with considerable loss of aircraft and shipping was in some way a victory. Whether the Germans could have successfully invaded Britain if they had waited long enough and chosen their time is an interesting speculation, but fortunately for the West Hitler decided to launch an attack on Russia in June of the following year (1941). Russia, of course, was a bigger prize, but in the event this attack proved to be Hitler's biggest mistake.

As one disaster succeeded another during the second half of 1940 the outlook for Britain seemed bleak indeed. There were a few brighter spots in the gloom such as the superb performance of the Royal Navy and the Royal Air Force; and Churchill's matchless oratory created hope where bewildered defeatism would otherwise have prevailed. But in September we lost 160,000 tons of shipping, in October the Germans were able to seize the Rumanian oilfields without hindrance and in November 4,500 civilians were killed in air raids on Britain. One of the curiosities of the 1970s is that most people are not only unaware of the battles which took place overseas in the Second World War but they are also quite oblivious of the fact that hundreds of people died every day in houses and streets of this country. One might have thought that on the ugly blocks which pass for architecture today there might be room for a memorial plaque or two for the brave, but now forgotten, citizens of the recent past.

These were the people for whom the victory of Alamein would mean so much. Day after day they heard the ominous wail of the sirens – one of the most depressing noises bureaucrats could possibly inflict – and every night most of them went to their crude shelters sleeping, when possible, through the thump and crash of air raids. Their men were seldom there to comfort them when the bombs shook the buildings in which they sheltered. Their children were often far away, evacuated to the countryside or even another country. There were brave slogans, among them 'Britain can take it'. 'Taking it' is all very well if there is a hope of eventual victory, but taking it when it seems a mere prelude to defeat is another matter. News of a victory – any victory – would make all the difference, even though you might not even know the name of the country in which the all-important event had taken place.

At the same time – and later – the men in those far-off countries often talked to each other of 'home'. Their homes might be slums in Whitechapel or Newcastle, Newport or Glasgow, but they were something worth fighting for. Unfortunately none of the post-war planning know-alls were present to hear their conversation before much-loved streets were demolished to make way for twenty-storey rabbit-hutches. Most people looked forward to having a slightly bigger home than the one they were born in with a bit of a garden, and friendly neighbours and a nearby pub. No soldier, even in a nightmare, imagined living in a tower block.

Few people if asked to place Egypt, let alone Libya, Tobruk or Benghazi, on a blank map of Africa would have been able to do so accurately. When the news came in that on 4th August the Italians had advanced from Abyssinia into British Somaliland this was meaningless to many, although resignedly they felt it was probably another petty defeat. In fact it was the start of the chain of events which led to Alamein and eventually to the fall of Mussolini himself. For the 'Sawdust Caesar', as Mussolini had been nicknamed, felt he must do something to impress his more powerful partner and ally, Germany. Hitler made little attempt to conceal his contempt for the Italian dictator and the fact rankled with Mussolini. The Italians themselves had scant liking for campaigns in distant arid countries, much preferring life in their own territories. However, they had over half a million troops available for this venture, and with little in the way of British opposition to stop them it seemed that victories must be inevitable. General Wavell had just over 80,000 troops to defend an area which included Palestine (Israel), Egypt, Sudan, Kenya, Cyprus, Aden and Somaliland. There were a few RAF squadrons equipped with ageing and outdated Gloucester Gladiators. The Italian line of communication was protected by ten modern battleships.

However Mussolini's plans went sadly wrong. In November the Italian fleet was crippled by a raid on Taranto Bay and on 9th December Wavell opened a desert offensive by attacking Sidi Barrani. By mid-December the Italians had been driven back over the Libyan border while Cunningham was busy rolling up the Italians in Abyssinia and Eritrea. By April of the following year (1941) the Italians had lost most of their best naval craft in sea battles, over 130,000 prisoners, and all their territory in battles ranging from the Red Sea to Benghazi. This was all heartening. However, they were Italians, not Germans. It was the Germans who had thrown us out of France and were now sinking our ships and bombing our towns. What was needed was some form of successful counter-attack against the Germans.

But it was not to be. Instead the news from the Middle East took an ominous turn. The number and size of the Italian defeats in Africa had impressed Hitler with the need to do something to bolster up his erratic ally. If his Axis partner continued to be defeated on such a scale there might be a revolution in Italy. Hitler already had work enough for his troops without wanting to use them in suppressing a national uprising on terrain as difficult as Italy. Fortunately for Hitler the Italians still possessed Libya (then called Tripolitania). Hitler therefore sent Erwin Rommel, who had distinguished himself while commanding 7th Panzer Division in the French campaign. Rommel's 'army' initially consisted of two divisions, and this was the beginning of the 'Afrika Korps'. It went into action for the first time on 24th February.

It was soon abundantly clear to all that Rommel had a genius for desert warfare. He was too far away for Hitler to be able to interfere with his strategy and he was therefore able to indulge in a variety of tactical ploys, feints, changes of direction, sudden withdrawals, unexpected attacks. He had an advantage in that he possessed new and up-to date equipment in both tanks and guns. The German 88 mm gun was widely respected wherever the Germans fought. Like our own 3.7 inch, it was originally an anti-aircraft gun but the Germans found it could be put to many other uses from anti-tank to harbour defence. The 3.7 was, in fact, a better weapon but its use was severely restricted. Two factors helped Rommel enormously. One was the fact that British troops were weary after a long and adventurous campaign; the second was that our tanks were by now in poor shape mechanically. Sand and dust shortened the working life of a tank considerably in the desert. Troops and supplies which could have settled the desert campaign, and even the elusive 'Desert Fox' (as Rommel came to be called), once and for all, were now diverted to Greece to help a hard-pressed ally. In the event the Greek venture proved a costly failure.

Rommel probed and struck, backed by full support from the Luft-waffe. He was by no means always victorious, but he succeeded in pushing back the British line to Sollum and isolating Tobruk. Some British losses, such as that of 3rd Armoured Brigade which was captured at Derna, and 2nd Armoured Division which suffered the same fate at El Adem, were crippling, for these were the units which might have carried the offensive back to the Germans. The supply and reinforcement position was made worse by a revolt in Iraq on 3rd April. Until it was checked there was considerable danger that the Germans might be able to establish themselves in that vital area – where oilfields and pipelines lay. This meant even more diversion of limited supplies and men. By June 1941 the reinforcement position had deteriorated so much that Rommel had over twice as many tanks as the British opposing him, in fact 160 against 70.

Gradually Wavell fought back. The situation in Iraq was restored. Other problems in Syria and Iran were settled. However, the attempt to relieve Tobruk in June 1941 failed. The British forces had nothing to match the PzKw IV tank with its 75 mm. gun and were at an even greater disadvantage against the German 88 mm. The latter showed its power only too clearly when used in the anti-tank rôle : a shell from an 88 would not merely check a British tank – it would go clean through it.

Quite unjustly, Wavell was blamed for his failure to relieve Tobruk; he was criticised for not waiting longer! Wavell had achieved miracles with insufficient troops and was certainly due for a rest. However, the move which sent him to India, which he did not know, and his replace-ment by General Sir Claude Auchinleck, whose experience had been almost entirely in India, seemed a strange one. Auchinleck's special knowledge could have been invaluable in the Burma campaign which would open five months later. However, in the subsequent argument as to whether Auchinleck should or should not have been replaced by Montgomery a year later, nobody ventured to suggest that the desert war had received anything but benefit from Auchinleck's appointment. The desert army was now re-formed as the Eighth Army and put under the command of Lieutenant-General Sir Alan Cunningham. Cunning-ham had 450 tanks to Rommel's 412 but was heavily outnumbered in anti-tank guns, of which he had only 72 against Rommel's 194. In quality the German arms and armour were more effective. Over half Rommel's force was Italian.

Eighth Army was made up of XIII Corps (one Indian division; one New Zealand division and one tank brigade) and XXX Corps (one armoured division [7th], one armoured brigade, one South African division and one brigade group), plus the Tobruk garrison, the Army reserve of one division and a brigade, and a small RAF component of 27 squadrons.

In November this force went on the offensive and, after stiff fighting, cleared Cyrenaica and relieved Tobruk.

In December Japan came into the war and vital reinforcements were diverted to the Far Eastern theatre, mainly Burma. Rommel meanwhile had received much-needed supplies of men and materials and came back to the offensive. By 21st January 1942 he had advanced to the Gazala line (west of and close to Tobruk). His plan was to force the

British to withdraw to Egypt, but he was not so foolish as to risk having his army destroyed in the process. The stakes were high for the British, for Rommel would threaten the very heart of Allied Middle Eastern power if he once entered Egypt and it was vitally important to recover the airfields in Cyrenaica and to be able to use them to defend Malta. Malta had been under tremendous pressure from the Germans, who realised only too well the vital importance of this Mediterranean island. From Malta the RAF and Royal Navy could defend Allied convoys, but equally the RAF could intercept and destroy convoys of German and Italian supplies to North Africa. The task of the RAF in North Africa was not easy, for many of the German bombers were faster than our fighters. The balance of power – and morale – was partly restored by David Stirling's 'Special Air Service' (the renowned SAS), whose members swooped deep behind the German lines in heavily armoured jeeps and destroyed 350 German aeroplanes on the ground. (The SAS also attacked other targets than airfields and dislocated the German supply system by such activities as destroying railway lines and telegraph exchanges.)

Auchinleck, viewing the position from the Middle East, felt that the situation in the desert should be kept stable with existing materials while any available reinforcements should be sent to strengthen the lines in the Far East and prevent the Japanese breaking through into India. Churchill, looking at the war as a whole from No 10 Downing Street, felt that Auchinleck should take the attack to Rommel and stabilise the North African situation that way. The men in the tanks and the fox-holes – as will be seen in the following accounts – were blissfully unaware of the conflicting opinions of higher strategy and were merely concerned with keeping flies out of their food and the sand out of the machinery.

The impatience of Churchill and his War Cabinet may be explained by the fact that since the previous January supplies had been pouring into the Middle East and that by now the Eighth Army was superior in numbers and equipment to its opponents. Cunningham had used the breathing space to 'dig in' the Eighth Army along the Gazala line. 'Digging in' meant laying extensive minefields, and grouping troops in 'boxes'. A box was a strongly fortified position which had the function of a medieval castle. It would be difficult to reduce, dangerous to bypass and would serve as a base for either offensive or defensive operations. However, history has all too often shown that an enterprising general can usually find a way through fixed-line defences. Rommel decided to take the initiative and by a series of ingenious hook movements in which he managed to encircle and destroy British concentrations, he moved on to threaten Tobruk. By this time he was in a position to lure most of the British tank strength to destruction either by anti-tank guns or superior fire power. The battle had begun on 26th May and by 20th June Rommel was able to watch his bombers and his gunners pounding the outer defences of Tobruk itself. A day later, after relentless bombardment, the Germans were able to smash their way through the remainder of the Tobruk defences. It was a magnificent triumph for Rommel and an appalling disaster for the British, not least because it was so completely unexpected. The garrison was small, and, as is the way with garrisons, contained large numbers of inexperienced administrative troops. But it was Tobruk and it was full of stores; it was a major disaster.

Furthermore, because Rommel was not a man to let a chance slip, the fall of Tobruk was by no means the end of the matter. Two days later Rommel was over the Egyptian frontier with a force of 44 tanks. He scattered the resistance which General Gott hastily organised with XIII Corps at Mersa Matruh and moved on. By this time he was in front of many of the retreating British units. From the outside the position looked even worse than it was. It appeared that there was nothing to stop Rommel forcing his way on into Egypt, Cairo and Alexandria. But there was. It was at a place called El Alamein.

II

The Battles

El Alamein is a ridge on the coast approximately half way between Mersa Matruh and Alexandria. A road and a railway run along the coast. From the Alamein ridge to Qaret el Himeimat, twenty-eight miles to the south, there was a natural defensive position, for south of Qaret el Himeimat there was an impassable barrier in the shape of the Qattara* depression. The Qattara depression is a salt marsh two hundred feet below sea level. Although light vehicles have been known to cross it, it is quite impossible for normal military traffic. There is no way of skirting around it, for to the south-west it links with the Great Sand Sea. What became known as the El Alamein position (although it covered much more than the coastal ridge) was this twenty-eight-mile stretch between the coast and the Qattara depression. This blocked that part of the desert which was suitable for military vehicles, for it was mainly of rock.

Desert is a wide term. To most people it means endless shifting sand under baking heat. In practice it may mean rock, salt marsh, hard sand, soft sand or gravel. It could be bare and flat or undulating and covered with scrub. It could be suffocatingly hot or (at night) bitterly cold. It could, at times, be quite pleasant. In spite of its drawbacks it is possible to become very fond of the desert.

Along this defensive line there were various features which were destined to play a significant part in subsequent battles. An ordinary tourist would probably not notice them for they were neither beautiful nor impressive. However, the history of warfare has shown that minor slopes, which in peacetime could scarcely be noticed, become vital objectives in wartime. Hill 70 in Northern France is typical of such features.

The Alamein position began on the coast (salt marshes) and was most strongly defended around Alamein station with what was known as the Alamein box. This was where most of the German attack was expected. The Alamein box made a semi-circle some six miles in

* May be spelt Quattara.

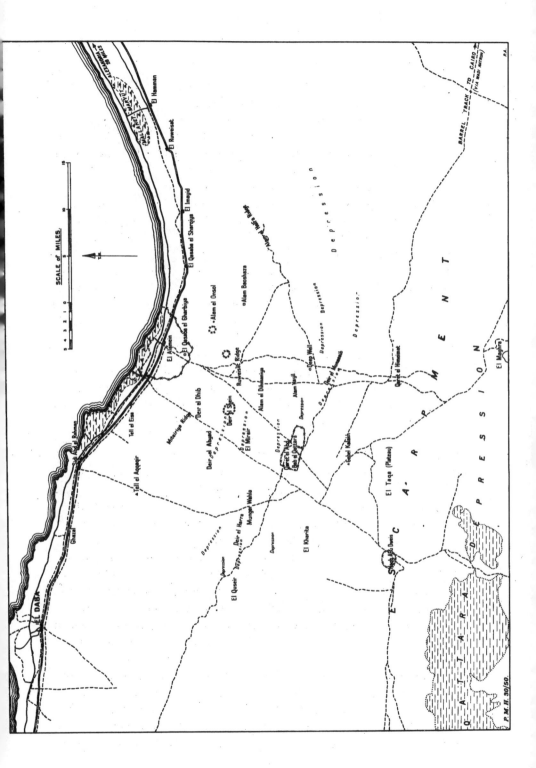

diameter and at the southern point was level with the Miteirya Ridge. This ridge included the famous Kidney Ridge, a misleading feature since it was not a ridge at all but a depression.

Eight miles farther south lay the Ruweisat Ridge, running east to west. In advance of it (i.e. to the west and slightly south) lay the El Mreir Depression. Seven miles south of Ruweisat Ridge lay Alam Nayal and five miles south of Alam Nayal was the Munassib Depression. A further twelve miles south would bring you to the mountain (seven hundred feet high) known as Qaret el Himeimat. As well as these main features there were minor ones which would not be noticeable unless they were part of the area in which you were going to fight. Likewise, distances on a map are not the same as distances in war. A mile is a different matter to an infantryman carrying his battle kit than it is to a tank commander, occupant of a staff car, wounded man, or unit trying to find its way through a minefield. Self-evident, of course, but like so many aspects of battle unappreciated except by those most immediately concerned.

For the past year work had been proceeding on the Alamein line as this might – it was felt – perhaps be necessary to the defence of Egypt. The forecast was correct; had there been no defences along this line in July 1942 the outcome of the war might have been very different. Even so the defences were a long way short of ideal. The Alamein box was reasonably well defended and there were brigade boxes at close intervals to the north of Ruweisat Ridge. With the exception of the Munassib Depression, which was occupied by the New Zealand division, the boxes were disposed in a south-westerly direction up to 9th Indian Infantry Brigade which was positioned on the northern tip of the Qattara Depression. The construction of these boxes is detailed in the accounts which follow – by the men who made them.

It has been suggested that First Alamein, of which the critical period was 1st-5th July 1942, was not in fact an Alamein battle at all but only the end of the battle of Gazala which had taken place between 11th and 15th June. It did, of course, mark the end of Rommel's Gazala thrust, but to dismiss a battle which took place at Alamein as part of one which took place two weeks before many miles away would be as confusing as it would be illogical.

However, the effects of the previous battles were very evident on both sides. Rommel's army was tired, but he assumed, rightly enough, that victorious troops would be less tired than defeated ones. He therefore tried to push through the gap between the Alamein box and the Miteirya Ridge, hoping that one half of his army could then turn north

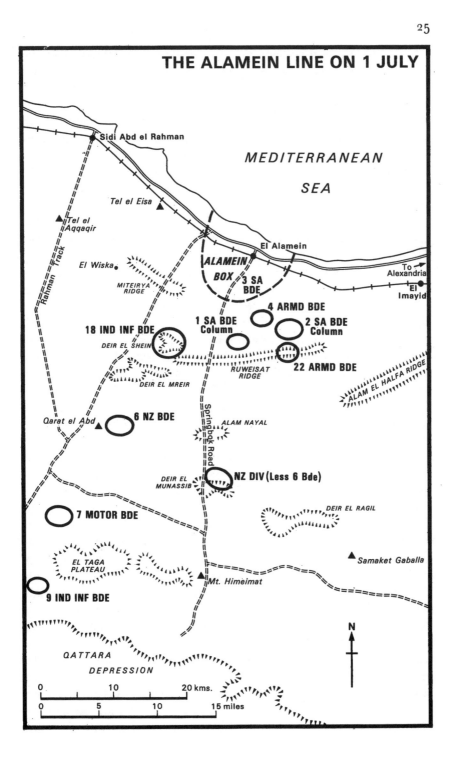

THE ALAMEIN LINE ON 1 JULY

MEDITERRANEAN

SEA

Sidi Abd el Rahman

Tel el Eisa ▲

▲ Tel el Aqqaqir

El Wiska •

MITEIRYA RIDGE

Rahman Track

El Alamein

ALAMEIN BOX

3 SA BDE

To Alexandria

El Imayid

4 ARMD BDE

18 IND INF BDE

DEIR EL SHEIN

1 SA BDE Column

2 SA BDE Column

22 ARMD BDE

RUWEISAT RIDGE

ALAM EL HALFA RIDGE

DEIR EL MREIR

Qarat el Abd ▲

6 NZ BDE

Springbok Road

ALAM NAYAL

DEIR EL MUNASSIB

NZ DIV (Less 6 Bde)

DEIR EL RAGIL

7 MOTOR BDE

▲ Samaket Gaballa

EL TAGA PLATEAU

▲ Mt. Himeimat

9 IND INF BDE

N

QATTARA

DEPRESSION

| 0 | 10 | 20 kms. |
| 0 | 5 | 10 | 15 miles |

isolating the Alamein box and the other could turn south and take the other boxes in the rear. However, events did not go according to plan. The northern thrust ran straight on to the Alamein box instead of by-passing it; this was due to lack of reconnaissance. They then found themselves confronting the South African brigades (1, 2 and 3), from whom they received such a hammering that some units turned in head-long retreat. The other thrust did little better, for although they captured the Deir el Shein box they received such a battering from the British twenty-five-pounders and six-pounders that the attack was blunted.

By the afternoon of 5th July Rommel's thrust had been contained and was encircled although he still held one half of Ruweisat Ridge. The fighting did not end at this point, for all through the rest of the month there was thrust and counter-thrust. It became, unintentionally from both sides, a war of attrition. The entire area became littered with corpses, burnt-out tanks and destroyed equipment. Both sides received reinforcements. Rommel had fought a brilliant campaign up to this point, but now that further advance was blocked he began to show signs of the strain he had undergone. Adding to the general pressure on the Germans was relentless and accurate bombing by the RAF. The part of the RAF, whether in bombing, dealing with enemy bombers, or in delivering reinforcements, is usually undervalued in land battles. The deeds of the opposing air force tend to be more vividly reported than those of our own.

It has been said that in the July battles Auchinleck was badly let down by his subordinate commanders. This, of course, refers to those holding the higher ranks. Brave, indomitable and devoted as they were they lacked the ability to co-ordinate forces in the field. Unit after unit would fight heroically only to see its efforts wasted because of lack of co-ordination and in the general plan. The War Cabinet took the view that Auchinleck should now be replaced by someone with a flair for choosing the right senior commanders for the battles of the future. On the other hand, many who served with Auchinleck felt he was the right man in the right place and should never have been removed from it. Nevertheless, when Auchinleck informed the Cabinet that he saw no prospect of a general offensive till mid-September, Churchill and the Chief of the General Staff (Sir Alan Brooke, later Lord Alanbrooke) then visited Cairo. On 6th August the Hon Sir Harold Alexander was appointed Commander-in-Chief, Middle East. General Gott was given command of Eighth Army but was killed by a German bomber two days later. The post was then filled by Lieutenant-General B. L. Montgomery. Alexander's Chief of Staff was a tank specialist named Major-General Richard McCreery. Montgomery's Chief of Staff was Brigadier Francis de Guingand.

There was and is much sympathy for Auchinleck for being replaced just when the tide was turning. He had done better than was realised until recently, for he had been supplied with little information from Ultra, the Bletchley Park decoding of German signals system, which at this stage was not keeping up with the pace of events. In contrast, Montgomery was well supported by Ultra when it came to Third Alamein, for it not only provided confirmation that the planted deception plans were working but valuable information was supplied to the Admiralty which enabled Rommel's supply convoys to be sunk. Montgomery, of course, had the three hundred Sherman tanks sent by Roosevelt. Had they been delivered earlier, Auchinleck's position would have been transformed.

The high regard in which Auchinleck was held comes out in various personal records. His personal courage and dedication were admired by all. It was said that he neglected the military axiom of concentration of force – or allowed his subordinate commanders to do so – and that he was too gentlemanly and not sufficiently ruthless with people who had failed him. Montgomery was a gentleman by birth and upbringing, but no one accused him of being over-gentlemanly in his treatment of those whose abilities had failed to come up to expectation. Nevertheless, Montgomery was often much more forgiving than he is thought to have been. However, he never forgot the remoteness and incompetence of many generals of the First World War, and was determined the same processes should not be repeated in the second.

A good example of Montgomery's impatience with incompetence concerns 4th Division. This arrived in the Middle East at the beginning of August, but no plans were made to send it forward till mid-August at the earliest. Meanwhile it would be engaged in becoming acclimatised and in training. Montgomery dismissed this policy as nonsense. Both these could take place where the division was needed. He needed it. The division was sent up immediately.

Montgomery was determined not to repeat the simple tactical mistakes of his predecessor (and others). Rommel usually showed himself and then fell back. This then turned the British tanks on to the German anti-tank positions, usually equipped with 88s, and our tanks were picked off before the German anti-tank positions – if known – were within range of the tank's guns. (The Americans paid a fearful price for ignoring this lesson at Sidi Bou Zid and the Kasserine Pass.)

During August both armies were rebuilding and preparing for the next round. On 31st August Rommel launched a new attack, this time in the south. The area was mined much more effectively than Rommel had envisaged. Furthermore the German attack did not come as the surprise it was meant to be. From Ultra, Montgomery had been informed of the direction and date of this attack. From the same source came information about the German morale and supply position. Rommel's plan was to make one of his famous hook moves by which he could swing wide of the main defences, attack a vulnerable point and then receive any counter-attack on his well positioned anti-tank guns. The main thrust was just north of Himeimat.

Battles are usually obscured by what is known as 'the fog of war', and this means the inevitable confusion resulting from dubious intelligence, broken or misunderstood communication, false assessments, and so on. In the desert any battle or skirmish had the additional hazard of the dust of war, for thick clouds drifted around any movement or disturbance. Although this was bad for both armies, it was obviously worse for an attacker who was moving into unfamiliar country. A misleading map had been 'planted' for the Germans to capture. A further handicap to Rommel was the fact that he was now operating in a narrower area, and the broad, sweeping hooks of the past would be impossible.

The final blow was that Montgomery, having sized up Rommel's special tactics, decided to employ these against him. In consequence, the Germans ran into solid opposition from guns and hull-down tanks on the Alamein Halfa Ridge.* The battle became a morale-raising triumph for XIII Corps, which had been so heavily mauled earlier at Mersa Matruh. This battle, although strictly speaking a second battle of Alamein, has gone down in the official records as the Battle of Alam El Halfa.

After Alam El Halfa the Eighth Army was not merely convinced it could win defensive battles, but that it could think in terms of attacking and pushing the Germans right back. This had been Montgomery's view since his appointment but the view of the Army commander is not necessarily the view of the soldier in day-to-day contact with the enemy. Eighth Army was an excellent formation with an admirable record but by September 1942 it had had 80,000 casualties. Fortunately the replacements were full of enthusiasm for showing they were as good or better than their predecessors. For an army it was somewhat unorthodox in

---

* The Sharpshooters (CLY) checked the point of the German attack although losing all twelve of their tanks in the process.

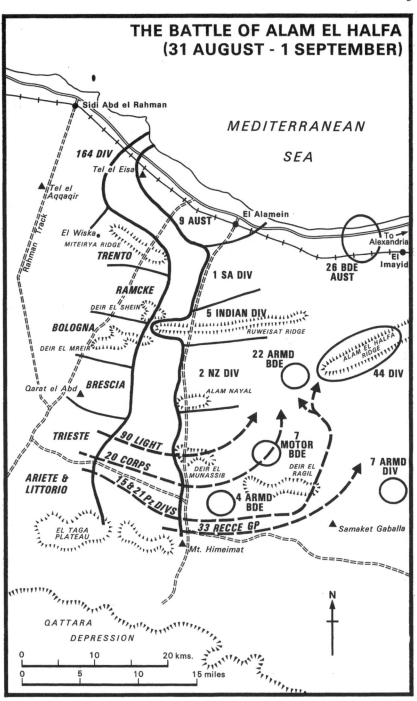

THE BATTLE OF ALAM EL HALFA
(31 AUGUST - 1 SEPTEMBER)

MEDITERRANEAN

SEA

Sidi Abd el Rahman

164 DIV

Tel el Eisa

Tel el
Aqqaqir

9 AUST

El Alamein

El Wiska

To
Alexandria

MITEIRYA RIDGE

El
Imayid

TRENTO

1 SA DIV

26 BDE
AUST

RAMCKE

DEIR EL SHEIN

5 INDIAN DIV

BOLOGNA

RUWEISAT RIDGE

DEIR EL MREIR

22 ARMD
BDE

ALAM EL HALFA
RIDGE

2 NZ DIV

44 DIV

Qarat el Abd

BRESCIA

ALAM NAYAL

TRIESTE

90 LIGHT

7
MOTOR
BDE

7 ARMD
DIV

20 CORPS

DEIR EL
MUNASSIB

DEIR EL
RAGIL

*ARIETE &
LITTORIO*

15 & 21 Pz DIVS

4 ARMD
BDE

EL TAGA
PLATEAU

33 RECCE GP

Samaket Gaballa

Mt. Himeimat

N

QATTARA

DEPRESSION

| 0 | 10 | 20 kms. |

| 0 | 5 | 10 | 15 miles |

Rahman Track

dress. All sorts of individual whims, such as corduroy trousers, coloured scarves, and suède boots, were to be seen. Nevertheless, although including large numbers of 'hostilities only' soldiers, its professional skill was second to none. Gunnery was of a particularly high standard and so too was the repair work in REME and RAOC, transport in the RASC, mine-laying and detecting by Royal Engineers and communications by Royal Signals. On the efficiency of those units – who were sometimes engaged in fighting Germans themselves – the abilities of tanks and infantry depended. Fictional war films have given a somewhat unrealistic view of armoured warfare by showing apparently invulnerable iron-clads lurching forward spitting death before their handsome and immaculate crews step out to be greeted by cheers from liberated people. However, tanks are cramped, hot, uncomfortable, vulnerable and claustrophobic. While on the move they can spray a target with machine-gun fire but if their larger weapons are to be used accurately the tank must stop. Between stopping and firing it will be a perfect target for an anti-tank gun – or for another tank hull down (with everything concealed except the muzzle of its gun). Surrounded by ammunition and fuel, tank crews prefer not to think of their chances of being burnt to death while trapped. But now famous cavalry regiments became highly respected tank regiments. Many of the same qualities were required. Curiously enough the strength and weakness of the arm had been similar ever since cavalry had been introduced to the battlefield. Centuries before, horses were trapped in concealed trenches or stopped by pikes. Now the trenches were anti-tank mines and the pikes were anti-tank guns. As in the past, 'cavalry' was at its best in reconnaissance, encirclement, and breaking through a weak position and pursuit. *Plus ça change. . . .*

By 22nd October Montgomery was ready to move and to win. He had 220,000 men and just over 1,000 tanks. The Germans had 108,000 men, of which half were Germans, and 600 tanks. Rommel had gone home sick and his place had been taken by General Stumme. Because of its disastrous record in the earlier fighting, it is customary to dismiss the Italian component of Rommel's force as ineffective and a possible liability. That view is far from the truth. Many Italians fought with tenacity and courage. Their artillery was good and their best units were as good as the Germans, especially at night. Rommel, having been frustrated in his drive for Cairo, was now determined not to give up ground. In consequence he had ordered the construction of a defensive position five miles deep along the entire Alamein line. German tanks were superior to the British and their guns, from the renowned 88 to the

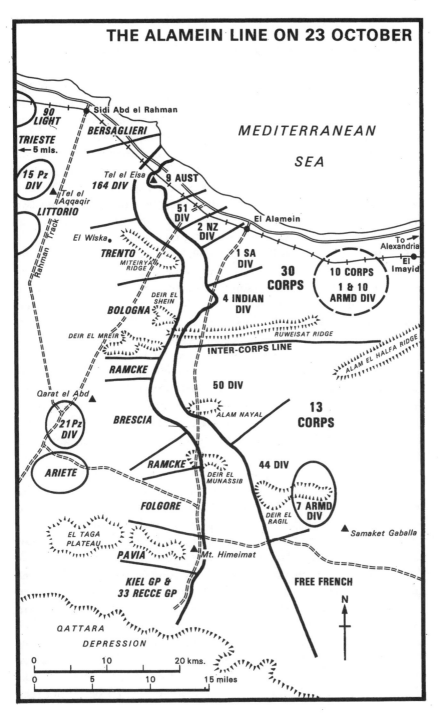

THE ALAMEIN LINE ON 23 OCTOBER

MEDITERRANEAN

SEA

90 LIGHT

Sidi Abd el Rahman

TRIESTE
← 5 mls.

BERSAGLIERI

15 Pz DIV

Tel el Eisa

Tel el Aqqaqir

164 DIV

9 AUST

LITTORIO

Rahman Track

El Wiska

51 DIV

El Alamein

2 NZ DIV

To Alexandria

TRENTO

MITEIRYA RIDGE

1 SA DIV

30 CORPS

10 CORPS
1 & 10 ARMD DIV

El Imayid

DEIR EL SHEIN

BOLOGNA

4 INDIAN DIV

DEIR EL MREIR

RUWEISAT RIDGE

INTER-CORPS LINE

ALAM EL HALFA RIDGE

RAMCKE

50 DIV

Qarat el Abd

ALAM NAYAL

13 CORPS

21 Pz DIV

BRESCIA

ARIETE

RAMCKE

44 DIV

DEIR EL MUNASSIB

FOLGORE

DEIR EL RAGIL

7 ARMD DIV

Samaket Gaballa

EL TAGA PLATEAU

PAVIA

Mt. Himeimat

KIEL GP &
33 RECCE GP

FREE FRENCH

N

QATTARA
DEPRESSION

0   10   20 kms.

0   5   10   15 miles

vicious Spandau machine-gun of the infantry, were also better than the Eighth Army weapons.

There was no doubt in anyone's mind that a British offensive was imminent. In this context the two great military virtues of surprise and concentration of force could hardly be expected. However, the former was achieved by the creation of a complete deception army in the south with all the paraphernalia of guns, dumps and supply lines. It was all string, tin and canvas but it gave the impression that an army of 150,000 was mobilised and poised in that area. A second deception was achieved in the starting date of the battle. The Germans were 'leaked' information that the British offensive would not start until 8th November at the earliest. The effect of finding that the battle had begun two weeks earlier than expected and in the north rather than the south was too much for Stumme, who had a heart-attack and died.

On the night of 23rd October XXX Corps pushed forward to Miteirya Ridge, the Australians made some headway in the north to what was nicknamed 'Thompson's Post', and the whole line advanced an average of five miles. Finding a way through the Axis minefields was a slow and dangerous task. Because of Stumme's death and disappearance there was no counter-attack. A day later he was replaced by Von Thoma and a day after that Rommel returned to the scene. On the night of 24-25th October, our 10th Armoured Division tried to break through opposite the Ruweisat Ridge but were held up. Montgomery was awakened in the middle of the night and asked if he wished to change his plan. He did not; and went back to sleep. The next day 10th Armoured had broken through the minefield which had been holding it up.

On the 26th the battle seemed to have become static (although fierce fighting was still going on). Rommel therefore decided to throw in his reserves and retake the north-westerly extension of Miteirya, which was known to the British as 'Kidney Ridge'. Here he encountered unexpectedly heavy resistance in a theatre in which the Rifle Brigade (now Greenjackets) distinguished itself. Details appear later. On the 29th the Australians pushed up from Kidney Ridge towards the coast. Here they encountered a strongly defended German outpost, the above-mentioned 'Thompson's Post'. It was a formidable position but the Australians lived up to expectations and by indomitable persistence took it. Rommel, as expected, threw his remaining reserves into a counter-attack. The Australians held firm. Rommel had now lost four-fifths of his tanks.

As the British line began to roll forward on 3rd November the Germans were already beginning to retreat. An order from Hitler then forbade retreat, but twenty-four hours later the order was cancelled. As the Germans renewed their withdrawal the British made a final desperate effort to catch up, encircle and capture. The ambition was defeated by rain which began on 6th November and made movement almost impossible. The only person it benefited was Rommel, who was able to withdraw along a metalled road while attempts to cut him off floundered through the mud.

So that was the end of the battles of Alamein and is, in outline, the story which goes into the history books. But for many these battles were not like that at all. They did not know of the strategy, nor the tactics, nor the presence and movements of other units. They were unaware of conflicts in the higher command, and oblivious to peripheral matters. The men who fought at Alamein fought a clean though bloody war far removed from the pleasures of civilisation; they lived mainly on dull concentrated rations such as bully beef and hard biscuits and they had at best four pints of water per day. That four pints had to cover drinking, washing and cooking. They fought a rugged and tenacious enemy led by a commander of genius. And they won. But what they thought about it all was quite different from what is generally written about the battles, and that is why it is here. For the most part they are rightly proud of their army and the part they played. Some consider that the 'official history' is either wrong or distorted and produce evidence for their views. They may well be right for official histories are by no means perfect though usually regarded as sacrosanct. Most of them merely feel that their experiences, though neither important, heroic nor spectacular, might be interesting nearly forty years later. And they are right.

PART TWO

The following letters and diary extracts show the Alamein battles from many angles. There is a considerable measure of agreement – most people emphasise the leadership and skill of Lieutenant-General (as he then was) B. L. Montgomery although there are many who consider that Lieutenant-General C. Auchinleck never received the credit he deserved for stopping Rommel at Alamein in July 1942.

A good proportion of the writers were what the Army used to refer to as 'other ranks'; attempts to remove this slighting term have not been entirely successful even today.* In the Eighth Army officers and men lived very closely together and shared the same flies, food, dangers and discomforts. There is not much 'Them and Us' anti-officer feeling, although any setbacks are usually blamed on the Higher Command rather than the Germans. Excerpts from the life of a wartime soldier are provided by Mr B. Cole's diary. His experiences were similar to those of many others, but few soldiers were as articulate. His army 'life story' is given as it shows the typical Army career of an Infantry private who eventually arrives at Alamein. Conditions on most troopships were fully as bad as on the one he describes : nobody who travelled on one will ever forget the appalling stench of the lower decks, crammed as they were with thousands of troops. Most were hastily converted liners – deathships if torpedoed – carrying a miscellany of units, and with ugly, mutinous situations sometimes very close to the surface. By the time they marched on board most soldiers were reasonably hardened, but when they left the troopship a few weeks later everyone needed some form of re-training.

The letters from 'other ranks' effectively dispose of the view that soldiers think nothing but beer, women and cigarettes. Many, as has been shown by their subsequent careers, had much more ability than the Army could discover and use to best advantage at the time – there was after all 'a war on'. A few rare beings may have been elated and not frightened by battle, but most people merely hoped not to be killed or badly wounded, not to show fear and not to let their comrades down. Mr Cole had no desire to achieve military glory and emphasises his fears

---

* Army Public Relations has made some headway with the term 'soldiers'.

and doubts; nevertheless any soldier will immediately recognise that he was made of sterner stuff than he cares to reveal. There were many like him – and they made the finest infantry in the world.

In peacetime the Army – and the general public – tends to revert to an old-fashioned and snobbish attitude to its regiments. It is more distinguished to be in, say, the Guards, Greenjackets, Hussars or Lancers, than Signals, Royal Corps of Transport, Royal Electrical and Mechanical Engineers or Royal Army Ordnance Corps, as if somehow one required more courage to be in the 'teeth' arms, as they are called. In fact the modern army trains everyone in the basic military skills of a fighting soldier. Following this some of the 'services' tackle assignments which would make others shudder. The Royal Army Ordnance Corps specialises in bomb disposal and REME collects and repairs tanks from highly dangerous situations. Signals are responsible for communication on the battlefield, are often isolated and exposed and have a continuous task. Royal Corps of Transport (then Royal Army Service Corps) have the task of delivering petrol and food, without which no modern army can perform for long. Royal Engineers have many tasks, but the worst at Alamein was clearing minefields. Any miscalculation in a minefield would lead to instant death or appalling mutilation. The interdependence and mutual respect of one arm to another was never more clearly demonstrated than during the Alamein battles.

It seems from these letters that the Eighth Army was refreshingly clear of snobbish nonsense, and that rank was respected because it was earned and justified, or lost.

The letters are arranged to give the reader an appreciation of the function of various arms on the battlefield. However, no unit can act in isolation, thus a tank crew will rely on Intelligence and Signals for information; on sappers to clear minefields; on gunners to give covering fire if needed; on the medical corps to evacuate casualties; on the service corps (now Royal Corps of Transport) for ammunition, fuel and food; and ordnance corps and electrical and mechanical engineers to recover and repair the tank itself. At Alamein everyone was dependent on the sappers clearing the minefields and opening up a way to advance. References to sappers are scattered throughout the letters .(The term 'sappers' to denote Royal Engineers dates from the days when engineers were required to dig saps [long trenches] up to fortifications and often to mine underneath the walls.)

In spite of the widespread belief, both within and without the Army, that organisation is chaotic, it is clear that the planning and administration which can deploy 220,000 men on a battlefield must be of very high quality indeed. Most of the organisation is based on past experience, sometimes bitter experience. However, the Army's continued use of obsolete and often meaningless terms is often absurd and leads to confusion. Mixed among them may be modern jargon such as 'casevac' for casualty evacuation. DAAQMG is an abbreviation for Deputy Assistant Adjutant and Quartermaster General; the term dates from the Napoleonic wars and denotes a staff officer, probably a major, whose job is to collect information about unit strength (for reinforcement if needed) for 'A' branch and about material needs for the 'Q' branch. Other staff officers will be found in 'G' branch dealing with general operational requirements. Thus G1, G2 and G3 as referred to in the letters. The Commanding Officer, a lieutenant-colonel, commands a battalion (then about 950). Within the battalion will be companies commanded by majors or captains who are OCs (Officer Commanding). Casualties were evacuated via RAP (Regimental Aid Post) to ADS (Advanced Dressing Station) to MDS (Main Dressing Station) to CCS (Casualty Clearing Station); however, most of these would still be in highly dangerous areas, not only from shelling and bombing but also from small arms fire.

The 'Order of Battle' denotes the list of units concerned. It does not mean the order in which they began to fight.

'The Benghazi Run', to which there is an occasional reference, was the term used by desert veterans to describe the journeys forward and back across the desert before the arrival of General Montgomery and the stabilised front. The term 'front line' became obsolete in mobile warfare and was replaced by FDL (forward defended localities). In spite of this Alamein with its minefields was a near approach to the trench warfare of the First World War. At night vehicles formed up into *laagers* (or *leaguers*), a term which dated from the Boer habit of drawing their wagons into a defensible square at night.

As with other battles of the Second World War, many who fought were wounded and permanently disabled. At the time of writing (October 1978) the pension for 100% disablement for an Other Rank, i.e. regimental sergeant-major down to private, is £29.44 weekly for the former and £28.60 for the latter. In addition either is allowed 50p per week for his wife and 37½p for a child. The officer is little better off although his pension is set out as an annual figure: a general gets £34 per week and a lieutenant gets £30. Even the general's pension is under half the national average wage and many people today would consider £34 a week starvation wages. Perhaps they are right.

I

In the Tanks

From Mr T. I. L. Powell

I was merely a trooper, a member of a tank crew in the Alamein campaign and certainly in no position to have any overall appreciation of the strategy and tactics of the battle. A good start is sometimes said to be half the battle, and certainly two things raised the spirits of the British forces before the Alamein battle was joined. The first was the appearance of the American Sherman tank on the scene. Here, at last, was something so vastly superior in both fire power and protection that a general feeling of optimism was generated in tank crews. Secondly all the preparations seemed to be so thorough, with nothing that could be foreseen being left to chance. As armour and vehicles moved forward, tracks literally were covered – track and wheel marks being obliterated from the sand by rolling sweepers. Concentrations of dummy tanks were scattered here and there to deceive enemy spotter aircraft as to the position and extent of the real forces.

The feeling of its 'being our turn this time' seemed more and more to take hold of one's mind. As to the fighting itself; a tank crew is a tiny world on its own. Part of a regiment – of course – and a division and an army; but for all that, five men shut up in their little protected, lethal box, strangely isolated and on their own.

When the time for action came it was with dramatic suddenness. I remember sitting outside my tank when the call came, 'Tank commanders to Command Tank.' The rest of us sat about, chatting and idly speculating what it meant this time. We were soon to know. Back they came in a very few minutes with the terse message, 'We're operational at one minute's notice.'

So, for the first time in my life, I went into battle. The tank commander, a regular army sergeant, a good-natured fellow and an inveterate borrower who in the past had always seemed hard up and had small loans from all of his crew, emptied his pockets and repaid every penny he'd borrowed. I remember him saying, 'Better pay my debts, you never know.' In less than half an hour he lay body and shoulders on the tank floor, his head and brains spattered on the surrounding walls.

As day by day the battle continued, my three strongest recollections are: the heat, sweat pouring and oozing from me, until I ached and itched with it. The strange lack of fear (and I make no pretence of being a hero, there were other occasions when I was acutely afraid) when engaged in combat with an enemy tank or possibly gun emplacement. It was, I think, simply a case of being so busy trying to ensure you knocked out him before he knocked out you that the whole of one's determination and concentration excluded all other emotions. And, most vividly of all, the seemingly endless hours and hours of utter boredom, observing a low ridge about 2,000 yards away with nothing moving, nothing happening, except the sun beating mercilessly down and one's eyes straining (as I remember our gunner putting it) 'at miles and miles of f . . . all'.

On the lighter side, incidents such as the order, over the radio, to brew up, which meant the spare driver had to nip out to what protection the rear of the tank offered and make tea. Frequently this would be observed by the other side and bring down a hail of mortar fire and back he would scurry to be greeted, 'Get in quick, but let's have the tea first.' Also radio procedure had its memorable moments. When a message was not completely heard, the receiving operator would reply, 'Say again all after . . .', or, 'Say again all before . . .', so that on occasions one heard an anguished request to 'Say again all after "Bloody Hell" '; or, on one occasion, 'Say again all before "Jesus Christ".'

Humour, generally, was either rough and bawdy, or sardonic. A typical example of the sort of thing that amused us was the story that Hitler had secretly contacted Churchill with the offer to remove Rommel from his command in return for Churchill retaining all his generals in theirs. Or the comment about a new major joining a unit who was so stupid that even the other majors noticed it. Of the cigarettes issued it was stated that the manufacturers were most annoyed that it should be believed they were made from sawdust and camel dung, and had indignantly denied that there was any sawdust in their product.

Eventually the tank I was in was knocked out. I clearly recall the driver, a phlegmatic little Yorkshireman calling to us in the turret, 'My visor's gone. Next one we've had it.' His tone was conversational, almost casual. In a matter of minutes the tank was engulfed in flames. What surprises me is that I was not conscious of any explosion or sound, just realising I was in the middle of a fire and myself on fire. The gunner was killed, the rest of us escaped. I do remember ripping the leads of the commander's earphones from the radio set so that he could fling himself out and hurling myself to the ground the moment his feet vanished through the hole above my head.

*

From Mr F. A. Lewis

Perhaps it would help if I first give a brief summary of myself. I was born 1911 in Bethnal Green and went through the various stages of a very poor upbringing until joining 10th Hussars 1928. I served seven years colour service including Egypt, India, etc., and to Army Reserve Class A 1935. My parents had moved to Dagenham (much falsely maligned) where I went to work for Ford as a sump washer and crankshaft grinder, etc., until August 1939 when I was 'called to the colours', as the Army puts it. In France 1940, we formed part of the rearguard and fought various actions. I think what was left of us returned to Britain about early July. Then I went to the Middle East with all the various campaigns you know about. At the very end of the African Campaign I was wounded for the third time; it was third time lucky and kept me in hospital for more than a year. My first two wounds were slight and I just received treatment from our MO in the field. I was twice mentioned in dispatches and awarded the Military Medal in October 1942.

I returned to Ford in 1945 and continued in various jobs and retired (early) in 1971 when I was then Manager of Ford Publications.

October 1942

It seemed an interminable journey to the regulating point where we were to have a final filling with petrol and remove the muzzle covers from the guns. As we progressed one caught glimpses of military police controlling the traffic where necessary and away to the left I could see an immense line of lorries racing parallel to our own column.

We were very silent for most of the journey until, just as we were approaching the first of our own minefields, the very skies seemed to open and become one leaping, dancing, frenzy of gun-flashes as the artillery opened its barrage. Soon we were among the guns, and stopped for a few moments among a battery of sixty-pounders. A few yards to my right the long snout of one rose from its pit, and suddenly with a terrific white flash it sent its shell flying over towards the enemy. In the momentary light one could see the stark silhouette of the steel-helmeted gunners standing motionless in the pit.

Another short move forward and we were at the regulating point, and flying up the long line of tanks came the RASC lorry with our petrol, and the barrage was ignored while we were busy filling up. Here we were to stay until two o'clock when the barrage would cease and the infantry we hoped had gained their objectives and smashed the gaps to be blown in the minefield for us to pass through.

To increase the inferno of sound came the Air Force, first with flares and then quickly after the heavy crump of bombs came to our ears. The whole night sky was alight with gun-flashes and bomb-flashes, and streams of red, green, white and yellow tracers lifted like questioning fingers towards the unseen aircraft above.

Suddenly, from the north came the father and mother of all gun-flashes and the resultant explosion seemed to rock the very earth. My driver grinned. 'The Navy?' It certainly seemed like it, as I am sure we had no gun of that size in the whole Eighth Army.

A jeep came speeding down the line of stationary tanks – the Colonel – shouting for everyone to start up and get ready to move. I noticed that the roar of the engine woke those members of the crew who had been snatching forty winks inside. Looking down into the fighting chamber, I could see fairly well in the red glow of the radio pilot light. The gunner was easing his long legs and settling himself more comfortably in his seat, while the operator with his feet on my bottom seat was dozing fitfully with his head on his chest. Seeing me climb in and adjust my headphones, they looked enquiringly at me and when I nodded, there was a general air of wakefulness. We lurched forward and entered the passage in our own minefield and I spoke on the intercom and reminded the driver to keep to the right and close to the green lights.

The operator who had been watching the outside world through his periscope suddenly spoke: 'Looks like Regent Street.'

This was followed by a weird babble of sounds in the 'phones and we knew our second driver, a Scotsman, was speaking.

Gunner: 'What's that bloody savage talking about?'

Driver: 'He wants to know if anyone is hungry.'

Operator: 'We're starving, tell him to get busy.'

From the dark recesses of the driving compartment soon came a ghostly hand passing through an almost constant stream of jam-covered biscuits.

Driver: 'Hope Jerry can't see those lights.'

Operator: 'Windy?'

Growl from the front : 'No, just careful.'

Steadily we moved through the gap until gleaming in front we could see the lamp marking the end of our own territory and in a few moments we were through and entering the first enemy minefield. One could see dim figures of infantry pacing along the route, and occasionally a stretcher party with its grim blanket-covered burden winding its way slowly to the quickly established casualty clearing station. On the ground could be seen the white tape laid by the task force which marked the route through the enemy minefield. Some local shelling was taking place, but on the whole things were pretty quiet and we made our way steadily forward without interference. The sky was paling for dawn when we emerged from the second obstacle, only to find our way blocked by yet a third one about which nothing could be done as it was now too late, being nearly daylight.

The squadron deployed, but to our dismay we found that we were jammed into a shallow depression while around us lay our forward infantry, and the whole movement forward was blocked by the minefield in front. Behind this the ground rose away to a respectable ridge behind which lay, if our information was correct, the 15th Panzers. It was this same ridge that we had taken for our first objective and from which we hoped to have the advantage in the ensuing tank battle, but our plans had gone astray and daylight found us in a very sticky position. As far as the eye could see were vehicles of all descriptions indescribably jammed together, and the Boche was not slow to take advantage of this fact and shells from his batteries soon began to fall thick and heavy.

For some hours we sat under this bombardment with absolutely nothing we could do until late in the morning the expected tank counter-attack was put in by the Germans. Over the ridge they trundled, a tight bunch of a dozen first coming into my view and showing black against the skyline but too far away for us to be able to do much about it. They stopped at about 3,000 yards and two or three K4s* began to shell the infantry lying around the tanks. All the while we watched them closely through binoculars and, holding our fire, hoped that they would grow bolder and move in closer. This they refused to do, but one or two K3s skirmishing round the others suddenly came within range of Shermans on our right and in a couple of minutes one of them was smoking furiously and the crew racing for cover, while the other tank lumbered off up the ridge out of range.

* German tanks : PzKw IV.

We now spotted a tank which we thought might be in range and the troop leader of 2nd troop asked permission to engage, which he received, but before he could start a terrific bang from my left rear caused me to turn and look in that direction. My B tank commander, with glasses glued to his eyes, was already ranging, but on my signalling him he very reluctantly stopped and made rude signs with his fingers in the direction of the enemy. Don 2* with his third shot scored a hit on the back of the opposing tank but we were all disgusted to see the resourceful Hun begin to tow the cripple away. All this took place at an extreme range, and we were only beginning to feel our feet in the new Shermans.

Shelling continued throughout the afternoon until at 3.30 an infantry attack was launched at the ridge supported by tanks, and one vivid memory of that was seeing a shell burst on the back of one of the advancing Valentines among the infantrymen clinging on the back. The attack was successful and about one hour later a gap had been made in the obstacle in front and we pushed our way through. Two of the tanks of the squadron here struck mines and we left them to be fixed up by the fitters following closely behind in their truck. Once through, we found the sappers busily clearing yet another obstacle under very heavy shellfire, so we stayed where we were, occasionally putting down a few shells when we saw any movement to the front.

After the sun had gone down, we received orders to get through the final obstacles and I was given the doubtful honour of leading the squadron through. The tapes marking the gap could be clearly seen in the moonlight as I made my way carefully through, and in a few minutes I found myself on the other side and in the clear. Seeing a Bren carrier making towards me, I halted and dismounted and waited for them to come up to me. A very tired and dirty subaltern jumped off and asked me where the hell I thought I was going. Didn't I know that I couldn't move to the left as it was mined, and did I know that another minefield was suspected in front?

Before I could answer, a sharp report away to the left, and a bullet struck the curved front of my tank and missed my head by a matter of inches. I quickly took a couple of paces to the rear, placing the Sherman between myself and the sniper and turned to speak to the subaltern who I found crouching with the rest of his men round my feet. He began to swear very monotonously, but effectively, and I could not but admire his racy invective all directed at the sniper who, it appeared, had already bagged two of his men. I decided to pass the information I had

* Don was the name given to each fighting troop.

to the squadron leader, and, not fancying presenting myself as a good target again, I shouted for the gunner to drop my mike out of the turret. Not hearing very well, he raised his head above the cupola ring the better to hear what I said, and I screamed at him to get down, but not before a bullet had whistled dangerously close to his head. I began to feel sorry for the sniper, and had to smile when the mike appeared over the edge and dangled in front of my eyes. There is certainly something very persuasive about a sniper in the moonlight.

Having passed the message, I waited while it passed to the Colonel, who quickly decided to bring us back, and one was treated to the spectacle of a dozen massive Shermans reversing through the narrow passage which I had just negotiated. I suddenly remembered that I had not warned the squadron against the sniper, and thought that they might think it rather ridiculous to be told to be on their guard against one rifle, so said nothing about it, for the moment anyway. Having a profound respect for his marksmanship, I was undecided as to how I was going to regain the turret without exposing more of my anatomy than was absolutely necessary. But no more shots welcomed me as I climbed in and we accomplished our return journey and formed up on the Colonel's tank into a double line laager when I was warned that my troop was responsible for guard duties that night. Having seen to this, I reported for orders for the next day. These were quite simple, namely, to continue the movement which we had interrupted that evening and to deploy away to the right, picking the best ground that we could in the circumstances.

The night was rather noisy, but no more so than usual, although both the Luftwaffe and the RAF were on the prowl and many flares were dropped. I distinguished myself here by getting the most enormous rocket from the Colonel, who was firing Very signals to denote bomb line limits. Against the stars I could plainly see a Ju 88 flying rather low in wide circles and, not being able to resist the temptation, I took a pot shot at him with the .50 calibre A/A gun, and as the tracer flew past his tail I was tickled to see him twist and bank in his flight to avoid the stream of cannon shells. Much to my disappointment the Colonel intervened rather violently, and to my disgust I had to stop shooting.

It was now within about an hour of dawn and everyone was rolling blankets and strapping them on their tanks and then standing shivering and talking in low tones, waiting for the order to mount. Suddenly from our left flank appeared a formation of motorised infantry with trucks and Bren carriers who made straight for the gap we were waiting to enter, and, true to the best traditions, halted and effectively blocked the opening to any further traffic. We were now ordered to mount and proceed and, as leading tank, I had somehow to push my way through the traffic, but the sight of 30 tons of armour was too much for the PBI,* who quickly made room for me to pass followed by the rest of the squadron. Once through the narrow passage, I quickly swung right for some five hundred yards, and was not very pleased to find the ground particularly unfavourable to us, but spotting a shallow little depression I halted in the centre of it.

Dawn was just glimmering on the horizon and a thin mist lay over the surrounding ground, but peering round me I could discern the dim figures of infantry in hastily scraped trenches, and thinking to gather some information, I dismounted. All I could gather was that the people I was talking to had taken over during the night and were not very conversant with anything which was likely to be of any use to us but, as the light grew stronger, I could see the bulky shapes of the regiment of Shermans on our right. This information I passed back.

The country we were now holding was still far from favourable. We seemed to be held in a shallow bowl which to the right moved smoothly away to a low ridge about 3,000 yards away. To the front was a small ridge which gave us no cover at all although the infantry were finding it useful and, in front of that, again the ground dropped steeply for some little distance and then rose away into a quite formidable crest. I had no doubt that the Boche with his usual low cunning would find the conditions to his advantage very quickly and put in a counter-attack, using his tanks.

As the sun mounted, we scanned the ground to our front very keenly and found that pockets of the enemy were still in possession and seemingly in quite good fettle. My operator here drew my attention to the corpse of a subaltern of the Gordons lying a few yards from the tank, and whom the whole crew could see quite plainly through their periscopes. I looked enquiringly at the gunner, who answered shortly, 'Flies.' 'Go to hell, I'm not being shifted from here for any bloody flies.' The driver's voice now drifted plaintively through the intercom : 'Big black flies, I can see 'em glaring at us, they'll be in here when the sun gets up.' A babble of sound in the 'phones denoted that the second driver was speaking.

Silence followed whilst we all waited for the first driver's interpretation.

'He says can he shoot up the little valley in front with his bow gun. I

* Poor bloody infantry.

think he's annoyed about that Scotsman in front.'

'No, he bloody well can't, not yet anyway.'

The operator here made everyone angry by speaking longingly of hot tea, and the driver suggested we pass the necessary equipment to a couple of the PBI occupying a nearby trench, and ask them to brew up for us.

This idea was abandoned as at that moment an enemy battery began to range on us and all the foot-sloggers disappeared into their various holes. Quite a lot of shelling was going on, and one could pick out the various types of gun by the shell explosions. Predominant was the whip and crack and woolly bear effect of the 88 mm and one seemed to hear the whistle of the approaching missile only a split second before it burst. Suddenly, from our rear came the hollow thump of our own tracked 105 mm and the swish of the shell passed directly overhead. This was followed by the whole battery loosening off, and there were many chuckles inside the tank at the continual thumps and swishes. Voice from the front: 'Well done, Robin, crash 'em in!' Robin, incidentally, was Captain Street-Smith of 'B' Battery, who were our supporting artillery, and for the first time were using 105 mm guns mounted on a tank chassis, making them as mobile as ourselves. My crew were always curious as to Robin's whereabouts and credited him with powers as an observation officer, which would certainly have embarrassed him if he had heard them.

Voice from the gunner's seat: 'Can't see the bursts, wonder where he's firing?'

Snort from the driver. 'You stick to your own bloody gun, you haven't hit anything yet.'

Operator: 'We would have done if we had a decent driver who could get us somewhere in time.'

Driver: 'Huh, I like that! How can we go anywhere when we never get any orders because that box of tricks of yours never works properly.'

Both of these insults were totally untrue, but the favourite amusement of these two was slanging each other.

Suddenly the radio began to hum and conversation ceased. 'Pip One, I've just been fired at direct to my front' – and the voice rose excitedly – 'and again, he's hit my cupola ring. Put down smoke, gunner, you bloody fool, put down smoke.'

This last was not intended for our hearing, but he had forgotten to switch over from transmission to intercomm. Seeing the smoke-shells bursting to my left, I had a long look through my glasses when the Squadron Leader's voice came through the 'phones: 'Pip four, can you see that gun? I think it's a tank dug in! Range 1,000 yards. Get on to him.'

Looking round I could see two tanks already firing AP (anti-personnel) shot, but they were warned off by the boss who told me to carry on. There was a scurry of activity in the turret as the operator slammed home a shell and the gunner swung the turret round on to the target.

I passed the order down the mike: 'Ten hundred one round.'

The answer came back: 'One round ready.'

'Fire!' and the AP shell went screaming towards the target. It struck just to the right, sending up a cloud of dust and I passed the corrections to the gunner, who relaid the gun and waited.

'Fire!'

'OK for line!'

The Squadron Leader's voice came through the 'phones: 'Change to soft stuff.' This meant HE (high explosive) and the operator nodded to me as he pushed home the bright yellow projectile.

'Fire!' A burst of black smoke obscured the target.

'Up 4 Fire.' Another burst, this time behind.

'Down 2 Fire.' This last shell scored a direct hit on the roof of the dug-in tank and burst with a brilliant flash of flame, throwing fragments of the enemy into the air.

Pandemonium broke loose inside the tank, congratulations pouring through the intercomm. to the gunner, who was grinning shyly. First blood to us and we felt quite jubilant. As the gunner was extremely fond of jam, we decided to open a fresh tin in his honour, and biscuits and jam were soon being consumed ad lib. The party was going well when a familiar whistle over my head caused me to scan the ridge to our right, where I could see one of the Boche tank chassis sporting one of their now long-barrelled 75s. As I watched, I saw the gun flash and recoil, and almost immediately came the whistle of the shell, this time much closer. I shot orders into the mike, and the gunner, pushing the tin of jam between his knees, swung the turret on to the enemy.

'75 Harry Edward Action', and the first shell went on its way to burst in front of the Hun.

The necessary corrections were quickly made and we saw the third shot score another direct hit and the carrier blazed merrily away to our general satisfaction. Looking down, I saw that the gunner was still holding a half-eaten biscuit between his teeth which he had been in the act of consuming when he received my orders.

A babble of weird jargon came through the 'phones and we waited.

Driver: 'He says "Keefik" has woken up and can we stop firing until he goes to sleep again?' 'Keefik' was our pup.

Operator: 'It's not our fault, it's those bloody Jerries.'

Gunner: 'Maybe he'll feel better if he can see what's going on outside.'

So with due solemnity Keefik was hoisted up to a periscope through which he gazed with great wonderment, until he saw a shell burst, when he broke into a frenzy of youthful barks. This display of offensive spirit impressed us all and he was rewarded with a slice of bully beef.

We were now asked, in code, if we wanted any ammo, and not having replenished what we had fired the day before, we took the opportunity of slipping back through the minefield behind us where we found the sergeant-major. He was busily unloading the shells from two trucks but, what was better still, he was making tea for each tank as it arrived. We jumped down and began to pass up the shells and I suggested that Keefik be passed out to stretch his legs and for other reasons purely biological. I must say my faith in the dog was ably upheld by him. The tea which was passed to us was like a pearl of great price, the first we had had since the battle started. Although carrying huge supplies, we got no chance of using it, to our great disgust.

It did not take us long before we had taken on our full quota of ammo and within a few minutes of doing so we were on our way back through the minefield again. As we moved slowly back, I had time to look around me and could see bodies of our own and enemy infantry still lying where they had fallen and some of them in the most grotesque attitudes. The flies were already at work on them, and one could smell that sickly sweet odour of death beginning to rise in the hot morning air. Back in our place again, we were relieved to see some of the Gordons digging a grave for the subaltern, who had lain in front of our tank, and as he was buried we swept the valley in front with machine-gun fire, partly to cover the burial party and partly as a last salute.

Shortly after this, a Boche tank attack was put in on our right flank, but 'stout friends on our right' dealt with this, and huge mushrooms of thick black smoke denoted the accuracy of their shooting. They did not escape scot free, however, and I could see one of their Shermans 'going up' in brilliant flashes of flame and, as the ammo exploded, throwing showers of sparks into the air.

It was by now late afternoon, and we were surprised to see an enormous smoke-screen being put down on our right front by the artillery and, sensing that something was coming off, I took a good look round. Moving up behind us came 'C' Squadron, who headed straight for the smoke-cloud, moving line ahead the better to negotiate the

'Monty' inspecting his men.

The barrage.

Tanks on the move. Note the dust clouds which blot out following vehicles.

British machine gunners (Vickers) in action.

narrow passage open to them. The air became alive with wireless messages, one of them to us to watch them closely and put down covering fire where necessary. We had no few trepidations at this manoeuvre, as the position they were about to attack was very strongly held and contained now a few of the infamous 88s – a gun which is a veritable nightmare to any tank personnel. What I expected happened. They were allowed through the gap without a shot being fired, then as soon as the last tank was clear, the Boche opened up with everything he had. With every vehicle silhouetted against the smoke, and at quite short range, the heavy anti-tank guns soon began to play havoc with the squadron as they tried vainly to deploy and engage.

In as many minutes three Shermans were soon blazing furiously and two had been knocked out but were not yet in flames, and one could plainly see the crew 'bailing out' and legging it for what cover they could find from the murderous fire coming at them from both flanks and also their front. We gave what help we could, putting down smoke-shells fast and furiously, but were handicapped by not being in a position to spot the guns which were doing the damage. The voice of their squadron leader came over the radio reporting the hopelessness of their position and his conviction that another few minutes would see his squadron completely wiped out. Acting on this information and what he could plainly see himself, the Colonel lost no time in ordering a withdrawal, and what remained of the squadron were soon rumbling back through the gap and one could see on the fortunate ones some of the survivors of the fight who had lost their tanks. These were clinging precariously to the outside of the Shermans and one could not help but sigh with relief as the last of them came through to comparative safety.

Evening was now upon us, and I was beginning to wonder where we would stay for the night. My thoughts were soon put to an end by the squadron leader informing us that we were to stay right where we were. I remember the Colonel saying we would have a quieter time, although I was a little dubious about this. It wasn't long before the ammo and petrol lorries were with us and the work of replenishment went on. Guns were cleaned and everything checked over ready for the next day. My B tank commander approached and informed me that his tank cooker was in working order and would it be all right to use it? The very thought of a hot cup of tea was more than we could resist and, mentally telling all in authority to go to hell, we were soon brewing merrily away, albeit taking great care to screen the small glow of the stove from the enemy. Great activity round and through the minefield in front led to some wild conjectures, but the next morning we were

soon informed that the enemy position which had wrought such damage
to C Squadron was now cleared. This being so, it was not long before
we were passing through the same gap, but this time without mishap,
and thus eventually were in position on the ridge which had been our
objective when the attack opened. I was left-hand troop and, having
swung the three tanks into position, it was not long before I jumped out
and walked forward to make a personal recce. Cautiously poking my
head over the ridge, I saw the most amazing sight.

Directly to my front at about 1,000 yards was a table and bending
over it a particularly fine specimen of the Reich seemed to be very busy
on some unknown task. To his right at some 500 yards was an 88 mm
gun pointing straight at me, and behind it was an enormous camouflaged hangar which was evidently being used as an MT workshop.
Hardly able to believe the evidence of my own eyes, I trotted back to
my tank and was soon checking up with the photographic map. Everything seemed to be correct, but I made sure by enquiring if any of our
people were in front of us. Receiving a negative answer, I told my crew
what I had seen, causing great glee and a powerful argument as to
which target we should engage first. Obviously, it should have been the
88, but I simply could not resist the tent and the figure outside it, so,
giving the necessary orders, the gunner was soon pumping streams of
bullets at it from the machine-gun. Satisfied at the results, we switched
the big gun on to the 88 and at the fifth shot completely wrecked it, the
long barrel sticking in the air like a signpost. We now turned our attention to the hangar and in a few moments it was blazing furiously.

An enemy scout now appeared on the ridge to our right, and I
signalled my B tank to engage. It was obviously an O Pip (observation
officer) and his appearance was the signal for a shower of shells to fall
among us, but my other tank now had his range and, as a lorry pulled
up alongside the Boche, he scored a direct hit on it and literally blew it
to pieces. This was enough for the enterprising Jerry, who leaped out of
his car and ran like hell down the farther slope of the ridge, leaving the
driver of his scout car where he lay, obviously wounded or dead. Things
were now warming up and we became the centre of a quite respectable
barrage composed mostly of 105s and 88s. I was rather worried at this
period at the apparent lack of protection on our left flank, and, being
myself extreme left troop, I spent not a little time scanning this part of
the country.

PS.   As you will gather from what you read, I was troop leader,
normally an officer's position. Young officers coming straight from

Sandhurst* were often the bane of senior field officers and also had a high casualty rate, though sometimes no fault of their own. In addition it made things very difficult sometimes with the rank and file, many of whom were battle hardened and retained no illusions. So, we continued through the rest of the war with troop sergeants in many cases and were not unsuccessful. Looking back I think someone very high up must have given a hint, or perhaps, as was once put to me in a Southport pub, perhaps they were needed for the second front. I don't really know, but I do know that for a back-street cockney with a Bog Lane Secondary Modern type of education I think I did reasonably well. I still get a warm feeling at the Regimental Dinner when generals address me, warmly I may add, by my nickname. Of course, I knew some of them as subalterns before the war, so perhaps that helps.

*

From Lieutenant-Colonel R. G. Green, retd. (late Royal Tank Regiment)

I think it is true to say that there were really three battles – the first (July), the 'Battle of Alamein Halfa' (30th August to 1st September) and the third and final, major, battle launched on 23rd October.

For the first battle I was navigator of HQ 4th Armoured Brigade in the south. For the other two I was Acting Brigade Major of the Independent (under direct command Eighth Army) 23rd Armoured Brigade Group. My Brigade Commander, Brigadier G. W. Richards (later Major-General) had earlier been my commander with the 4th Armoured Brigade. Unfortunately he died a few weeks ago.

In regard to the last battle (October) it has frequently been said that the main thrust into and through the enemy defences was effected by an entirely infantry force. This is not true. Perhaps the legend has grown up because so many of the previous battles had been dominated by tanks – on both sides – and so there may have been a desire to give all credit to the infantry divisions. After all, Monty was an infantryman!

In fact the four armoured regiments (Valentines) of the 23rd supported the four infantry divisions, actually carrying infantry on their backs in some cases, in both the initial assault as well as the breakthrough to facilitate the later passage of the armoured divisions. The four regiments, reading from north to south, were:

40th RTR (sometime Leeds Rifles) ⎱ in support of
46th RTR (sometime Liverpool Welsh) ⎰ 9th Australian Division
50th RTR (sometime King's Regiment) 51st Highland Division

* During the war Sandhurst was shortened to a three months' course.

| Nil | 2nd New Zealand Division |
| 8th RTR (Regular Regiment) | 1st South African Division |

Apart from the 8th the other three were ex-Territorial infantry battalions – I may have got their old titles wrong, but I am sure about the 46th.

For the initial assault the 46th were held in reserve, later to be committed to an attack together with the 2nd/3rd Australian Infantry Battalion on Thompson's Post – a very determined outpost held by the Germans to the north on the coast. This was a disaster (an unreported minefield) and the position was taken the next morning by tanks of the 40th without infantry support. The 46th suffered severely and took no further part in the battle except for providing some reserve tanks and crews.

Throughout this battle my Brigade Commander and I (in the same tank) maintained our wireless links open to all four regiments who were otherwise acting under the orders of their respective divisional HQ. Brigadier Richards nevertheless, much to my dismay (!), kept his small HQ well forward and in a central position so as to co-ordinate the actions of the regiments; acting as 'nursemaid' he was able to bring his own influence to bear at once. But for his prompt action, for example, Thompson's Post would not have been overrun so quickly.

So you will see from this that we were able to watch progress throughout the battle at first hand.

The attack on Thompson's Post was a nightmare – literally – it was attacked at night as the earlier break-in battle had been (using false moonlight provided by searchlight beamed on the cloud base). We were trapped in the minefield along with the CO of the 46th who was severely wounded. Altogether a nasty business.

Surprisingly, as I remember, we could get little response from the 8th RTR and I set off to find them. The South Africans had not advanced to the same extent as the other divisions, and the 51st Highland in particular; I found the 8th some miles ahead of their division all alone and shooting away like mad.

So much for it being solely an infantry battle !

After the 'break-in' phase was over and the armoured divisions had made their way through, the poor old 23rd Brigade received a signal from Eighth Army, which as BM (Captain) I handed to my Brigadier

(G. W. Richards). It required that we disbanded all regiments except the Regular 8th RTR so as to provide reinforcement tanks and crews for other formations.

'I see no signal,' said the Brigadier. 'Get my staff car, a wireless van, and the Humber [this was an armoured car, sometime Derbyshire Yeomanry, I think, which we had looted from the battlefield]. You, me and Tony [Major Tony Robarts, 11th Hussars and our DAQMG*] are going up to XXX Corps to sell some Valentines.'

And off we went. By the time we reached Corps HQ they were beyond Benghazi, confronted by determined resistance at Barsa Brega or Buerat – I forget which – and without any tanks. Such as they had were operating down south in the desert. Suffice to say that up came the 23rd, mainly by transporter. Thinking they would motor across the desert by way of Msus, the Brigadier sent me to meet them at Fort Antelat. I went in the Humber which broke down leaving me and my crew in the desert without food or water for five days. I was rescued by the Greek Brigade, which I mistook for Italians. Awkward.

When I got back my Brigadier's comment was: 'You're late.' But I got the Humber back.

The 23rd were the first tanks into Misurata, Homs, Tripoli, Ben Gardane, Mareth and accompanied the 51st Highland Division all the way to Tunis. They were also among the first tanks into Sicily, Italy and, later, Greece.

Talk about turning a blind eye!

While the Western Desert of Egypt comprised a good deal of areas of soft sand – the Munassib Depression in particular – the Libyan plateau was a fairly hard gravel desert and it was possible for light vehicles, scout cars, staff cars, etc., to reach speeds of 50 mph if need be. Tanks, too, could go at speeds limited only by their design.

Prior to Alamein, ground had not been a major factor. It mattered not – except to the press and the War Cabinet for reasons of war propaganda – whether we advanced or withdrew so long as we were weakening or destroying the enemy. Like the fleets at sea. But Alamein was a different proposition altogether; to lose the battle meant the loss of Egypt.

The desert could be both enemy and friend. As an enemy it brought to both sides lack of water, for drinking, washing and the vehicle radiators, sand storms – the dreaded *Hamsein* – and blinding sand from

* A staff officer. See preliminary notes.

the tank or vehicle in front. And burning heat. Our tanks got so hot that you would burn your skin off; fighting compartments became an inferno. The sand got into everything – one's hair, eyes, ears, tea (the blessed drink) and our food. If your tank was hit the first thing you would know would be the clouds of sand blown up from the floor of the fighting compartment. If a sandstorm came, and they would come without warning, you would hope that it would clear off you before the enemy; if the other way round he would be shooting at you well ahead of time. I was much concerned when first I went into the desert because I found that all my brother officers reeked of perfume. I came to think they had been there too long! Later I realised that they had raided all the Cairo hair-dressing saloons, men and women, for dry shampoo – requiring no water. I, of course, had none. If you were near the sea and had sea-water soap, there was no great problem. But I wasn't – the tanks seemed to live only down south.

But it could also be a friend. Apart from Egypt, where one found a good supply of flies near the coast, there was virtually no animal or insect life. Just the occasional jerboa – the desert rat (a nice, friendly little fellow) – the scorpion and an occasional gazelle. The Arabs and their camels kept well out of the way. The sand was clean too. When we found we had a case of athlete's foot the MO said simply, 'Take your boots and socks off and walk about in the sand – it will clear it up' – which it did. An officer who lost his leg below the knee having lost also his tank and crew used the sand to quench the wound before being taken prisoner by the Germans.

Either you liked the desert – its vastness and the reduction of human values to the barest essentials – or you hated it. I liked it. Navigation was all-important. The desert has no landmarks, or precious few; the maps were for the most part just blank areas with the odd track marked – if you could find them.

I do not recall ever being hungry. Disenchanted with the diet, yes. Mostly 'meat and veg' stews in tins. And those damned tins of peaches. Condensed milk. I used to like it as a child! The tea, which only soldiers can brew, was marvellous. In tanks we had an advantage; if you packed the tins close to the exhaust pipes you could cook as you motored! That we rarely went hungry was due to our echelon commanders and the RASC.

We spoke about fatigue. The distance between fear and courage is narrow. If you are fit, wide awake and on the ball things do not seem too bad; if you are exhausted and down, then nothing seems possible – just let it all end, for God's sake!

The danger of fear is worse for the private soldier than for the officer and NCO. The former has much time in which to think, sitting in a puddle of mud waiting to get up and, with a supposedly glad cry, after an interminable night spent in bitter cold and without even a smoke, to launch himself plus rifle and bayonet at the well dug-in and fortified foe. The latter, on the other hand, have so much on their minds, issuing orders, checking, etc., that they have little or no time in which to ponder on their likely fate.

War is an obscenity. No one knows this better than the soldier, sailor and airman, who see it in the raw. The hero is not shot in the shoulder for the heroine to bandage; he has his jaw blown off, or he is disembowelled. It matters not whether he is friend or foe – we were all in this bloody desert and this bloody war together. In the infantry it was worse; in tanks you did not always see the bodies – they were inside, burnt to a cinder.

Alamein was a great and very significant battle which no doubt changed the course of the war. It was not a great battle in terms of numbers on either side – each had some fifteen divisions or so – and in those terms cannot be compared with, say, Stalingrad.

But we didn't know it, at least not then. We had killed or taken prisoner a lot of people, but we hadn't destroyed the Axis armies. They had to be chased, all the way to Tunis, then Sicily, then Italy and so on. To us in the Desert Army it was just another flog; up the 'blue', as the BM had said that day.

To me Alamein had another significance. Prior to the battles and the arrival of 'Monty' (who was given so much that his predecessors had lacked), the desert had been the home of what could almost be described as a 'private army'. When first I had arrived at Abbasia Barracks in Cairo straight from a convoy from England, my 'draft' of RAC officers had been told by an immaculately dressed cavalry colonel (with only one arm and a DSO): 'Two things. Forget everything you have ever learned in England. And learn to do as you are told.' No Sam Brownes, no polished buttons, no 'bull'. Bush jackets, suède boots (later to be called desert boots), perfumed hair shampoo, silk scarves (to keep out tthe sand), little or no saluting, but know what you're on. No kit. Just a change of pants and vest, socks, two blankets and a ground sheet. We lived on our tanks, armoured cars, whatever; rank could count only to the extent that you could earn respect. All took their turn in cooking, rearming, refuelling, checking the guns, etc. All slept together under the same tarpaulin. Vehicles tied together with string, almost. Loot the battlefield – for extra wireless sets, batteries, ammo, water, fuel, anything that could come in handy. We listened to 'Lili Marlene' on the German's radio; our tune as well as theirs; there was an empathy with the other man 'on the other side of the hill'. Only poets can capture the feeling and sense of those days – or music.

After Alamein so much changed. We had the kit, almost in abundance, we were chasing and they were running. The old days were gone. Perhaps it might be fair to say that from now on commanders would be judged more upon their obeying of sound orders than upon initiative. I don't know.

*

From Mr W. E. Bowles, MC

In late 1942, there seemed to be a general feeling in my division (10th Armoured) that, having stopped Rommel dead in his Alam El Halfa attack, we now had a commander who knew the answers; we sensed that Monty didn't intend going on the offensive until he was sure of winning and when it could be seen that masses of reinforcements and modern tanks were rolling in we felt we were on a sure winner in the next round.

On the night the Alamein battle started the artillery bombardment was awe-inspiring. I think we felt that a few hours of that treatment would make minesweeping operations in the corridors unnecessary – how wrong we were it later proved.

At the time I was WO II in charge of Divisional HQ Protective Troop, and in battle the Divisional Commander (Major-General A. Gatehouse) used my tank as his means of visiting the forward regiments and maintaining radio communication with the various units, and with the Corps Commander. In the early morning of 25th October (about 0400 hrs) I had to call him to the radio (General Gatehouse) to receive a rocket from Monty for not being in the place Monty thought he should be. On going forward, conforming to Monty's wishes, we found ourselves two-thirds of the way down the southern mine-cleared corridor in an unholy traffic-jam of tanks, supply trucks (wanting to get unloaded and back out before daylight), Bren carriers, guns, etc., in an atmosphere reminiscent of the old-fashioned London pea-souper – in those corridors the heavy traffic churned up the sand as fine dust, which filled the atmosphere and brought visibility down to three or four yards. I think this made my most nightmarish memory: the way ahead was choked with vehicles, the way back was also choked with follow-up traffic; anyone foolish enough to try a detour round a broken-down vehicle was likely to hit a mine. There was the heavy roar of a score of tank engines, frantic shouts and messages, urgent calls on the radio telling one to 'do this' and 'go there', and into this blind maelstrom was falling a generous dose of enemy artillery fire. *That* corridor didn't open up according to plan and in fact it was abandoned and sealed off shortly afterwards.

Another of my memories was, as an experiment, towing with my tank a 3.7 in AA gun, with the gun crew hanging on up behind me. The idea was that at last light each day we'd dash out into no-man's-land and, on the command 'Action!', we'd do a 180° U-turn and halt, the gun-crew would jump down, lay the gun on to an indicated target (most likely a disabled enemy tank – probably track broken but not 'brewed-up') and give it the *coup de grâce* – this to prevent it being towed back and salvaged during the night. Unfortunately after two or three shots the gun's recoil – via the towing shackle – cracked the tank's transmission housing, and that stopped our bit of fun : I don't think the idea was popular with the infantry anyway – a flat trajectory shell at about head height is a bit disconcerting!

I think the most 'telling' event of the whole battle, from a tank soldier's point of view, was that after about ten days of the crumbling dog-fight, Monty, at an 'Order group', said that the final breakthrough would be achieved by 9th Armoured Brigade crashing through the anti-tank screen, regardless of losses. When the Brigade Commander ventured an estimation that this would cost 75% casualties, Monty replied that if it cost 100% it would still go in . . . and I saw the remnants of that Charge of the Heavy Brigade coming back in dribs and drabs – shades of Balaklava.

To me, and to my comrades, the big disappointment of Alamein was that in spite of our predominance, when the break came, with all our tanks, SP guns, etc., and our short supply lines against the very long ones of the enemy, yet the Afrika Korps got away without being trapped, and was able to fight a masterly tactical withdrawal all the way back to Tunisia.

*

From Mr B. H. B. Milner, MBE

Just before dawn on 27th October we advanced through the mines towards Miteirya Ridge. Delay was caused by a mix-up. Once we were all facing the wrong direction. It was practically light when we sorted ourselves out and led the way through more minefields to the ridge. We were to attack a tactical feature known as 'Shield' (also a dump) and to protect the Rifle Brigade. As we approached the ridge the battle began,

58

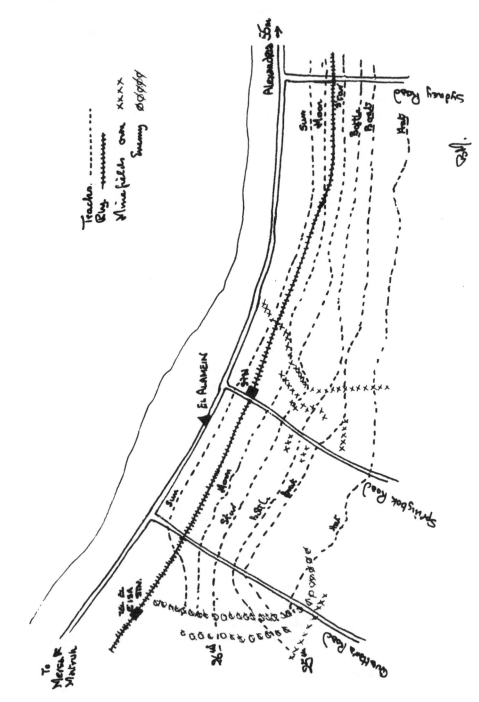

the ground was unfavourable for us and the shellfire very intense. Jerry had everything possible in front of us : AT guns, light field guns, 88 mm and 105 mm and some of our twenty-five-pounders. Mk III and Mk IV tanks. Fighting became very fierce. Orders came through that in spite of everything we must advance. C Squadron encountered enemy tanks and were fighting a losing battle as the odds were too great, many of our tanks were hit and put out of action. The Jerry guns seemed to be all round us. By now enemy HE shellfire, both impact and air bursting, was getting intense and in the dust and smoke observation was difficult.

Orders came through that Shield would be taken at all costs. 41st-47th Squadrons were to attack in waves, 47th leading. The attack was put in. Great toll was taken of our tanks, many were hit by close-range anti-tank fire, several caught fire. Artillery assistance was repeatedly asked for, but wasn't forthcoming, as the spots couldn't be pinpointed on the map. It was obvious that Shield could not be taken by storm, so the attackers withdrew to the ridge again.

While all this was going on, we were continually on the move following the CO's tank and dodging shells. Several Germans and Italians came 'out of the ground' and gave themselves up. Nobody knew what to do with them, so a trooper from B Squadron rustled them together and passed them back. As the column departed, others appeared and ran full-tilt after the retreating column. Mr Canfor, wandering amongst the tanks without a tin-hat, came across a Jerry and brought him over for us to have a look at. The RAF appeared and dropped a few bombs, then the artillery opened up with 105 mm from 'Priests', and so the attack died down about dinner-time and we came back from the ridge to replenish and check up.

I got the old stove going and made some coffee. We got out of the tank and examined our bruises. There were holes in the mudguard, blanket box, funnels, the bedrolls and sundry other things we carried on the outside of the tank, but nothing serious. The number of tanks still running in the regiment was only about nine – imagine our feelings when, just as the coffee was drinkable, over the wireless came the order that 21st Panzer Division were advancing from the south and were three miles away near Shield and we must prepare to meet them. So back to the ridge went our little party and waited.

The sun went down, but the attack never came. We just had a few shots at the old crowd, and as darkness fell we retired back to the head of Star track and went into harbour – and what an empty harbour. A few tanks kept on rolling in as the recovery section got them out of the minefields or from the ridge. We made ourselves an elaborate meal from our private store, then climbed aboard the tank and fell asleep for a couple of hours. We needed a lot of rest, though the pep tablets had worked wonders.

The noise of mess-tins brought us completely to our senses at three o'clock on Tuesday morning. B Echelon had arrived with food, water, fuel, cigarettes and sweets. We ate, and replenished the tank, and got down for another snooze. Before dawn I was rudely awakened and while still in a daze whisked off to 'Uncle' Brown tank. I didn't like it a bit. I was happy and very confident in 'Regina'. But 'orders is orders', so I made the best of a bad job. In our crew we all did a fair share and worked together. I'm sorry to say this cannot be said of every crew.

Now I became a 75 mm gunner; we were back to the ridge before dawn and prepared for action. We were in a fighting troop now and were known as Don 4. Strangely enough when the attack started Don 1, 2 and 3 were called up, but never Don 4, 5 and 6, so we went up and had a little do of our own, though I didn't fire many shots. I scored one direct hit on a Mk III or Mk IV and put it out of action and put down some very near shots on other tanks and transport. I had a shot at an 88 at long range, but didn't wait to see if I was successful. This 88 suddenly appeared on the skyline in a spot where a Red Cross van had been standing for a quarter of an hour.

Greater caution was exercised today and at lunch-time, much to our disappointment, the Brigadier ordered us back. We replenished the ammo stock and brewed up and awaited orders to return to the ridge. They never came. While we waited, over came the RAF – eighteen bombers with fighter escort. They never broke formation and dropped their bombs on Shield and passed on. Jerry ack-ack was very poor indeed. The artillery was putting down a barrage occasionally, so absolute havoc was created amongst the enemy. Ten minutes after the first wave of bombers was passed, another came. They appeared five times, then all was quiet; only a few shells were heard bursting.

Later that afternoon we were sent back through the minefields to the junction of Star track and Qattara Road, leaving the taking of Shield to the infantry.

*

From Mr H. Metcalfe

We were not a specialised unit but survivors of the Libyan battles making our way back (some with equipment, others without) to the frontier of Egypt, where the next stand was to be made. In the area of

Sollum this small column was formed, a fighting force to harry and keep contact with the enemy's progress. At this time the Axis forces were advancing very fast. The emphasis was on delay, to give our main forces time to reorganise into a defensive line. The column consisted of a composite squadron of the Queen's Bays and 4th Hussars, which were the armour. The artillery unit and infantry I cannot positively identify. It was under the command of Major Lord Knebworth of the Bays.

At Ruweisat Ridge on 2nd July a mixed force of the Bays, 4th and 10th Hussars and 9th Lancers repelled an attack, routing thirty enemy tanks. On 4th July this composite squadron, now under the command of the 9th Lancers, helped to repel an attack and Lord Knebworth was killed. There is no doubt he would have received a decoration for outstanding leadership and bravery but for this.

About the middle of July we re-equipped and a squadron of the 8th Hussars was joined with two squadrons of the 4th Hussars – now to be known as 4th/8th Hussars. We joined the 4th Light Armoured Brigade with the Bays and KRRCs at Himeimat.

In the attack on the enemy's rear on 2nd September we had been formed into a group consisting of 4th/8th Hussars, J Battery RHA, some six-pdr anti-tank guns and C Company of the KRRCs. Later in the October battle we were transferred from Munassib to the 2nd New Zealand Division for the breakthrough.

Through all this one must not forget the magnificence of the Desert Air Force. Who can forget those eighteen Bostons (bombers) flying in impeccable formation at regular intervals to bomb the enemy lines.

In my humble opinion, although much has been written about Alamein, the Eighth Army's finest hours were during the early days of July 1942 when those that had got back to Alamein after a gruelling retreat turned and stood and thwarted the Axis conquest of Egypt.

Recollections

Shadowing the enemy advance into Egypt was a British force consisting of sixteen light tanks (Honeys), eight twenty-five-pounders, carrier-borne infantry and supply trucks, a hotch-potch of survivors from the June battles in Libya. We ran part of the time alongside the enemy, separated only by a short distance of desert. Our object was to disrupt the enemy lines of supply.

Throughout the night we hid in the desert, listening to the rattle and rumble of an enemy column passing by. In the sky to the east, the signal lights of enemy camps soared, sombre proof of the enemy's success. At first light we broke camp, moved east on the prowl, sought out unwary enemy camps, shot up lorries and sometimes bagged a few tanks. Then away, to wait and ambush other columns moving up in the wake of their advance. Sometimes a few enemy tanks would be amongst them and so a small battle would develop for a few hours, thus creating delay, confusion and damage, scattering their lorries far and wide. We broke off any engagement in the early evening and retired into the all-enveloping black desert night.

There was no news of how our main forces were faring. The enemy flares moving farther and farther east was enough.

When we settled down for the night, a square was formed : tanks on three sides pointing outwards, twenty-five-pounders similarly on the remaining side, infantry placed between them, all other vehicles inside the square. Then would start the refuelling, servicing, etc., all done as quietly as possible. Petrol-tins, shells, passed from hand to hand, conversation was in whispers, a bite to eat, bully and hard biscuits and water, nothing warm, although the nights were cold. Every man did a half-hour's guard, so that every weapon was manned during the night – and so to a little sleep. All too soon came the call at first light to break camp. Another munch of hard tack and away. It was at mid-day that you got at the hard tack with a little comfort and leisure. The sun was blazing down and the shimmering heat haze interfered with accuracy of observation and fire for both sides, so a little respite was obtained and maybe a quick brew.

Late in the afternoon south of Mersa Matruh, there were sounds of a heavy conflict. We turned towards it and arrived in darkness to find some British troops trying to fight their way out of an enemy encirclement. So we took to the high ground outside the ring and poured fire of all arms into the midst of the enemy. Utter confusion enabled some of our troops to escape. These we escorted out of the area to safety and then left them to go back to marauding. This was a satisfying episode as we could see the direct result of our intervention.

In the Fuka area on 30th June, there was grave concern over petrol. Fortunately an enemy HQ was spotted resting in the sun – a big communication vehicle and many lorries, the guns amongst them still limbered up. In the tanks, accompanied by the carrier-borne infantry, went the twenty-five-pounders adding to the turmoil. The communication vehicles were destroyed and two petrol lorries captured. Lorries were fleeing in all directions, amongst them in a staff car a high-ranking German officer. The car was promptly knocked out, but he ran to a lorry and boarded it. This was disabled. The radio was screaming, 'Get him, get him !' – but he thwarted capture, being picked up by another vehicle. This coincided with the arrival of enemy tanks who stopped our gallop. Now on the defensive, the British column slowly retreated, the twenty-five-pounders deterring all attempts by the enemy to get to close quarters.

We now have petrol, the knocked-out staff car provides five hundred English cigarettes and twelve gallons of water, all shared out. The infantry have come back with thirty German prisoners.

That night we did not form a square but mustered double line ahead. It was time now to get back to the British lines some fifty miles away. At 11 pm we started off double line ahead, tanks leading, carrier-borne infantry at the rear. No shooting unless shot at was the order. The enemy lights and flares in the sky seemed to be all around us.

All that night we travelled, every now and again passing through enemy camps, some just looking on with hands in pockets, others leaping out of bed-rolls to avoid being crushed and shouting angrily. Our salvation must have been that the enemy were using so much captured material that they thought it was their own troops moving up. At seven o'clock in the morning we were recognised by a German observation officer. It would be about seven miles out from the British line, which had been alerted of our approach. The column was now racing through heavy shellfire, enemy forces were coming out to cut us off. Then the British guns opened fire and laid a curtain of fire around us. So the column arrived safely with its bag of prisoners at seven-thirty in the morning of 1st July at Alamein, weary but relieved that we had not finished up in the bag. As we picked our way through the FDLs, the South Africans' waves and smiles conveyed welcome and ours, 'Glad to be here.'

We re-equipped with reconditioned Honeys and were off to Himeimat in the south for vigorous patrolling and observation duties. Up before first light, we were through the FDLs and settled into the observation area before the dawn; we reported back over the radio every half-hour for enemy movement. We left at last light, coming in to our own lines turrets reversed – a sign that we were friends. When we reached the regiment's area, we got a cup of hot onion soup. Sometimes we had to ask over the radio for a tracer to be fired into the air to direct us to the correct area. 'Toffee apple' was the code word for tracer. You then heard over the radio a guttural German voice : 'Come over here, ve will give you Toffee Apple.' It becomes a bit of a lark this, and makes our day.

I remember the never-ending battle during the day with flies – eating and drinking became a work of art, one hand waving back and forth over the food, the other hand waiting, then a quick rush to the mouth before they pounced again. They were around mouth, eyes, face, anywhere there was moisture. They settle on the rim of hot cups of tea in dozens.

Warnings came of an enemy attack, so it was off to sleep fully dressed except for boots. Five days later, just before midnight, we were alerted. Heavy gunfire, and we waited for the signal in the sky that would denote a major enemy attack. Red over white over green. It was a major attack; we moved out to battle positions. Through the radio a message : 'There will be no retreat. You die where you stand.' That last bit didn't sound very encouraging.

The early-morning light revealed the enemy like a great black snake, its head getting on with the job of getting through the minefields. Now to the business of stopping him. The enemy was already suffering under the combined weight of fire from infantry, tanks and artillery, plus bombing. The enemy were through the minefields, the infantry came back under covering fire from tanks and artillery. The tanks and twenty-five-pounders alongside now took over. Slowly we retreated under the weight of the attack, but it was no walk-over for the enemy. Guns and tanks worked together – first one, then the other, retired, exacting a heavy toll. The enemy was moving very slowly; he was in very bad shape. Then he turned north, leaving us on his southern flank. Things were becoming less hectic now.

Once again we formed into a column of tanks, artillery and infantry, and moved south into the Qattara Depression, then moved west towards Himeimat and, when nearly back to our original front line, peeped over a ridge. Hundreds of enemy lorries lay in the valley preparing to move. In the tanks went. The lorries were laid out in lines like ships at a review. Down the lanes raced the tanks, every piece of armament being used. Lorries were burning, blowing up, the enemy rushing away to find cover. Lorries were scattering, but again the appearance of enemy tanks forced us to retire. Over fifty lorries were destroyed, many more damaged and of course we had our usual collection of prisoners. We got back to our own lines well satisfied, to learn that the enemy forces had been repulsed by our main forces and were retreating.

So it was back again to the fortification of a new line, the patrols, spotting, etc., and the build-up for the next battle. It was September now – June seemed decades away. More troops were coming into the desert and new equipment – it's getting rather crowded. Now began in October the exercise of advancing through minefields. There was now much troop movement and the French took over our part of the line whilst we move up a little. The big battle must be very near.

At mid-day on 23rd October we were told the balloon goes up tonight. At 9.40 pm the great barrage opened. The whole British front was a mass of rippling flame as you looked back at it – ear-splitting noise so that you could not hear the tank engine turning over as we waited for the signal to move forward. At 10 pm the barrage lifted and the columns of tanks, guns, etc., moved forward into the minefields. The gaps in the minefield were lit by small lamps. Tracers were racing through the night, also as a guide. Then there was a temporary stoppage – later it was found that the obstacles in front had bogged us down and we were not getting through the enemy minefields. It turned into a stalemate.

The regiment was withdrawn and sent north to join the New Zealanders. There were signs of a breakthrough, the gap was made and off with the NZs for the chase. El Daba, Fuka, Mersa Matruh, Halfaya, past Tobruk – all the familiar names again.

The Honeys were now nearing the end of their tether but they had served us well, and had proved excellent when used correctly. Whoever nicknamed the Stuart tank – 'Honey' – was not far wrong. It was the perfect vehicle for reconnaissance, but too often in the past it had to be used as a front-line tank and suffered accordingly.

*

From Mr M. Bailey

The Staffordshire Yeomanry went abroad to Palestine in December 1939 and served as cavalry for two years. We were then mechanised and at the time of Alamein we had one squadron of British Crusaders and two squadrons of American Grants with A Squadron having some Shermans.

We were in the 8th Armoured Brigade along with the 3rd Royal Tanks and the Sherwood Rangers, Notts Yeomanry. For the Battle of Alamein we were in the 10th Armoured Division, but after the break-out we were formed into an Independent Armoured Brigade Group. Our first real action came on 31st August, when the enemy launched an attack on the Alamein line. This attack failed and the Brigade was withdrawn on 14th September.

For us the Battle of Alamein started on 18th October. We were moved to the south of the Alamein line in order to deceive the enemy. On the night of the 21st we were moved out in darkness and dummy tanks were left in our positions. We moved north to a new concentration area east of the Miteirya Ridge where the tanks were disguised as trucks by having a canvas body placed over them.

On the 23rd, the CO briefed us on our rôle which was to break through and execute a flanking movement. At 1915 hours we moved forward for the first phase of the attack. We reached our report line at 2135 hours and five minutes later the great barrage which heralded the opening of the Battle of Alamein blazed forth. This was my first experience of a big battle and I did not know whether to be frightened by the noise or reassured by our fire power. At this time I was radio operator in a Sherman tank. The radio operator in a Sherman is also the loader for the turret mounted 75 mm gun and the coaxially mounted Browning machine-gun. As in this position one can only see out through a periscope, one can only judge what is going on by listening to the radio. We were on a regimental 'Net' at this time; that is, all tanks in the regiment were on the same frequency, so one could hear of the progress of all the regiment.

At 0200 hours on 24th October the regiment passed through the start line and through our own and enemy minefields, and by first light we were 'hull down' on Miteirya Ridge. The brigade was eventually counter-attacked by German tanks and anti-tank guns. The brigade claimed a total of over forty tanks destroyed.

On the 25th we withdrew into close laager in preparation for another advance to El Wiska. This was done during the night and we ran into intense 88 mm anti-tank fire. The regiment suffered very heavy casualties and were forced to withdraw having lost two Crusaders and fourteen heavies. Although I saw action many times in later years, I think this was the worst action I remember. We just could not see the enemy and could not take evasive action because of minefields. The 8th and 9th Armoured Brigades lost many tanks that night and the blazing wrecks illuminating the battlefield made us sitting ducks for the 88 mm gunners. To me it was a good example of how not to use tanks at night.

During the 26th we were able to get some rest and reinforcements in men and tanks arrived. On 28th we moved back into the line to relieve the Bays and took up battle positions opposite the 15th and 21st Panzer Divisions. On 29th the Notts Yeomanry were heavily attacked and we went to their assistance.

On 1st November the first signs of a breakthrough were becoming apparent and on the 2nd General Montgomery's orders for Operation Supercharge were received. The regiment moved along the Coast Road and down the 'Diamond' Track through the minefields. Some opposition was encountered but by the 4th the regiment was through to open country.

*

From Mr J. Ruane

I can honestly say that in retrospect I am glad I was there and that I lived with so many wonderful people. Fear was there all right, but everybody was the same and one could even joke and laugh.

Prior to the battle when Montgomery arrived it was clear to us that this was to be the final battle and – if we lost it – it would be every man for himself, an overland trek up through Palestine, Syria and Persia. The Navy had left Alexandria and this was the final curtain. Monty certainly imbued everybody with confidence and we trained hard with new Sherman tanks.

The day before we had a last open-air service with the padre and I looked around as we stood wondering how many of us would be alive tomorrow. I remember the last preparations, the issue of rations, the benzedrine tablets to keep us awake, the mounting excitement and tension as the hours crept on.

The terrific barrage of twenty-five-pounders started at twenty minutes to ten on Friday night and the noise was impossible to imagine. We moved off under the barrage to get through the minefield by first light and on to the first enemy-held ridge. I found the only way I could follow the tank in front was to follow its exhaust flames, as I could not see the tapes or lamps marking the gap in the churned-up dust. This journey I think was about fourteen miles and was a nightmare of noise and confusion and shelling. To give you an idea of the extent of the barrage on the first ridge, one could almost step from one shell-hole to the next, but the enemy were dug well in and far down.

However, as the dawn appeared they came out in thousands to give themselves up, mostly Italians, screaming and holding rosary beads and prayer-books. It was a scene from Dante's *Inferno*. The order came over the air to stop shooting at them. I distinctly remember the Germans refusing to sit with them and keeping to themselves in groups.

As the light became full day, the sky overhead became black with fighter planes and bombers trying to shoot each other down. I saw instances of pilots being shot whilst descending by parachute, both by our fighter pilots and the Germans. This was indeed war with a vengeance. I remember jumping on top of the turret on my tank and asking Major Everleigh, who was trying to shoot down a plane with the .5 machine-gun, to let me have a go. The excitement was terrific.

Then as the day wore on the sight of sappers lining up and going over the ridge to probe for mines with bayonets was terrible and awe-inspiring to watch. Every one of them deserved a medal, as they seemed to go to certain death. They no sooner 'went over' than bursts of enemy machine-gun fire seemed to wipe them out; then another line would form up, stub their cigarettes out and move over the top. It was a privilege to be in the company of such men.

The distance to the main enemy defences was, I believe, about a thousand yards and this ground was fought on and contested until the final assault on 2nd November. In the interim period the losses were immense. We tried attacking by first light on several occasions and on different sectors and I can remember with pride the courage of all concerned.

The 9th Armoured Brigade was under direct command of General Freyburg, who I think was the greatest soldier of all time. At the final battle on 2nd November we were given the task of breaching the enemy line and, after the battle, Brigadier Currie told us that when he was allocated that task Montgomery had told him he would accept 100% casualties and indeed this is practically what happened. If I remember correctly we were left with seventeen tanks in the whole brigade and ceased to exist as a brigade. The Germans broke and ran. I have a distinct memory on 5th November we were limping out to the rear and had stopped for a few moments. I was dismounted and talking to another tank driver, Trooper Sweeting, who was showing me a perfect AP shell-hole right in front of his seat, when, out of the sun with engines switched off, came a bunch of Stukas who strafed us with cannon fire.

We reformed at Mena, re-trained at full strength and subsequently joined the fighting in Italy. I had previously taken part in the invasion of Teheran, but the Alamein battle was a sheer slogging match over open sights, brutal and horrifying. I can remember dust churned to a fine powder moving back and forth like liquid away from the tank tracks as it swirled over the bodies of men.

I remember the sheer exhaustion as we laagered up at night and filled up the tanks with fuel, drew rations, etc. Then the benzedrine tablets and the move again at first light. Each night was the same – so and so had bought it, such and such a troop had bought it. Even so, the spirit was marvellous. For men to live in those conditions for twelve days with the noise of constant battle was unbelievable. We nearly all had our fingers and knuckles septic and filthy from the attention of the damned flies who feasted on us, on every little cut and scratch.

I remember broadcasting home to my people (with others of course) and being introduced on the air as a member of the famous 9th Armoured Brigade who helped to breach the line at Alamein. I could write for hours of the laughs we shared before the battle and then the misery of losing all those wonderful brave lads who failed to return.

But the desert was the place to fight. It was clean and beautiful till we despoiled it with the hell of war. But it was man to man, and women and children were sacred to our minds. This altered horribly in Italy and I can still see a young woman crouching in a ditch holding an infant in her arms, completely insane with fear. This was my first day of war in Italy and one I shall never forget.

In conclusion then – I am glad I was there and believe I am a better person for being privileged to have met some real men at that time and to have shared with them those frightening and, for all that, very great days.

*

From Mr L. Devenish

As the driver of a Matilda tank fitted with flail attachment I took part in the first wave of the main Alamein offensive. Our flail broke down in the first minefield and our tank was subsequently destroyed. I took no further part in the offensive.

Prior to this I was involved in a rearguard action when we were falling back towards the Alamein line. We were on detachment from our unit, 42nd RTR, and had been sent to join 'The Rash Force', named I think after its leader. I do not know where we fought, but it must have been fairly close to the final defensive position.

*

From Mr G. Parlour

Alamein was not exactly a comedy show, but still we managed to get a few laughs. I was a tank driver with A Squadron, 40th RTR, and it was always my big ambition to get a job with a mobile bath unit – they used to come up the blue and give us a shower once every so often – but I never made it.

So there I was – lumbered with the job of driving this tank. The tank was a Valentine with (don't laugh) a two-pounder and a Besa machine-gun! The Jerries, of course, had 75s on their Mark IVs and on the Tigers – which luckily for us didn't get to Africa in time for the Alamein do – had 88s! Mind you, the Jerries had the 88s at Alamein all right and some time after it was all over we were driving along the coast road – still in pursuit but a long way behind – when we came across what I thought was a bloody great naval gun sticking up in the air which had been knocked out by the side of the road.

'What the hell's that?' I asked the chap looking out of the top of the tank.

'Oh,' he said, 'that's an 88.'

Well, this was the first time I had seen one close up. 'Jesus Christ!' I said, and stalled the engine.

But let me tell you about the mess-tins. In those days we had no plates and we ate all our grub out of these mess-tins and even drank our tea out of them, too, if we lost our mugs. Well, mine were getting a bit rusty and rumour was that the stores had just received a batch of new ones. So I put them down on the sand and ran over them with the tank. But, of course, when I got round to the stores the rumour was false and so I had to straighten them out again. And what a job that was.

Then – this was before the actual battle took place – they actually had us going round the desert picking up pieces of paper! Well, this got up everybody's nose and I wrote home saying that our lot wanted the desert looking nice and clean for when Rommel arrived. But the mail was censored and they didn't like that bit, so I had to cross it out. And got another bollocking.

This next bit is quite true and I have told it to many people but I don't think one of them ever believed it. Jerry was stonking hell out of us and I was beginning to think, 'Hell, it's only a matter of time,' when our tank commander – I'll never forget his name, it was Corporal Shaw – said to me, 'Take it up about twenty to thirty yards.' So I took it up twenty or thirty yards and one fell right where we had been. Then he said, 'Go back to where you were.' So I reversed back and a second one landed right on the spot we had just vacated. Shaw said, 'You're OK now, stay put.' How in hell did he know that? It's something that has puzzled me ever since.

Our adjutant was killed in one action. His gunner – a corporal – received the MM and the driver twenty-eight days' jankers.* I forget what the jankers was for, but it was all in the same action.

They say it's better to be born lucky than rich – so these days I never complain about my luck. After Alamein our tank had more holes in it than a string vest. The easiest way to knock out a tank, of course, is to knock off the track. And if only one of the lugs on the track is knocked inwards this brings off the track automatically. Well, they had hit our track once or twice but – lucky again – the lugs had all been knocked

* Jankers = punishment.

outwards! So, of course, the track stayed on and it still went round. How lucky can you get?

After it was all over we were taken out of the line and other mobs went through to take up the pursuit. The prisoners started arriving in droves and we would go over to have a shufti at them. I will always remember one little Itie who was pleased as Punch. Pointing ahead with a big smile he was saying, 'Alessandria! Alessandria!'

And when we finally got back home – on leave from Austria in '45 – people wanted to know about Alamein. I remember one afternoon my rich aunt came round to tea and she was asking what it was like in the desert. 'Oh,' I said, 'it was just miles and miles of f-f-f-fairly flat sand! Phew!'

And, finally, I went to only one Alamein reunion at the Festival Hall and never recognised a bloody soul.

*

From Mr J. W. Telford

I suppose I can safely confess now that I kept diaries! The 1942 one is stained with sweat from where I had put it inside one of my socks one night when we felt sure we'd be in the bag before morning. But we got away, with me then realising that there wasn't a hope in hell of the Jerries not finding the diary!

1st August: Out of hospital, made way to Amirya. 'Beer-up' in 'Rising Sun' (a marquee – awful fug). On the beer with a Grey's Sergeant and a Royal Sergeant, had no money but we got on fine when I told them my father was a Grey for his '21' years!

4th August: Some re-forming on. We're now 1st/6th RTR and 4th/8th Hussars! Four squadrons in and two in reserve?

5th August: To Alexandria. To Marconi for cable home. To United Services Club and YMCA. Cinema. Old chap tried to have me involved in a 'gold' ring. Gold?

8th August: Suddenly we are to move up into the blue! Off 2 pm. Flies terrible. Past roads to Hamman and Burg El Arab. Truck broke down. We slept out. Griff is that Churchill is out here. ['The Griff' was rumour, usually believed. And in this case the Griff was right.]

9th August: Not going up after all! Left the Chev derelict. Hung about till 2.30 waiting for a B Squadron officer. Joined up with 'Basil' again [Captain B. Forster of the 'columns']. Back to Mariopolis. We had a lot of this stop/go sort of activity. [We could take bets then and later that if we were warned that we could expect 'trouble' we would have an easy time and if they said 'this one will be a piece of cake' that was the time we knew we would be in real trouble!]

12th, 13th, 14th, 15th August: On leave in Alex.

16th August: I become the most popular bloke in B Squadron! I don't know how they had my address, but I got a parcel. Three hundred cigarettes from a Miss P. Davidson at a New York address and I don't smoke! When they had all been shared out I was adjured to write and say a thank you and maybe she'd send us some more!

24th August: Now training very seriously. Churchill at Alamein on 21st? Seemed very hopeful. Got to smash Rommel. Jerry attack expected 23rd-26th. All Allied supplies diverted to us in Middle East.

25th August: Gunnery training hotted up. To be ready too for gas. No Eighth Army allowed in Alex during this full moon. Jerries starting again? Football matches. Suddenly *flap on*. Sudden 'Stand to' to repel paratroops!

26 August: 'Stand to' at 5.30. Flappish now. Shifting people round a bit. First am Wireless Op for 'Monty' Dawson's anti-paratroop radio truck. Later restored to Driver-Op on Stubby's [Corporal Stubbs] Grant tank. 'Stand to' 7.30 pm.

28th August: Away at 10, after getting up at 5 am. To Hamman and along C Track. Flies and heat terrible. Found 1 RTR after a struggle. Stubby may not get a tank now. Not enough tanks! Crew commanders go up for a recce.

29th August: Lying about all day. Flies are very bad. They say Jerry has green fly nets for head. Wish we had! Concert party began 6 pm within sound of artillery! Very good really, particularly one chap's facial expression and characterisation. Another time we had two girls and a driver and they did classical and other dancing – again with a background of firing. All the lads thought them super and they even did the 'Seven Veils'! [A striptease act.] Reminds me. My wife would write and say she had heard on the radio some comic that made her feel close to me since he was just back from entertaining the troops in the desert. Desert my foot! The big names never got nearer us than the snooty Officers' Clubs on the Nile – till after Tripoli fell.

31st August: Crew commanders all back. Jerry attack 2 am? Now we aren't going up! Attack seems to have fizzled out. Bags of aerial activity. Bombers in swarms. Sudden move north at 11 pm.

2nd September: Bombers must be plastering Jerries. Going over in eighteens, each lot with twelve fighter escorts. More excitement. Jerries bombed with a mile of us.

3rd September: Griff is that Jerries pushed fifteen miles into our southern flank and then stopped. Redraza (Major OC B Squadron) thought we were going up. Later not going up! Another disappointment. 44th Division left here, rest back.

4th September: Back to Mariopolis. Tents 'lats', etc., by 5.30.

8th September: Sure sign we will be moving shortly – started inter-troop soccer and basket ball leagues. Competition for cleanest and best organised tent spaces! Bluddirot! Childish. Beat 7 Troop at soccer. Local Shafto cinema show, *Love comes to Andy Hardy*. We thought it quite good!

9th September: Sudden decision – B Squadron to go up. Tentage to Amirya. Arrived at B Echelon 5-ish. News of fighting. Dixie Dean – pal of mine from 43rd Tank days in Britain – burnt on top of tank, had been wounded as he tried to get out. The corporal who got him out recommended for MM, we hear. Glad Dixie's OK.

11th September: About twenty Stukas bombed a mile west of us. Had a tour of the battlefield! Taken round to see smashed Mark 3s and Mark 4s. Saw some wicked-looking high-velocity guns knocked out. Griff – Jerry 121 Brigade smashed up – caught a packet. That was their 'reconnaissance in force'.

14th September: Our ack-ack and machine-gun ack-ack can be relied on to fire on our own planes – some fool always does – even on Bostons in formation! Which reminds me of the CO – then Lieutenant-Colonel

R. M. P. Carver – 'on the air' to our liaison officer with the artillery, 'Why do the ack-ack bursts always exactly follow the Jerry planes and never catch up with them?'

18th September: Griff is that we are an armoured box to hold off a Jerry attack before Eighth Army is ready – there are only us among our Armoured Brigades – rest back refitting in a hurry. Slight enemy air activity.

22nd September: 51st Highland Division on a scheme round us. Coming up soon. Just out and in very good spirits.

[*The diary contains interesting and evocative comments on day-to-day life in the desert, but in order to conserve space and retain a balance, we continue with the period of the 3rd Battle of Alamein.*]

20th October: Jerry recce planes over. MEs? Going like fun about 500/700 feet chased by dozens of ack-ack bursts and stacks of machine-gunning. Reminded us of fox and hounds! On the whole we were for the Jerries! Odd thing – we found low-flying things hard to hit. Speed, we supposed. We are a bit worried about the state of the tanks. And now we hear we are to take them into action. We drew this one on the 17th and it's pretty duff. Rumour has it this one was sent back to stores by C Squadron as US [unserviceable]. Anyway, we are working hard on it. ['We' are B Squadron.] And we have been warned so often that we were expecting imminent action that we just shrugged it off. But there was a vague expectancy. Some distant bombing and an air crash.

22nd October: Checking of equipment going on. Rumour – no chloroform or morphia? The expectancy always produced 'funnies' like that. But it was no rumour that there were no wireless spares. Which made my tank operator job a shade difficult. An ME shot down in our regimental laager after what seemed like a suicidal bombing attack. Three of them. All down. Were they after a nearby AV [Armoured Control Vehicle]? Pep talk from CO. 'The party is about to begin.' We were invigorated not because any of us were VC hunters but we were anxious to get the job done so that we might get home and get on with living! The chaps I was with were very pro-Monty. So was I and am! But our regiment was originally Regular and in the desert *ab initio* and they were disillusioned by all those Gazala Gallops, first westwards and then driven back eastwards with only the prospect of same again.

23rd October: Lull all day. Unnatural. What's on? Sent airmail letter-cards and Christmas cards home. Advised to. Now we are told we are to get through minefields, ours first, 'May', 'June' and 'Nuts', then theirs 'January' and 'February': tremendous artillery barrage. Strange sort of echoing as if we were under an immense dome. And the continuous gun-flashes made a most weird sort of nightmarish light. We set off. Exciting, breathless. And that sort of orchestral music of the continuous guns in the background. We wondered if the Jerry saw it that way! I remember seeing a captain walking behind a Scorpion. Intent on supervising the job. This tank had a barrel fastened across its nose which revolved. Fastened by one end were chains which whirled round and thumped the ground ahead. Supposed to blow up any mines in its path. Something seemed to worry the captain and he literally screamed at the crew and someone nearby. On edge, poor devil. Some job! I wondered later why there was very little of the terrific excitement that I felt the very first time I went into action. Living dangerously palled fairly soon I suppose. Our chaps and the chaps on the ground looked a bit grim and a bit drawn. I suppose it was all that sand that made it a sort of ghoulish nightmarish day by the seaside! Enlivened by Lieutenant Adams' tank almost burning. We were stopped in the minefield 'cleared lane' and they decided to have a brew up inside the tank. Imagine! For a brew up the Eighth Army had ex-petrol four-gallon tins filled with sand soaked with petrol and lit from as far away as possible. These clots were doing it inside the tank. Something came unstuck and things went on fire a bit. What worried us was that any fire might bring down Jerry firing on all of us around. They got it out. I've always been amazed and amused by the Eighth Army's thirst for tea. We called it *shy* – we thought that arabic for 'tea' but I'm not sure. Most of the arabic we learned came from the cookhouse, where there might be Arabs working. And I never could be sure that the words we used were likely to be swear words. But whatever the Eighth achieved, and we thought it pretty considerable, they did on tea. Beer? Tinned, I think from India, and very warm. Terrible stuff. Of course, if you were a sergeant or above you were allowed whisky. I wasn't then such a superior being!

24th October: Had about ten minutes' sleep, then bags of shelling and some Italian prisoners. They looked stricken and utterly weary. Then a lull except for very big guns longer away. Then the news that the Greys and 5th Tanks had got through. Then our planes came over to do some bombing. Then one of A Squadron's tanks was hit by shelling. Then at

11 am we are to have a daylight go at getting through the minefields. Only did one, principally because A Squadron leading lost five tanks on mines with Itie infantry on hand to shoot up the crews. Hotly debated – had they or had they not cleared the mines? Then news of 4th CLY and 1/5 Queens (our lorried infantry) catching a packet. All rather apprehensive. Two hours' sleep.

25th October: Warned that Germans were to counter-attack. We – B Squadron – went on with attempt to get through by daylight. Lost a Grant. Terrible lot of just hanging about. Attempt cancelled. Didn't eat or drink till around 1500 hours.

27th October: We are to remain here. The advance seems to have petered out rather. The BBC says 'we are hanging on grimly to our gains'. To which we ask, 'What gains?' We did a practice flap. Which means we are to pretend we are suddenly attacked in laager and we are to make a good getaway. What a shambles! Were there rockets! (Tried again on 28th. Much better.) Now they say things have in fact gone well. Watched tank buster planes near Himeimat.

4th November: Away early on plan of chasing Jerries. In Deir El Murra we ran into M13s, Mark IIIs and anti-tank guns. Three abreast! Real action. Lost a Honey commander killed and another Honey and Grant knocked out. So much stuff swanning around that replenishment was very difficult. Finding our own supply vehicles was only the first hurdle. Then a mini-tank battle. Bostons joined in with two raids. We broke off action – we guessed it was so that we could dash on and cut off the Jerry stuff heading/streaming west. Late in the afternoon joined a battle line of tanks. Had some shooting. Hearing good news from all sectors.

6th November: Another chase – nineteen miles north-west. CO says on radio we are racing to 90 Light Division – old rivals of ours. We hope to cut them off and cut them up. Running fights very exciting, firing with everything at armoured cars, half-tracks and transport. Got some of them. PM. A big tank battle – my first real one. Jerries have made a line behind which they hope, we think, the 'soft' transport can get away. A downpour. Why does the rain lie on the surface? You'd think the ground would be like a sponge and soak it all up. Trouble with our crew not fighting as a team. We were knocked out. I got a gash on the wrist and another in the thigh. Evacuated. Later heard Sergeant Page was in trouble. Sorry. Wish I could have been there. Thought him good. Losses – Denny, Jury, Nicholson, Carter dead. Jones, Swift, Pyne, Tait and me wounded. We lost three tanks.

*

From Mr J. E. Delhanty

In the desert we received thirty Sherman tanks and on the 22nd we went 'up the blue'. Our C Squadron went in with Crusader tanks to persuade Jerry to come out to play, but when we arrived they had been rubbed out. We attacked on the southern sector for a couple of days, then on the central, and finally on the northern.

The night before the 27th we were given our instructions to go straight through Jerry's lines and take no prisoners.

The first trenches we came to were packed with Ities. We made short work of them, ran alongside their trenches and dropped in grenades, shouting : 'Eggs for breakfast, you bastards.' We then went back, with one track on the edge, and gave them a quick burial.

As we rolled down into the *wadi* we spotted eight Mark IVs and promptly engaged them; we were in hell's delight at the thought of a battle at close quarters, we were eighty yards apart. We received one on the turret; the one that sent it received a couple from me straight in the guts; we got all the crew as they baled out with the Brownings. I polished off another, then we were hit with a shell from a squeeze gun. The barrel only fires forty rounds, then it is kaput. The diameter of the shell is two inches and leaves the barrel measuring only one and a half inches. It came straight inside the tank just behind my back and set the AP ammo on fire. It was like breathing hell-fire, so we decided to bale out as we had ten cwts of HE in stock. As I rolled off the deck I went up in the air as Jerry dropped a few HEs around us. I felt a knock in my back. I rolled into a small depression and I was sure my legs had gone, then I had terrific pins and needles and found they were in working order. I heard Blackie, our radio op, screaming from the side of the tank, so I crawled back to him and pulled him away from the tank as I knew she would blow up any second. We were only fifteen feet away when the turret flew straight up in the air. It appeared to slowly turn over and dropped back on the tank.

I was taken prisoner as I was tying my hankie around one of Blackie's legs. One was snapped off and the foot on the other leg was twisted around and was only hanging on with a bit of sinew. It was two hours of terrible agony for him before he died. I held him while the doctor in their First Aid Post cut off his legs. He had given him four shots of the needle, but the shock was too great for him to go unconscious. The second driver had terrible burns on his face and arms.

There were only seven of us out of the one hundred and fifty. We gave name, rank and number, then the Jerry officer told me the day I had left England, the date we arrived on the desert and the instructions we had received the previous night. He said you took no prisoners and although you have obeyed your instructions to the letter, you have broken the Geneva convention, so will be shot at dawn. The seven of us were put in a trench and guarded with four machine-guns, but at first light the 51st Jocks were coming. The officer came to us and said we were not to be shot but handed over to the Ities. He could not wish a worse fate for anyone.

The Afrika Korps were a fine body of men, good clean fighters and well led. We ourselves were proud to be under the command of dear old Monty. None better!

II

The Infantry

From Mr Bill Winchester

As a prelude to El Alamein one should have an introduction to the terrain over which the battles were fought, for here was the ideal spot to organise wars, where armies could fight it out away from the cities, and without destroying towns and innocent women and children. Our first look at the mythical East began in the desert. The stinking horrible desert. The amazing and fabulous descriptions set out in tour journals of the mysterious desert and exotic cities of the glamorous East must have been written by someone who had not been farther than his local cinema to see a technicolour production, for their imagination is a million times more creative than nature intended these sand-swept, sun-parched, insect-infected, diseased, desolate, barren lands ever to be.

Summer 1941, and an HM troopship docked at Basra to unload on to the quay an assortment of men that were later to help in weaving the intricate pattern of history from Baghdad to Trieste. We journeyed across the desert through Baghdad, coming to rest on the shores of Lake Habbaniya, where we underwent intensive training in desert warfare. Several months later we left for the Western Desert ('up the blue', as it was called), to take up defensive positions at El Duda a few miles outside Tobruk. Here we helped in the defence of Tobruk until the middle of June 1942, when the German offensive was well under way, and we received orders to withdraw.

Our battery commander at that time was Major Allfrey, who had to all outward appearances been a pre-war gentleman farmer, and I believe would have much rather have been on horseback leading the hunt than in a jeep leading our battery of artillery. He was hardly ever seen without his familiar jodhpur breeches and riding boots, and a horse's tail switch in his hand. A hunting horn hung in the cab of his truck.

Everything except our guns and bare essentials were destroyed at El

79

Duda and at dusk on 17th June we withdrew with Major Allfrey at our head and the Afrika Korps at our heels. During the night we were fired on by enemy artillery, and dive-bombed by Stukas, suffering heavy casualties in both men and equipment. Our retreat eastward came to a halt at dawn, when enemy forces were sighted blocking our way directly ahead, and further unidentified forces were sighted directly to the north. A bren-carrier and crew were sent out to reconnoitre and find out the identity of the troops to the north. These proved to be hostile, thus making it clear that we now had the enemy behind us to the west, in front to the east, and on our left to the north. The only direction now appearing clear of the enemy lay on our right to the south.

This direction was taken, but, as we had been observed by the enemy, the forces to the east and west swept round and kept pace in parallel lines with us, and the forces to the north gave chase at our heels. It was not long before a halt was again called when more troops were sighted again directly ahead to the south. With the aid of field-glasses these were quickly identified as German from the markings on their vehicles, and further observation showed them to be still closed up in their night laager. Orders were given for the trails of our remaining guns to be dropped ready for action, and the three sections of pursuing Germans, having apparently watched our movements, also halted and took up positions more or less boxing us in. If ever I thought that my number was up, this was it. For remnants of our battery to take on what at that seemed to me to be Rommel's complete army would certainly have been suicide, and to my mind it would have been far better to have swallowed our pride, raised our hands above our heads, shown a white flag and surrendered, becoming live cowards and not dead heroes.

Major Allfrey had other plans. Before a shot could be fired by either side, he gave orders for the guns to be immobilised, to remount our vehicles and head for the German night laager to the south. Leaving the German troops to the north, east and west preparing to annihilate us in battle, we sped southward with such speed that the troops in that direction were taken by complete surprise and as we smashed into their laager, except for a few tired guards, most of them were still sleeping. As we went through their lines we saw them tumbling from the backs of trucks, and clambering out of slit-trenches, grabbing their rifles and revolvers as they did so, more confused than aggressive. It was then that I heard it loud and clear, a triumphant, defiant challenge to the sound of the German firing – Major Allfrey's hunting horn. This time it was cheering on the hunted and not the hunters.

As we lurched over the sand through the enemy positions I was lying

Looking ahead. Lt-General B. L. Montgomery.

The Luftwaffe comes down to earth.

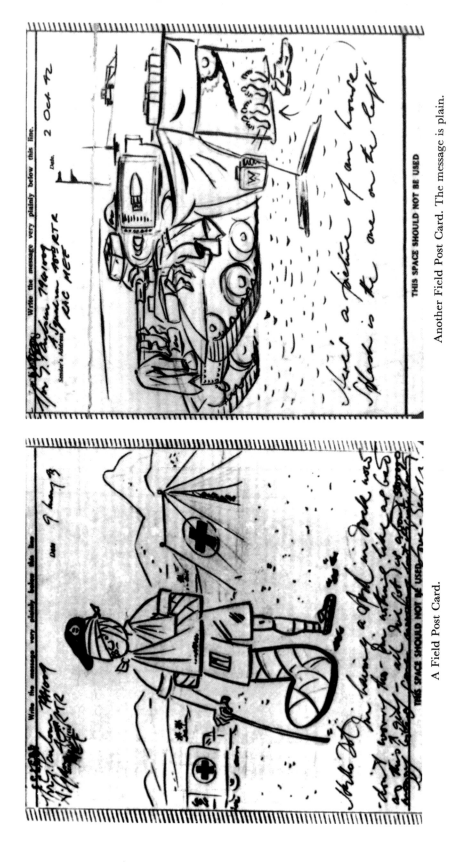

A Field Post Card.

Another Field Post Card. The message is plain.

flat in the back of a truck trying to immerse my whole body into the floorboards away from the flying bullets, but crawling to my knees and gingerly peering over the top of the raised tailboard of the truck I saw the Major. There he was, slap bang in the middle of the German lines, sitting on top of his halted truck, waving us on with one hand, while his other hand held to his lips the bellowing horn, his ginger moustache engulfing the mouthpiece like a ring of fire. Our truck got safely through, and, looking back before the scene was obliterated from view by a miniature sandstorm flung up from our spinning wheels, I could still see the Major cheering his battery on. Major Allfrey was later awarded the Military Cross.

Tossing everything out from the back of the truck to make it lighter, we sped across the sands not knowing into which direction we were heading, intent only on winning the race to freedom. At long last all signs of other military vehicles were left behind; our truck alone was the only moving object to be seen in the sea of sand. By dusk we were almost out of petrol, were tired, hungry, thirsty, unarmed, scared and completely lost when suddenly, like a mirage, there loomed ahead in the near darkness a fair-sized gathering of vehicles and troops which we assumed to be German. Having only our fists to fight with, untrained in unarmed combat, and outnumbered by a heavily armed party of men, we reconciled ourselves to spending the rest of the war in a prison camp and came to a halt some fifty yards from the group. We dismounted and began to walk towards the others, but when about fifteen yards distant an enquiring voice came from the back of one of their vehicles: 'Arst 'em if they could do wiv a cuppa cha, Taff.' They were men of the South Wales Borderers.

After a night's sleep we were given some petrol and rations, bid farewell to our hosts and set off for Cairo. While we were going back the few remnants of us that were left were gathered together by an infantry officer, and under the reorganisation of General Auchinleck were formed into rearguard positions at El Alamein. On 1st July, Rommel's troops hit this line with everything they had, but our battered troops fought back and held on. The Afrika Korps made a vain, desperate attempt to crack what was left of the Eighth Army and stream on to Cairo, but failed. This proved to be the turning point of the war, for the battle of El Alamein was fought and won. By August we had been reformed and were once more in the desert. On 23rd October, under the command of General Montgomery, we moved forward from El Alamein and the enemy retreated before us. In such a short space of time we were to be elevated from vanquished to victors.

From Mr B. Cole – 'A Front Seat'

I was a private in the 4th Battalion Royal Sussex, of 44th London Division, and in C Company. I was wounded in the action, and you could say I had a front seat. The section I was in was doing a standing patrol on the road between the minefields when the spearhead of Rommel's armour rolled up the road towards us.

Most of the credit for the defence of Alamein went to Montgomery; it should have gone to Auchinleck. The overall plan, the minefield box, hinged at the south of the Qattara Depression, with the approaches covered by the big guns firing from the semi-circular ridge at the back of the position; this was Auchinleck's idea. The overall defence plan, as I say, was excellent; the particular action in which I was engaged was a balls-up, and cost the lives of young men, and, since I have had time to think about it, I think they were sacrificed brutally, and unnecessarily.

I do not remember the names of my fellow soldiers too well; the only real officers that stick out in my mind from the war were a Major Upton, to whom I was batman for a time, and a certain Lieutenant De Manio,* but both these came later in the desert war when I was with the 1st Battalion Royal Sussex. Jack De Manio, of course, became a radio celebrity. I wasn't in his company so he would not remember me, a lowly private. I remember him though, a flamboyant charecter with a penchant for coloured neckwear, always racing off somewhere into the blue† in a jeep.

I suppose of all the reluctant heroes that were called to the country's defence in 1940 I was the most reluctant. The politicians having failed to save the peace, and having through their own greed, stupidity and lack of co-operation turned the people of Germany over to Hitler, we were once more faced with a world-wide conflict.

Being possessed with a modicum of intelligence, I knew that war was a most uncomfortable experience. Having been regaled with stories of blood and terror of the First World War, and the possibilities of violent death and worse, I regarded the immediate future with extreme foreboding. Not being cast in the heroic mould, I found it difficult to be even partly filled with patriotic fervour. Those rolling speeches about us 'all being in the same boat' didn't seem to help very much; to me the war seemed to be a great hostile sea, and I was on a raft in the middle of it, and every bomb, bullet and shell was aimed at me personally.

Well, having failed to convince my medical examiners that I was

* Jack de Manio was awarded the Military Cross.
† 'Into the blue' means into danger areas.

tubercular, epileptic or insane, I found myself inducted into the armed forces as a private soldier with a travel warrant and instructions to proceed to a place called Pheasey Farm near Perry Barr, Birmingham, where I would become a member of the King's Own training regiment, of the fourth battalion.

Here I was then on a train travelling north in company with several other nervously articulate young men, all individuals, shortly to be moulded into warrors; well, in appearance anyway. As the coachloads of recruits from the station pulled up alongside the whitewashed kerb-stones of the camp, they were met by tough-looking NCOs with knife-creased battledress, and mirror-shined boots. Each NCO had a paper clipped to a board, and no sooner had we alighted, clutching our personal luggage, than we were sorted out into alphabetical order and were soon shuffling down the road and into the camp, following behind the ramrod back of our guardian. On looking around I observed that the camp was part of a new housing estate that had been taken over by the Army, the empty houses serving as offices and also as billets for the men. In a field adjoining the estate a large marquee had been set up as an administration centre. Having been sorted out into several files, we were lined up opposite a table just inside the entrance. When my turn came I was duly documented, given an AB 64 part one,* a paybook, and an army number. Incidentally, if you were to ask any man or woman what their army number was, they can always tell you. They can forget the name of their first love, or the house where they were born, but their army number? Never!

After our documentation we were once more gathered together like sheep and followed meekly behind the sergeant to a large nissen hut where we were issued with several items of clothing, and a mess-tin. We were adjured to look after these possessions assiduously, and told the penalties for losing them. Later on several of us noticed that the over-coats and battledress suits were damp, and in some cases blood-stained; also they had what appeared to be bullet holes in some of them. They had apparently been salvaged from the debacle of Dunkirk. Hardly the sort of thing to encourage the timid embryo soldier. Anyway, after all this chasing about on top of the long train journey from home, we were all pretty tired, and so after a meal of corned-beef sandwiches and cocoa we found our billets and were soon fast asleep on the straw-filled palliasses under the rough blankets.

* A small pocket-book given to all soldiers containing details of the soldier's name, rank and next of kin.

The last thing I heard was the familiar strains of the 'Last Post', a sound that always brings a lump to my threat, I suppose because of its associations with Remembrance Day and the many who died in that war that was to end all wars. Instead of which, I thought, 'Here we go again, how long this time before we start chiselling out the names on the cenotaphs?'

There is no need to dwell on the next six months near Birmingham. With winter approaching, we were moved out of our camp, put into coaches and moved south. Our destination proved to be Lewes in Sussex, where we arrived after an extremely uncomfortable journey by road. We had been informed beforehand that we were going to join the Royal Sussex Regiment and that we would continue our training as members of that renowned and glorious regiment among whose battle honours was one for the storming of the Heights of Quebec under General Wolfe. It was to be hoped that we would prove ourselves worthy of the honour bestowed upon us.

The coaches had been pulled up just outside the town of Lewes, and we were marched up the main road and into the playground of a large school. 'This is it,' we thought. 'Nice comfy billets right in the centre of town.' We were soon to have this notion corrected. We were lined up to the satisfaction of the new RSM and addressed by our new Colonel: 'I don't want you men to imagine that these' (indicating the school with a sweep of his swagger-cane) – that these are going to be your billets.' He paused to let this fact sink in. 'Dugouts have been prepared on the South Downs, and these will be manned twenty-four hours a day.' It was a cold wet day and it did not require a great deal of imagination to foresee that we were in for a very uncomfortable time.

I have always been a great fan of horse-racing and spent many happy hours watching my money go round on various tracks in and around London. I had, however, never before been on Lewes Racecourse and could have wished it had been on a much happier and sunnier occasion than the one in which I now became acquainted with that establishment.

All through that wet and cold winter we manned dugouts on the downs overlooking the racecourse. The grandstand and tote buildings served as cook-house and sleeping quarters, the stewards' house was used as an officers' billet. Why we did not all go down with pneumonia, I do not know. One or two of the less hardy ones did. One of the chaps in my platoon always seemed to have difficulty in breathing if he had to run or exert himself at all. The corporal was always yelling at him,

'Keep up, Brown, or you'll find yourself on a fizzer.'* Well, Brown disappeared one day; I imagine he just ran away. We heard later that he had been picked up by MPs in London, but had died of TB later in hospital.

If there is anything calculated to disprove the statement 'we are all in the same boat', then the troopship I now found myself on certainly did just that. The *Christabel* was a ship of about nine hundred tons, and there were about three thousand troops on board. As usual, we had not been told where we were going, but at that time the Middle East was the main theatre of war and it was a pretty shrewd guess that Suez was our destination. This meant a journey taking about eight weeks since we would have to go via the Cape, the long way round. This convoy was the largest that had ever left England, and there were about forty-two ships, not including escorts, of which besides the battleships *Rodney* and *Nelson* were four corvettes.

The two battleships stayed with us until we got past the Azores, and then mysteriously they left us. One didn't know what fate may have had in store for them, but I hope I shall never spend another eight weeks in such uncomfortable conditions as I did on board that trooper. It also brought into sharp focus the difference between 'them' and 'us'. 'They', the officers, had cabins; we were crammed into bunks stacked four high in rows, with about two feet between each row, down in the bowels of the ship; by the smell down there bowels is a very appropriate word. The toilets were usually ankle deep in water and spew, the heads (the navy name for lavatories) always blocked up. Since there were only a limited amount of heads, the poor unfortunate victims of sea-sickness chose the most convenient place to be sick in, and fortunate was the soldier in a lower bunk that did not get spewed upon.

There were no mess-decks to eat your food; we started to queue for meals about half an hour before time, and the queue which started outside the galley used to wind up through several decks and finish before the roped-off area which was the sun-deck reserved for officers. It was nothing unusual to queue up for an hour before reaching the galley, and receiving the mess-tin full of greasy stew and inevitable currant duff. This was only half the battle; now one had to find a few inches of space somewhere to sit and eat it. So, clutching the mess-tin with one hand and grabbing the rail with the other, one climbed over and past other blokes all likewise engaged. If the sea was rough, the whole opera-

* On a charge, i.e. charged for an offence under the Army Act.

tion was made even more hazardous and half your dinner was lost by the time you found a place to eat it. In contrast to this, the officers sat at tables in ship's dining-hall, with silver and white tablecloths, with stewards to wait on them. I'm quite sure that if the ship had been torpedoed very few of us sleeping down in the hold would have survived, since in the normal way with no urgency or panic it was practically impossible to get from one part of the ship to another because of the terrible overcrowding.

It was summer-time and when we reached Sierra Leone on the coast of Africa the heat down below was unbearable, and so many of us took a blanket on deck to sleep at night. This did not go down very well with the Yankee captain, who issued orders that no one was to put their bed down on the top deck; however, we were all past caring and ignored the order. So the captain had the crew sluice down the decks every morning at about five o'clock – anyone not up by then got a soaking.

Conditions were so bad that there was talk of mutiny, and groups of soldiers were having discussions on how they could force the officers to put us ashore at Sierra Leone. At one point the captain had the machine-guns (which were normally mounted for aircraft) turned around so that they covered the decks. I don't think an English Merchant Navy captain would have gone that far, but being an American captain he probably regarded us as a load of aliens anyway.

It was a miracle that we only lost three men on the eight weeks' voyage on our ship. One man jumped overboard in the night. We could only guess why the poor chap took this way out. Another soldier had been missing several days. A search was made and his body was found beneath a lorry down in the bottom of the ship. He had apparently died as a result of sea-sickness through neglect; he had crawled under there in search of some comfort from heat and crowds of bodies everywhere. The other chap died of sunstroke. Someone should have told him that the mid-day African sun can kill you. Well, all bad things come to an end : one day in early June we docked at Port Tewfik – we had arrived in the Middle East.

I called my personal account of the war *A Worm's Eye View* deliberately to stress the fact that the writer was ever a nervy type, and not your bold warrior. When shells were bursting and bullets flying, no worm ever loved mother earth more passionately than I did, so I suppose I should really call this section a lizard's eye view.

We landed up in the 'blue' late in July 1942 and we took over a system of box defences at Alam El Halfa. 'We' were the 44th London Division, 4th Battalion, Royal Sussex, of which I was still a lowly private in C Company. The idea was fairly simple : a series of boxes with barbed-wire all round and minefields laid out in front. The roads entering the boxes could be quickly closed by mining them, in the event of an attack. On his last big push Rommel had stopped at El Alamein, and was now regrouping his forces ready for the thrust through into the Nile Delta. The bigwigs in Cairo had the wind up and rumour had it they were poised ready for flight.

Alam El Halfa was down in the south with the vast Qattara Depression beyond it. The depression was soft sand and no tracked or wheeled vehicle could get through it; hence Rommel would have to thrust right through us if he were to reach his objective, which turned out to be the case, or nearly the case. As history has shown us, Hitler never gave Rommel the support he asked for; that is one side of the coin, the other is the fact that the Navy and RAF took their toll of the vital supplies Rommel needed to maintain an attack on this scale. In the event Rommel's attack ground to a halt through lack of petrol, water and all the other necessities to keep up the momentum of an armoured attack. We were badly mauled being right in the path of the attack, and I was one of the many casualties.

However, I find once again I have jumped ahead of my account, so I will get back to the point where we moved into the position. We roasted throughout the day in our slit-trenches; the terrific heat was draining our bodies of moisture which we could not put back. We were allowed a pint and a half of water a day for all purposes, which of course included washing. We could get tea from the cook-house; a large depression in the ground had been roofed over with corrugated iron and sandbags, and this served as a cook-house. The cooks were sterling blokes, and managed to provide us with three meals a day in spite of being bombed almost daily. Jerry got to know our meal-times, because just as you had got your place in the queue, over would come a Messerschmitt to bomb and strafe us. Sometimes a squadron of Stukas would come over and dive down screaming towards the gunners surrounding the ridge, releasing their bombs at the end of the dive. It took a brave man to keep his Bofors gun firing whilst they dived at him; however, a chap told me he had lost his lance-corporal stripe because he had ducked at the last minute. I felt sorry for him. The instinct of self-preservation can be stronger sometimes than the fear of not doing your duty.

It was at this time that 'Monty' took over from 'The Auk' (General Auchinleck) and issued us with an order of the day which we were to become familiar with – in effect we were to prepare ourselves for an attack by Rommel, we were to stay in our positions, dead or alive, but we would not retreat again. He was right, we did not retreat again. However, I did not write this narrative to praise generals; they can do that very well themselves. What made an impression on me was not victories, large-scale battles, but incidents which left an indelible impression. Such as the poor devil with his legs blown off spitting out a mouthful of sand and with it the morphia pills which had been given to ease his agony. Private Bradshaw laughing and shouting excitedly because his rifle had blown up and blown off his finger when he had fired his sand-filled weapon at a diving Messerschmitt. With envy we watched him leave in an ambulance for the cool green Delta. Such as Corporal Brown giving orders to Tich Evans, telling him to 'turn off the tap underneath the Bren tripod'. Fantasies about water had led him to the point where he could see an imaginary tap pouring priceless water into the sand. Such as poor Tomlins, already wounded, lying on a stretcher waiting to be evacuated and being wounded again by a mortar bomb.

There were sometimes incidents that had their lighter side. Mail reached us, the first we had since landing out here, and one of the first letters I received was a demand note from a firm in London from whom I had purchased a banjo on the HP. The banjo had fallen to pieces very soon after purchase and so I felt under no obligation to continue payment. I wrote a letter to the company expressing my regret for defaulting in my payments, and went on to say I would gladly settle up the account if they would send their collector to my present address. They never bothered with me again.

On the night before the battle of Alam El Halfa, my section, in charge of Corporal Wright, was put to guard the road between the minefields, the road that led into the box. Two of us out of the section would stand guard for two hours whilst the other four slept nearby, huddled up in their overcoats. The nights in the desert can be very cold, and we were glad of our overcoats then.

The chap sharing my two-hour stint was a scholarly sort of bloke; why he was still a private I don't know. He could quote long speeches from Shakespeare, and poetry at great length. I hope he survived the war. Anyway, there we were talking in whispers, when in the light of the full moon we saw some shadowy figures moving up the road towards us. We yelled out the customary challenge, and it turned out to be one of our own patrols coming back. The lieutenant in charge of the patrol told us that he had heard a lot of activity going on near the German positions, and we might expect to be attacked the next morning come daylight. Sure enough, about five o'clock as the sun was coming up we saw great columns of dust in the distance, and truckloads of NZ soldiers and soft-skinned transports came rushing past us. They were mostly ancillary units who would be in the way in an armoured battle. It took about an hour for these vehicles to pass us, and then all was quiet for a while, and then we heard the drone of aircraft. Several squadrons of Stukas were overhead and they peeled off one by one and plastered the guns inside our position. We hugged the ground as it rocked with the impact of the bombs; we felt very vulnerable as there was no cover out there on the road. We tried to dig in with our mess-tins, but it was hopeless, the ground was rock-hard. We simply had no cover, and that was a grim thought with what we knew was coming our way.

When things quietened down a bit a Royal Engineer chap came with some mines; he and his mate got to work with pick and shovel and planted the mines across the road, covering them with loose sand. It seems a bit daft now looking back that we did not borrow the tools to dig ourselves a bit of cover. But perhaps it did not occur to us even then that we were to be left there to cover the mines when the Jerry tanks arrived, in case they thought of getting out and lifting them. Anyway, no one troubled to put us in the picture, and Corporal Wright was a bit of a donkey, a brave donkey though as it turned out.

Well sure enough there we were with our little pop-guns when the first German tank with a dirty black cross on it came rumbling up the road towards us. My knees turned to water as I waited for the hell that I knew was now going to be let loose. The tank stopped and fired its machine-guns at us and plastered the road behind us with several rounds of HE. I was lying there feeling sort of helpless with bullets buzzing past my ears, like a swarm of bees. Two of the chaps were firing at the tank with a Bren gun, like David taking on Goliath. And then the incredibly brave, stupid Corporal Wright got up and walked towards the tank, his rifle held at the correct 'high port'. He fell dead, riddled with bullets before he had got many yards, such a useless way to die.

I saw the poet crawling back up the road, he had been shot through the ankle. There was a terrific explosion, and something flew past my head; it was a leg with a boot on it. A round of HE had taken Chalky White's leg off. He was looking at me with astonishment and pointing to the raw bleeding stump with the white bone sticking through. I went towards him with the idea of helping him, I think. Just then the machine-gun opened up again and poor Chalky got it full in the face. A bullet smashed into my hand causing me to drop my rifle. I felt something boring into my shoulder and a taste of blood in my mouth. Nearly everyone seemed to be dead or dying, and I ran away from the senseless slaughter, unable and unwilling to stay and let myself be shot full of holes like a colander. I dropped into a slit-trench at the end of the road, and fell on top of two sergeants in the bottom of it. I stayed there quietly bleeding whilst my companions looked on. Later on a young lieutenant came up and helped me out of the trench and into a Bren gun carrier.

He took me back to our dressing station where my hand was dressed and a piece of plaster was put over the hole in my shoulder. The medical orderly entered it on my evacuation label as a flesh wound. Fifteen years later a chest X-ray showed up the bullet which it had been host to all those years. We were evacuated to an advanced dressing station, spent a night there, and next day we were on our way back to the sweet green Delta.

I have looked back on that action many times and I can never regard it as anything but a stupid, wanton waste of young men's lives. Those mines in the road could have, and should have, been covered by snipers inside the box firing from prepared defensive positions. The First World War had more than its share of donkeys for officers; we had more than we could afford too.

*

From Colonel L. C. East

My most vivid memory of the battle was the opening of the barrage of over eight hundred guns at 2140 hours on 23rd October. I was a regular commanding my battalion – a TA battalion of 'heavy' infantry – was in reserve but waiting to go into action and we were therefore naturally somewhat tense. To me the sudden lighting up of half the horizon behind us and the crash of the guns was awe-inspiring in the extreme and gave me a feeling of confidence in the Royal Regiment that I have never forgotten.

The two main lessons that I learned were the value of leadership and the 'guts' of the British soldier.

I cast no slur on anyone, but the difference between our two arrivals in areas of the Middle East was out of all proportion. The battalion arrived in camp at Katatba sixty miles east of Cairo on disembarkation from Suez after its journey from England via the Cape, when nothing but a few tents were provided, not even rations for twenty-four hours: the battalion moved forward at twenty-four hours' notice to join the Eighth Army after General (as he then was) Montgomery had taken over command and could not have been better received. From then on we invariably knew what we had to do and every private soldier was as far as possible kept fully informed on the general intention.

Most of my battalion had been in France for a short time in 1940 and had served after that in SE England, so did know what it was like to be under fire. The Battle of Alamein was an entirely different experience. We were lucky to start with the occupation of a defensive position on the Alam El Halfa ridge, when we were partaking with the RA in putting down defensive fire. The attack on the Deir El Munassib was different again. The job of the brigade was to straighten out a salient in the Italian lines, and my battalion unfortunately suffered heavy casualties in its advance. On 24th October the battalion again advanced to capture bridgeheads in the 'January' and 'February' minefields already cleared by the Sappers. The companies never flagged and reached their objectives. I put this achievement down to the leadership of the company commanders and to the guts of the NCOs and men.

My first meeting with the Desert Rats was before the main battle when I went forward with the Divisional Commanders Recce Group. As taught in England, I was in full battle order complete with tin-hat and gas-mask : I had, of course, very white knees. I felt a complete fool to see the officers of 7th Armoured Division in jerseys, corduroy trousers, flowing scarves, berets and desert boots : their only weapon in a few cases being a revolver strapped round the waist. I never wore a tin-hat again !

I should like to emphasise the value of the TA soldier. All ranks were volunteers and the officers were hand-picked. I believe they were all steeped in the 300-year-old tradition of the regiment. They used their brains the whole time and were not able, as regular soldiers are, automatically to carry out their tasks as a result of long training. They learnt very quickly and were quite first class. I believe that the whole country owed a deep debt of gratitude to the Territorial Army. I should also like to pay tribute to the really magnificent divisions that were in the desert before our arrival. I am thinking of the members of not only 7th Armoured Division and their great commander General Sir John (now Field-Marshal Lord) Harding, but also of the Australians, New Zealanders, the Rhodesians, the South Africans and the Indians.

Possibly the biggest bugbear of the fighting was the mines, obviously because they could not be seen or heard before they blew up. I should particularly like to pay tribute to the Sappers. I was never brought up to believe that the Royal Engineers led the infantry into battle. In the desert they did.

To my mind the desert is an ideal terrain in which to fight a war. Though sorry for the odd Arab and camel that gets killed, it in no way compares with the number or desolation caused in a civilised country to people and animals. The desert itself is not just a flat plain of sand. Certainly sand and flies are the chief plagues, but it is broken up by escarpments, wadis and undulations generally, while to the south the flowers with their really attractive scent in the early morning, before the sun gets up, are a sight to behold. After the breakout at the beginning of November the Queen's Brigade as lorried infantry of the 7th Armoured Division moved across the desert in artillery formation! Shades of the Plains of India over twenty years before!

*

From Mr P. B. Kingsford

I was a platoon commander in 1st/5th QRR, 131st Brigade, XIII Corps, at Alamein. I, as a lieutenant, had the rear platoon of the forward company, but after the forward platoons had been pinned down we ended up with them on the night of the 24th. We had had quite a number of casualties in February minefield – from A/P mines and from artillery falling short (or counter-battery work?). The 1st/6th QRR was on our left. They were also held up and were being mortared during the day of 25th October. No tanks had got through to support us as, I believe, the gap in the minefield was being enfiladed from El Himeimat (two 'pimples'), which had been recaptured by the Germans.

The first sign of hope was in the evening when the Italians (a parachute regiment) in front of my platoon surrendered. I was short of men and sent my runner (Keohane by name, I believe) back with about twenty-odd POWs!

After their surrender, we (1st/5th) got all the mortars on to us – and had very severe casualties. We could not go forward as German parachutists had taken over the pill-boxes from the Italians at the same time as the latter had surrendered. The Colonel decided to make a dash back when darkness came, but things got so bad that he and a handful more men left before dark. I was wounded and was picked up early next morning and taken to trenches in our rear (which our attack must have inadvertently avoided). When I got up, I noticed a mortar bomb stuck in the rock about three inches from my head! It had not gone off and, in retrospect, I realised that I had been temporarily dazed when it had landed!

After a hair-raising journey in an ambulance, which was dodging shells, I was flown to Italy where I spent ten weeks in hospital.

From the Reverend Charles W. K. Potts

The Reverend Charles Potts had gone out to the Middle East as a chaplain. However, after seeing various 'flocks' going up to the front he could no longer resist taking a more active part himself. He therefore resigned his chaplaincy commission and joined the Sherwood Foresters as a private. He was soon commissioned and served with the Buffs, with whom he won a Military Cross.

He wrote a book called Soldier in the Sand, *from which the following extracts are taken:*

Sticky Bomb Party

The inferno that was the great battle of Alamein continued unabated. The appalling din of guns firing and of shells bursting, the grim sights of mangled men and twisted corpses, the nauseating smell that was a mixture of sulphur and rotting human flesh, the mental strain from sleeplessness and responsibility, the fear of breaking down in front of the men : all these became everyday things. I suppose that we grew accustomed to them, for as time went on we noticed them less.

Either Met [another lieutenant] or I were generally at Advance Headquarters of the Notts Yeomanry. Their commanding officer was then Lieutenant-Colonel Kellett, who was commonly known as 'Flash', owing to his habitually elegant attire. He always looked the epitome of smartness. His clothes were spotlessly clean : every day he donned a freshly ironed and starched shirt and freshly creased trousers. His batman carried starch, flat-iron and ironing-board all through the desert campaign as far as Mareth, where Flash was killed.

On the afternoon of the second day of the battle I was at tank headquarters, ready-to-hand in case the services of the motor company should be required, when Flash called me over to him. He pointed ahead to where between twenty and thirty derelict tanks, knocked out in battle, were scattered over the desert. They were mostly burnt-out hulks, ugly monstrous black shapes. Flash explained that the Germans were using these as sniping posts, from which they were trying to pick off our tank commander in their turrets. He asked if we could do anything about them.

'I think that we might have a crack at them,' I replied. And I jumped into my Jeep and hurried to tell Met. He decided to send Bill Stanbury with one or two carriers. I suggested that I had better go with them to show them exactly what was required. Met laughed : he could see that I wanted to be in on this party, and he told me that I could go.

We took with us some 'sticky bombs'. These are a form of anti-tank grenade, shaped like a huge 'toffee-apple'. One holds it by the stick. The underneath part, which is round, is covered with glass, coated with a sticky substance. When the bomb is thrown, or banged hard, against a tank, the glass breaks, and the sticky stuff makes the whole bomb adhere to the side of the tank. The release of the handle, which is primed, starts the fuse to set off the bomb. The bombs are packed in a metal container which looks remarkably like a week-end suitcase.

Bill and I decided that the best procedure was for him to take up a position on the flank with two carriers, from which he could give me covering fire, whilst I investigated the derelict tanks.

I felt rather foolish while I walked part of the way forward, carrying the little suitcase. I could not resist playing the fool a bit; it was a crazy game that we were playing.

It is a common experience of men in action that one's moods vary considerably. There are times when one is horribly frightened, and there are times when one does not care a fig what happens. The latter was my present mood.

Before I reached the nearest tank I put down the suitcase. I had already primed the bombs. I went forward now with only one bomb in my right hand, and my revolver in my left hand. It amused me to think that I should be a very poor revolver shot left-handed – not that I was much good with my right hand.

We had not expected to find any snipers in the nearest tanks, but I had a look around just the same. I banged on the door of the first tank.

'Excuse me,' I said, with a rather feeble attempt to be witty, 'but is there a sniper in there?'

And at the next tank : 'Good afternoon, Jerry. Anybody at home?'

About twenty tanks I searched, going more warily as we went farther ahead of our own lines and nearer to where we imagined the Germans' forward position to be. I was suspicious of one tank, so I crept up and slapped a bomb on it. Finally there were only three tanks left. I went over to Bill, who had been working forward on my right flank.

'What do you say to having a crack at those?' I asked.

'I don't think you should go at them on your own like that,' he replied. 'Let me go forward in my carrier, and give them a burst of Bren-fire first. If there is anyone there, they'll probably return fire or clear out.'

I agreed. These last three tanks were some distance forward of the others. Bill set out while I walked forward, keeping a little to his left. He opened fire with his Bren from the carrier, then ran right round the nearest tank and came back towards me. His carrier was not more than about fifty yards away from me when there was a loud report and the carrier was lost in a black cloud of dust and smoke; then flames leaped up. Three figures came dashing out of the cloud and ran for cover behind another derelict tank, the last that I had searched. I thanked God that Bill and his crew were safe.

Meanwhile enemy machine-guns had opened fire and their bullets spattered the ground. I ran as fast as I could over to Bill.

'Are you all right?' I asked. But then I could see that all was not well. All three of them were badly burned and I saw that they were in great pain.

'Can I help you back?'

'No, don't touch me – these burns . . .'

'I'll get the other carrier,' I said.

'No, for God's sake, don't bring them up here.'

Then I saw one of our tanks, about two hundred yards away to the left rear. It was well ahead of all our other tanks. I ran to it for help to get Bill and his crew to safety.

Anxiety lent me wings and I ran like a hare. I have a vague recollection of machine-gun bullets shooting up spurts of dust round my feet as I ran. I do not know if the Germans were aiming at my legs, which are thin enough to make a very poor target even if they were stationary; on the move I reckon that they are well-nigh impossible to hit.

I was panting and exhausted when I reached the tank and took cover behind it. I climbed on to the back of it and banged on the turret. It was rare for our tank commanders to fight with the lid down. After what seemed to me to be an unnecessarily long interval, the lid of the turret opened a crack and the tank commander peered out.

'What's up?' he asked.

I told him about Bill and the other two. I was panting hard still and could hardly gasp out my words. Could he rescue them in his tank, I asked.

'Sorry, old man,' said the tank commander. 'The only reason that I am in this damn awful position is that I've had one of my tracks blown off. I can't move.'

I was disappointed: I might have noticed this, if I had not been in such haste.

I asked him if he would send a message back on his wireless, requesting help from another tank. He agreed to try and he reported the situation back to his headquarters.

'They'll see what they can do,' he said.

Feeling that I could not count on a rescue tank being able to reach them, I looked round desperately for other help. I could see nothing that would serve.

It was beginning to get dark. I ran back to where I had left Bill and the others. Again I drew the enemy fire. I reached the place but I could not see them. I wondered frantically if I had lost my sense of directon. Perhaps this was not the right place. Perhaps they were behind one of the other derelict tanks. I ran around looking for them. Then I ran back to where we had left the other carrier, waiting behind cover. I sent it back to report to Met what had happened.

I was feeling responsible for Bill and his crew, and I was distracted by having lost them like this. In the course of my search I saw away back on the right a small Red Cross flag sticking out of the ground. I thought at once that perhaps Bill had seen this and managed to get there for help.

It was practically dark by the time that I reached the flag and tumbled into a large trench.

The Vicar's 'At Home'

Those who fought in the Battle of Alamein will know that location of this episode when I say that it was in the area of 'Snipe', 'Woodcock' and 'Kidney Feature'. 'Snipe' and 'Woodcock' were the code names given to two pieces of rising ground. 'Kidney Feature', a contour-marking on the map in the shape of a kidney, was presumed to be also a piece of rising ground, but was later found to be not rising ground at all, but a falling away; not a low hill, but a depression. This resulted in a certain amount of confusion of plan for the commanders in that area of the battle.

The trench into which I fell was one of those large, deep trenches, commonly dug by the Germans: there were trenches nearby of the same sort. British infantry were now holding them, men of a territorial battalion of the Royal Sussex Regiment. I was welcomed cordially.

At first I was too exhausted to speak. When I did try I gasped so much that I was practically incoherent. Mine host of the trench was a doctor, the battalion medical officer.

'All right, old chap,' he said, 'just take it easy. Have a rest for a bit, then tell us all about it.'

My panting eased up after a minute or two and I told him what had happened.

'Well, there's nothing more that you can do about it now,' he told me. 'We haven't seen your friends; and you'll never find them now in the dark. You'd better hang on here until it gets light in the morning.'

It was a huge trench, very useful for its present purpose as a Regimental Aid Post. In it were also one or two medical orderlies. Soon we were joined by two other men, the padre and the mortar officer of the battalion. They explained to me that they were part of the Battalion HQ, that they had a company forward of them, but that they had lost touch with it. The enemy had counter-attacked, and recaptured the forward positions. It seemed that the forward company must all have been killed or captured. This was now their forward position, manned only by a doctor, a padre, a mortar officer and a handful of men. They were all remarkably cool, considering their predicament. The mortar officer did not stay for long, but went off to another trench. The doctor and the padre remained chatting calmly and amiably, as though I had dropped in at their country residence for a social call. The padre was the coolest man that I ever met. He talked in a kindly way, very much after the usual style of a benevolent vicar in the course of his rounds of parish visiting.

Periodically he scrambled out of the trench and went over to one or other of the nearby trenches. We could hear his cheery voice greeting the men there.

'Well now, and how are we all?' I half expected to hear him call them, 'My dear brethren.'

There could be no better padre than he was. It was obvious that he loved the men and that they loved him. Confident and unperturbed amidst the pandemonium of front-line warfare, he radiated goodwill, restoring our faith in God and humanity. The very sight of him, cheerily brandishing his walking-stick, was a perpetual tonic.

The doctor too was one of the best. I should like to meet him again one day – I did, as it happened, meet all those three officers not so long afterwards in Alexandria, as I shall mention later, but only for one evening, and I am ashamed that I cannot even remember their names.

During the night a battalion of the Highland Division came to our relief, counter-attacked the enemy, and made our line secure once more.

All night the shelling, mortaring and machine-gunning was fairly intense, and Jerry, as usual, put up a continuous succession of parachute flares and Very lights. It was only necessary to show oneself for a second to draw enemy machine-gun fire. They were watching us like a cat outside a mousehole. It was therefore the more credit to the Sussex padre that he so unflinchingly carried on his visits from one trench to another.

When the morning light appeared, I went over to another trench that had been taken over by the Highlanders, and there I contacted a major of the Seaforths. I pointed out the farthest derelict tanks, and told him of my concern for Bill and his carrier-crew. The major assured me that he had seen nothing of them, but he had not been that far forward yet.

'Were you out by those tanks last night?' he asked.

'No,' I said. 'That was yesterday afternoon.'

'Good Lord!' he said. 'I don't envy you. They are less than a hundred yards from the Jerry positions.'

'Fortunately I did not know that when I first went out there,' I said. 'I only realised it when they opened fire.'

I despaired of finding Bill and the others. Hoping that a tank had managed to rescue them, I decided to return to the company and make my report to Met.

I found my Jeep, which to my relief was unharmed, hopped into it and drove away. I called at tank headquarters, but was disappointed to hear that they had heard no more of Bill.

When I arrived back at Company Headquarters, I found that the Colonel was there with Met. They had given me up as lost, as well as the others. I heard that the carrier that I had sent back to report had also been shot up and the sergeant in it had been killed.

I expected that I should get a 'rocket' for my mishandling of the whole business, but the Colonel was very good about it. He decided that if neither I nor any of the Seaforths nor Sussex had been able to find Bill and his crew by day, they must either have made their own way back to safety and have been evacuated as casualties, or been captured, or else had concealed themselves in trenches. It was unlikely, we thought, that they should have made their own way back, for then we should have heard news of them. On the chance that they were still concealed in trenches, the Colonel decided to send out a fairly strong patrol that night.

I insisted that I should go with the patrol, but the Colonel firmly refused me.

'You've had enough of that for a bit,' he said. 'You'd better rest here.'

I pointed out that I knew better than anyone else where to look and it was granted that I had better go up with the patrol commander by daylight beforehand to show him the place, but the Colonel still refused me permission to go out on the patrol.

One or two volunteers, as soon as they heard that there would be a search patrol out that night, came forward without being asked. One of them was Corporal Care, who had been one of the section commanders of the first motor platoon that I had commanded. He was a magnificent type of regular soldier, tall, well-built, smart and hard-working, always ready to volunteer for extra duty if it would ease the burden of another man. At first his slow deliberation had irked me, but later I discovered that he was painstakingly thorough and completely reliable. My admiration and affection for him was equalled by the respect and liking that the men of his section felt also for him.

'Let me go on that patrol, sir,' he said to Met. 'I've got a score to settle with those Jerries. They killed two of my section yesterday.'

That day was much the same as the previous days of the battle, intensive shelling on both sides; but we were becoming more accustomed to it. Being close to the tanks we had quite a lot of solid, armour-piercing shells coming our way. They were liable to bounce in any direction and to perform the most extraordinary acrobatics. Sometimes they ended up by rolling sideways along the ground. I remember on one occasion seeing Private Hawkins being chased by one. It was a most comical sight. Hawkins was a tall, red-haired lad, with a fairly pronounced Adam's apple and big teeth, and he had a great sense of humour. He was running with long, bounding strides and looking over his shoulder, with a most amusing expression of mock terror on his face, at the shell which was rolling and bouncing along the sand behind him. All the spectators were howling with laughter and Hawkins joined in as soon as he had evaded his pursuer.

At night the patrol went out. They searched the area very thoroughly, but their efforts were fruitless. The next morning we were told that a rescue tank, in response to the wireless request for help, had gone forward that evening while I had been looking for further help and that Bill and his crew, after crawling a part of the way back themselves, had been picked up and later evacuated to hospital. The tank commander had forgotten to notify us through his headquarters, which was a grave mistake, for he could thereby have saved us much unnecessary anxiety and trouble.

On the fourth day of Alamein, when we were moving to a different sector, one of the fifteen-hundredweights broke down. I commandeered the services of a three-tonner to tow it. We were delayed in starting and the rest of the company had gone on without us. I went in front in my jeep, leading the three-tonner and the towed fifteen-hundredweight. We drove a mile or more back out of the front line and then turned off at right-angles. We were passing some artillery 'wagon-lines', three-tonners full of twenty-five-pounder shells, when some Stukas appeared and dived on us.

I had no time to stop my Jeep completely. I jammed on the brakes and rolled off the seat on to the ground. I did not fall quite clear of the car and the right wheel went over my ankle. It caused me to limp for a day or two afterwards.

But the trucks had the main force of the bombs. Out of the fourteen men in this small party, following only a few yards behind me, five were killed and seven wounded.

Corporal Care had been driving the three-tonner. His head had been blown clean off. It was gruesome to see his body sitting upright, dressed in a greatcoat, with his arms, marked by the corporal's stripes on the sleeves, still holding the steering-wheel. I threw a blanket over him. He had been one of our finest soldiers.

Barely ten yards away, an artillery truck had been hit and was on fire. The shells caught one by one and exploded, sending out a shower of jagged metal splinters that whirred through the air past us.

The only two men who had escaped unhurt, one of whom had been sitting beside Corporal Care, helped me to lift the wounded down off the trucks. It was a difficult business because of the shells bursting alongside, but we managed to carry them all to comparative safety.

One of them was a man who, during our training periods, had been the despair of officers and NCOs. He had always looked untidy and seemed incapable of looking smart. Now he was showing us that we had misjudged him. He must have had amazing courage, for he was sitting up, and with calm and even cheerful assurance he was advising us as to the correct bandaging of his leg-stumps. He had had both feet blown off.

Our valuation of men's characters underwent some drastic changes during those days of action. Often the soldier who had seemed to be the very epitome of smartness, ability and energy might become a nervy wreck, or even perhaps a cringing coward; whilst the regimental ragamuffin, the habitual drunkard, the mousy weakling or the 'awkward duffer' turned into a hero. It was proved beyond doubt that no man has the right to judge, or condemn, another, being unable to see into his very heart with the eyes of God.

                                 *

From Mr H. B. Harris

Having served with 1st/7th Middlesex Regiment (DCO), attached to 51st Highland Division at Alamein, my most vivid recollections are of fixing bayonets and advancing in box formation, after having spent the previous twenty-four hours 'dug in'. At first light after walking throughout the night, we were instructed by our company commander (Major A. J. Hughes) to dig Z-shaped trenches (douvers), owing to the fact that nobody really knew where the enemy now was.

Our battalion commander, I believe, at the time was Lieutenant-Colonel J. W. A. Stevenson, the Essex and England cricketer, who exhorted us to throw cricket balls at the enemy should we exhaust our ammunition.

*

From Mr P. B. Ewing

I was part of 44th (Home Counties) Division in the second and third battles, and we never seem to get recognition in any of the reminscences which are published from time to time. Because we were so badly knocked about during the twelve days of battle between 23rd October and 4th November, we were taken out of the line at Mersa Matruh. From there we were all sent off (we survivors) to other units and the division was never re-formed; that's why it attracts so little attention.

Although commissioned later, I was only a lance-corporal at the time of these events, and this is necessarily a worm's eye view :

On 20th August we moved into position on the Ruweisat Ridge, at the south of the Alamein positions. It was known that Rommel would try to push through towards the Nile at any time, and we were supposed to head him off. When the attack came at the end of the month, however, we were merely spectators, although we held firm to our positions in the face of much shelling and dive-bombing. But we had a perfect vantage point for the whole proceedings, and saw Rommel's tanks gradually driven back beyond the minefields and knew that we were a little safer.

Further manoeuvres then took place and we were in a position farther north, near the coast, when the big move began on 23rd October. Before then, however, we had been allowed several week-end leaves, and had savoured the delights of Cairo and Alexandria in a small way. We had also driven to and fro collecting supplies from the Canal Zone, and enjoyed the almost-empty coast road into Alex, and the Halfway House restaurant on the busier road south from Alex into Cairo (six eggs to a plate – manna to all of us who had endured years of rationing at home).

On the night of 23rd October, we moved up closer to the minefields which separated our positions from those of the enemy, and at ten at night all hell broke loose : the biggest barrage heard anywhere in the world up to that time, we were later told. We were very grateful for the little white rubber ear-plugs which had been issued, and managed to keep going. Our task was to breach the minefields at certain points and to set up bases on the other side, ready for a further push when daylight came. In some areas, this succeeded, but in mine it was a failure; just as we were getting somewhere, a huge ammunition dump was hit by shells and hundreds of men were killed. I was so near to it, I couldn't understand how I escaped, but was told later that blast goes upward at first, then comes down again; I had been in the nearby shelter-zone. So we retreated, picking up many wounded on our way back and delivering them to field stations, where they were quickly tended.

We then settled down to ten days of stagnation. The guns fired night and day and the Stukas came over, attacking our positions, but there seemed to be a mutually agreed siesta every afternoon; between one and four little of importance happened, and stretcher parties were able to go out and collect some of the many bodies lying in the no man's land which separated us. Many, however, could not be reached and the stench was often unbearable in such heat; and the flies sometimes became unbearable too. It was incredible where they came from; you would arrive in a new empty area and within minutes they would be there, buzzing around and stinging arms and legs quite painfully. At night, we had a green-coloured ointment to protect us against mosquitoes, but by day nothing seemed to work. Mepachrine tablets (bright yellow and full of quinine) were issued to prevent malaria, and for those of us who obeyed instructions and took them daily they did the trick.

I had had a bad scare on my first-ever night in the desert. We had all obeyed instructions and dug slit-trenches, and I fell asleep in mine very early, because it gets dark about seven in those latitudes. About midnight I was awoken by a mighty roar and instinctively pulled my legs up under my chin. It was fortuitous that I did so; in a matter of seconds a huge Bren-carrier went across the end of my foxhole, just where my feet would have been, After that, I duly dug my trench to comply with regulations, but never slept in it – instead I put my sleeping bag underneath my truck, a thirty-hundredweight wireless van (I was a wireless operator, but seemed to be forever taken off duty and told to use my rifle instead, maybe because I was not as fast at morse as others were). On one occasion when I was sleeping like that in the middle of three similar trucks, the other two received direct hits from enemy shells. Moments like that made me wonder whether I had some sort of charmed life. I was very religious at that time and never lost a chance of attending an open-air service; in fact I played a piano for many a large-scale one before the battles got going in earnest.

Finally, on 4th November the enemy began to retreat and we followed him as fast as we could over the difficult terrain; in the end we hit the coast road, and that's how we got into Mersa Matruh safe and sound. Within a couple of weeks, the decision not to revive 44th Division had been taken and I considered myself lucky when chosen for Eighth Army HQ, to which I went via Tobruk and other interesting places, arriving in time to spend Christmas with them in Benghazi; pouring rain, red mud, poor rations and Deanna Durbin records. But that's another story . . .

*

From Major D. J. Watson

As a new lieutenant fresh out from England, I joined the 1st/5th Queen's Royal Regiment in Egypt just after they had lost two companies at the Battle of Munassib, just before Alam El Halfa. I held the surviving veterans in some awe, but my main fear, both then and later, was the fear of getting 'lost' in the desert.

The 44th London Division, which contained the Queen's Brigade, was briefed in the inimitable Montgomery style to stage a major diversion in the south.

So we set off late one evening, two battalions, two companies up in line abreast across a thousand yards of minefields, led by an officer on a compass bearing and Lieutenant-Colonel East using a stick as a result of a First World War wound. We were to advance behind a barrage of a thousand guns. There were casualties in the platoon on my right from one gun firing short or possibly from the enemy replying. I can still remember the shriek from one of my platoon when a booby-trap on the barbed-wire literally blew him to pieces.

Eventually our leading platoon and the 1st/6th Queen's on our left arrived in the middle of the Italian positions and some twenty to thirty Italians cheerfully gave themselves up and remained for the next twenty-four hours, withdrawing with us at the end of that time. The remainder of the Folgore Division, however, were made of sterner stuff and proceeded to inflict heavy casualties on us, using mortars and machine-guns, firing from entrenched positions. I remember young O'Connell, both legs severed by a mortar-bomb, screaming for help and then for his mother before he mercifully died. Major Capper, who led the advance, was hit and disappeared from sight, but called out deliriously at intervals during the day before he too fell quiet.

When the barrage stopped, the advance stopped; we had reached our objectives and were in close contact with the enemy. After a period of confusion in the darkness while we vainly attempted to regroup and advance farther, I found myself sharing a slit-trench with Sergeant Parkin in response to a shouted command to 'dig in'. We occupied that slit-trench for the next twelve hours and once daylight came it was dangerous to lift your head and suicide to stand up. We had biscuits and bully and water in our bottles.

Fortunately the sergeant and I found ourselves in a slight dip which meant we were safe from the enemy machine-gun fire which continued throughout the day. For some reason the mortar fire which had caused such casualties earlier did not recur, possibly because we were too close to the enemy lines or possibly because they had run out of ammunition. The only communication was by shouting from one trench to another. An officer runner (Lieutenant Opperman) was sent back before first light to ask for tanks to come forward in support, and he was awarded an MC for this hazardous task.

As dusk approached those forward of us who were in a position to observe the enemy reported they were gathering in force for an attack. The plans for a rearguard action were overtaken by a sudden rush of Italians, so we got up and ran. I can still chuckle at the thought that not only did our prisoners run with us but a few of the attackers joined us as well! I could not at the time recall crossing the thousand yards of minefields again or two considerable wire fences but can still see the welcome line of our tanks who 'started up' and opened fire as we approached. Next day the Folgore Division discovered that the Germans had taken all their transport, so the rest of them had no option but to lay down their arms and become prisoners of war.

I think I was more frightened after the battle than I was before or during. During the advance I was keyed up to meet the physical demands made on me and once in the slit-trench, the dynamism of the advance having been lost, I had rather a dumb acceptance like a cow in a slaughterhouse.

*

From Mr A. M. Campbell

My field ambulance was part of an infantry division which was involved in the initial attack at El Alamein on 23rd October 1942 and it was part of our function to prepare beforehand an underground advance dressing station just inside the British minefield. This consisted of three square chambers with connecting passages and sloping ramps for entrance and exit. We had to do the digging for this (manually) during the hours of darkness in the ten days or so before the battle and then lie up underground under camouflage during daylight as the area was under direct observation from the German lines. This digging and equipping was completed on the night before the battle commenced and the personnel who were to man the station were installed that night. The main part of my unit was bivouacked on the sand-dunes a few miles east of Alamein Railway Station and, as I had previously reconnoitred the best route to the dressing station, I decided myself to take eight ambulance cars forward after dark. The following is an account of the period of the battle taken from my diary.

At 1900 hours I left my headquarters at El Imayid with eight ambulance cars, proceeding along the main road to El Alamein, carrying an additional supply of rations, stretchers and tents for use above ground when circumstances should permit. On reaching the Qattara Track (leading to the Qattara Depression), I considered it advisable to go forward to the dressing station in one car to ascertain if the road was clear. Having done this, I returned for the other cars and we reached our destination at 2140 hours, just exactly as the artillery barrage commenced. As the guns were now behind us but not far away, the noise was indescribable, and the wind created by the blast and the shells screaming overhead was terrific and rather fearsome, while the heavens were lit up by the flashes which were almost continuous. There was a rising moon shining over all.

All the dressing station personnel were on their toes ready for reception of casualties, but of course there was a lull so far as casualties were concerned for a short time after zero hour. I then went on foot to check that the walking wounded post had been established as arranged – it was an eerie walk and rather frightening, floundering about in thick powdery dust which was mostly knee-deep, while the moon could be seen shining ghost-like through the dust of battle. Tanks, lorries, etc., were milling around in seeming confusion. There was also considerable activity by aircraft of both sides, bombing and shooting up tanks and lorries and an occasional one of those burning fiercely here and there. The planes were using parachute flares which further added to the unearthly glare and in fact it was so bright at times that one felt conspicuous even though on foot.

No particular rush of casualties was experienced at the dressing station until about 0600 hours on 24th October, when the stream of casualties became a flood and we were almost overwhelmed. The situation was relieved when a company from a sister field ambulance was brought up to assist. After the first day or two of the battle the rush of casualties diminished somewhat so far as we were concerned. During the week which followed a considerable number of the casualties admitted to our dressing station were from armoured units, which of course was to be expected as the battle was developing into an armoured clash on most sectors.

III

Signals

From Mr K. A. Nichols

In July 1942 I joined 7th Medium Regiment RA as their Signals Officer. The regiment was in action just west of El Alamein station, between the road and the sea, in the 9th Australian Division sector. The regiment consisted of two batteries, 27th/28th equipped with 4.5 inch guns and the South Notts Hussars Battery equipped with 5.5 inch guns.

The 7th Medium Regiment was a regular army unit that happened to be based in Egypt at the outbreak of the war, having previously been based in India. It had been in action from the opening of hostilities on the Libyan frontier and had subsequently served in Greece and Crete. The SNH Battery had joined the regiment to replace 25th/26th Battery which had been lost in those earlier campaigns.

The CO, Lieutenant-Colonel Joe Elton, had taken command of 7th Medium in 1941, after service in Keren, etc. In February he was appointed Commander of 5th Army Group RA with the rank of brigadier. The four medium artillery regiments then in Eighth Army were grouped under 5 AGRA, which was formed just in time to take part in the battle of Medinine, 6th March 1943. Joe Elton lost his life when the aircraft that was flying him from Cairo to the UK was shot down in North Africa.

The 4.5 and 5.5 guns were very effective weapons, the smaller calibre firing a 56 lb shell and the larger either an 80 or 100 lb. The 4.5 had a range of about 20,000 yards and could cover an arc of about a hundred square miles without moving the trail. Both guns were used as effective counter-battery weapons, being able to outrange most enemy artillery pieces.

The essence of counter-battery work was determining the locations of the hostile batteries. Whilst photo-reconnaissance by the RAF was essential, the unsung heroes who did so well in achieving this were the officers and men of the 4th Durham Survey Regiment RA led by Lieutenant-Colonel Whetton. Sound ranging was useful but never as effective as accurate flashspotting, which was done mainly from steel scaffolding towers erected at intervals on the front. The towers were accurately surveyed in and gave useful landmarks in the rather featureless desert. The flashspotters, protected by a few sandbags, lay on the tops of these towers with their binoculars and telephones. With skill and good communications, two or three flashspotters could pinpoint an active hostile battery whose presence could be confirmed from air photographs.

Co-ordination of the operations was in the control of the counter battery officer, a Major Brown RA. In the weeks before the Alamein battle, decisions would be taken whether to 'strop-up' the hostile battery there and then, or to leave it in blissful ignorance until H hour of D-Day. Efforts were made to decide whether it was a German or Italian battery. If the former, it would receive the heavier blow. It was often decided to give a second, though smaller, 'strop' after an interval of some fifteen minutes. The idea was that the survivors would by then have recovered their breath and would be back in the gun position, checking the damage, removing casualties, etc.

Although our flashspotting towers were so invaluable and subject to much harassment from the enemy, he never succeeded in following our example. I can recall only one attempt to erect such a tower by the enemy. It appeared overnight. Soon after dawn a single gun was moved out of one of our troops to a new position to engage this 'one-gun' target. Difficult though it was to demolish a target of this nature, it was not long before the scaffolding collapsed. This seemed to dissuade the enemy from trying again, although he had not succeeded in destroying any of our towers.

Coming to the actual battle of Alamein, forward gun positions for our batteries were prepared well in advance and carefully camouflaged. These were immediately behind Tel el Eisa, the feature the Australians called Jesus Hill. These were occupied on the night of 22nd October and we all lay very quietly under cover during the daylight hours of the 23rd. Ample quantities of ammunition had been stored in the gun positions ready for use at H Hour. Line communications had been laid in duplicate and triplicate, the cables been dug-in where necessary, so as to ensure good telephone communications for the forthcoming battle. All that could be done in anticipation had been done.

Our Regimental HQ was set up in an old gun position previously used by an Australian battery of twenty-five-pounders. This position might well have been noted by the enemy in previous weeks, so we knew we might well receive some retaliation in due course, but it was preferable to use it than prepare a site elsewhere which might well be spotted and disclose our intentions. The general deception plan of Eighth Army, which proved very effective, was to give every indication that the thrust would come on the south of the Alamein position, not the north.

When darkness fell we checked all arrangements, my particular task being a final test of all telephone and other communications. This being done, we had a meal and by 9 pm, Joe Elton and I found we had nothing to do until activities started, so, at his request, we played chess. We broke off the game about 9.30 and waited, watches in hand, for the gunfire to open precisely at 9.40. At that moment the artillery opened up all along the front. The carefully prepared fire plan which, in the case of the medium regiments, was to knock out enemy batteries, was put into effect. By the time the programme was completed, the enemy's artillery was severely battered and, except in few cases, unable to respond to the calls for defensive fire from their own infantry.

During that night and the subsequent days 7th Medium continued its rôle of counter-battery work and providing covering fire for our advancing infantry and armour, bringing down heavy concentrated fire on call on enemy strong points and assembly areas where counter-attacks were being prepared. I particularly remember our firing 'Stonks' – concentrated fire from many guns – on Kidney Ridge in support of 2nd KRRC and part of 76th Anti-Tank Regiment RA. Both these units had sailed to Egypt in the *Franconia* as I did, and in early 1942 I had been OC Signals to 76th Anti-Tank Regiment RA.

Whilst in our first position behind Tel el Eisa we suffered no retaliation from the enemy, who was far too busy endeavouring to hold back Eighth Army's infantry and armour. This was most unusual because we normally had our daily share of gunfire and bombing whilst at Alamein prior to the battle.

In a few days after the battle began there was sufficient room for us to use the XXX Corps corridors and move into forward positions so as to be able to strike deeper into the enemy's rear positions and to be able to extend our covering fire over a wider area of the front.

Once the breakout had been made, 7th Medium moved west of the Rahman track. One battery moved onward with the NZ division, the rest of us were left there for several days until we were called for in Libya.

A reminiscence has come to mind. A few days before the battle I had developed a whitlow on one finger. With all the preparations I was too busy to bother about it, but during the day of 23rd October, having seen the MO's careful preparation of his Regimental Aid Post, I decided to give his facilities a trial run. In a matter of seconds he had lanced the offending infection and, as I was his first customer at his new RAP, I favoured with a first sample of his medical comforts – straight from the bottle. It was my good fortune that this was the only occasion in over four years overseas that I had to attend the RAP and then only for such a trifling complaint.

P.S.   Joe Elton and I continued our chess game to the sound of gunfire on the night of 23rd October and were able to finish it before duty called. I won, for Joe, a first-class soldier and excellent CO, was not as able on the chessboard.

*

From Mr D. A. Norman

We were told that we would have to lay field telephone cables across the minefields so that the gaps to be cleared through them by the Royal Engineers would be in telephone communication with each other. One cable would be across the last British minefield and the other across the first German field; we were also warned that whilst the REs would first mark with tapes across the front of each minefield before we began laying our lines, 'the area in which you will be laying will still be a "mine marsh" ' – a term for an area where odd mines are laid rather than the concentration of a minefield, and that we would have to chance being unlucky enough to find one of those odd mines.

The Troop officer detailed my lance-sergeant, Les Kerr, with his party to lay the line across the German field; myself, that across the British field, and the other lance-sergeant, Sergeant Dennis Bullock, to see to all the inter-connections and the switchboard which was to be established in a dug-out at the entrance to one of the gaps. We, of course, then had to make sure communication was kept OK, and repair it as necessary, for of course as soon as tanks started moving across field cable laid on sand it didn't stay intact for very long.

I well remember moving up into position on the fateful night in October. All was quiet and very dark yet the night carried odd sounds and there was an air of expectancy as we sat in the dug-outs that we had been instructed to excavate and occupy. Then it happened – all hell broke loose. We had not known that we were surrounded by twenty-five-pounder gun-pits, and as the barrage started we, to a man, flung ourselves into our dug-outs as low as we could get, with the shock of not knowing what was going on around us. Earth and heaven burst into a cacophony of sound totally indescribable. Perhaps our thoughts naturally turned to the unfortunates, though they be German or Italian, who were at the receiving end, and certainly at that time nothing seemed to be coming back as return fire.

Eventually the barrage lifted and we got the word to move into position and begin to lay our lines. On moving up to the first minefield, we saw the gap that the REs had cleared – tapes marking each side of the gap, but the tapes running across the field against which our field cables were to be laid were non-existent: we had got there first before the REs had been able to lay their tapes, which of course should have been there to deter vehicles from entering the minefield at any point other than the marked gaps.

So there was nothing for it but to lay our lines by compass bearing, each section consisting of the Jeep driver, a linesman, and the sergeant; the Jeep towing the drum barrow, carrying a mile-long drum of D8 with other drums aboard the Jeep. My thoughts turned to the likely event and effect of the Jeep running over a mine: who would get the worst effect – the linesman walking just ahead with the compass, the driver of the Jeep, or the person pulling off the cable and making sure it was laid safely on the ground? This function I chose to do, resigned that, should we hit a mine, in all probability we would all be killed, perhaps the driver only standing any chance of protection. And so we set off into the dark of that night, lit only by the gun-flashes and now, to our further discomfort, some mortar shells arriving from the enemy.

I recall the driver, a lad from Yorkshire, certainly not looking as if he was cut out to be a hero; he had been brought up from birth by his Grandma, I remember – one Bernard Murray. So off went the Jeep and its shape and form became less distinct as with no lights it increased the distance from myself.

Suddenly I noticed the Jeep stop, and Bernard jumped out brandishing the shovel that was a standard part of the kit of every desert vehicle. I rushed up and as I drew near saw shadowy forms with strange shaped helmets. God, I thought, Germans! And evidently so did Bernard, hence his intended attack with the shovel. However, fortunately for us they were not Germans at all, but South African soldiers whose helmets bore a resemblance to the familiar German pattern; I don't think Bernard's shovel would have been much defence had they been Germans suitably armed.

We reached the next marked gap and found the command post manned by Royal Corps of Military Police, connected up the field telephone, and tested back to the exchange, which by now had been established at our start point by Lance-Sergeant Bullock and his party. Then we carefully turned our vehicle around and, all mounting, drove back as much as we could see in our own previously made tyre tracks. God had been good to us so far. On the way back we came up with the RE's vehicle, now laying and erecting on posts the tapes along the route of our lines – i.e. a total reversal of the intended arrangement. However, a noticeable increase in enemy fire, air bursting in the vicinity, deterred us from loitering, and we continued to our rendezvous and the safer environment of our dug-outs.

We learned that Lance-Sergeant Kerr and his party too had success-fully laid the cable across the German minefield and Lance-Sergeant Bullock that through the gap; all line communications were established and the field telephone exchange in the dug-out was now being operated by other linesmen of the troop continuously.

As dawn broke, hundreds of vehicles and tanks started to move up and through the gaps and the tank tracks started to make a sorry mess of our field cables. Faults began to occur in all directions, necessitating line repair parties going out to repair or replace some.

I suddenly realised that Lance-Sergeant Bullock and his Jeep were missing and was informed that he had gone off while still dark to repair a fault on the line running through the gap and had not yet returned though the line was now working. Then we had a call : in returning from repairing the fault Sergeant Bullock had strayed off course into the minefield, and found a mine. The explosion blew the vehicle apart, wheels and tyres totally disappearing, water-cans split at the seams and shrapnel perforated everything in the vehicle, including the bedding rolls – yet miraculously Sergeant Bullock and his accompanying lines-man were blown out of the Jeep by the explosion, dazed, shocked, bruised and superficially cut, but not seriously hurt.

They had, after recovering from the shock, pulled their perforated blankets from the wrecked vehicle and decided to kip down by its side until morning light came. Then they were able to retrace their steps in their own tyre-tracks until they were picked up by a returning vehicle and taken to a first-aid post to receive minor personal repairs before rejoining the troop, shaken and vehicle-less, but ready to continue their duties.

With daylight, return fire from the Germans became more intense and 88 mm shells were now air-bursting all around. First one would see the sudden appearance of that little intense black cloud of smoke, then would follow the crump of the shell that we'd just seen burst : no more effective lesson was ever given than light travels faster than sound, and we dreaded the one we wouldn't see burst, or that we would certainly not hear, for that one would certainly have sent us to our maker. One

Tanks on the horizon made superb targets for those with the guns and guts for the job.

A tank off its transporter in the left hook to El Hamma.

'Things that go bump in the night'.

Phosphorus was one of the most detested ingredients of shells and bombs.

such shell removed from this life one linesman who, just having returned from repairing a fault, was stooping to put on a brew when the blast and the deadly shrapnel removed all his lower parts. His colleague linesman escaped death but received a piece of shrapnel which entered through his shoulder and left somewhere near his shoulder-blade. We never saw him again and assume he got a Blighty; but I do recall his name, Signalman Newman, a jolly type. I wonder where he is now and if he recalls these events – on the assumption that he made it and is alive.

As the battle proceeded and the Eighth Army moved up, so we too moved up through that gap where our part that night had been played. We saw Germans looking no longer the proud Aryans, but disconsolate, being marched back under the direction of one British infantryman with rifle at the ready. As we emerged through the gaps the sight of tanks, both German and Italian, still brewing up with grotesque and terribly burnt bodies hanging half in and half out of the cupolas and lying alongside the shattered tanks, brought home to us not only the ferocity of the battle that had waged but also just how close those enemy tanks had been to us.

Life then took on a series of HQ moves as we followed in the wake of the advancing army, trying to keep telephone communications from forward units back to the base armoured command vehicles. I remember the night when, during a counter-attack, tank-shells started to rain on the unit. Several vehicles were hit and erupted into flame; panic resulted and an immediate move began. All telephone lines were disconnected from the ACV and we were given a new map reference to which to extend a link line from the present area now being abandoned.

To my shame, that night I took a chance and in the dark took our compass bearing in the vehicle, assuming we wouldn't be too far out. Many hours afterwards, and with twenty miles of D8 out and jointed, we thankfully saw in the distance vehicles which, when we drew closer, showed our familiar Fox's Mask Divisional sign. Connections were made, proven and so thankfully to kip.

Next morning, however, to our horror and through our binoculars, we saw no more than half a mile away our previous site, and shamefully we crept out with a fifteen hundredweight truck and laid a new line direct, taking no more than half a drum. During the ensuing day we went out with our three-tonner and cable-reeling machine and reeled in the twenty miles of cable we had laid that previous night in a very large, almost complete circle : the lesson was well learned that night.

Another incident to mind was the day we were dive-bombed by the dreaded Stuka Ju 87s. I was never really sure which was the more frightening – the scream of Stukas and the resultant explosions, or the arrival of bursting shells where it happened before you heard it.

Then there was the night that I, along with a linesman and driver in a Jeep, went off into the desert to try to re-establish communications in one of the many fault situations usually caused by tank tracks churning up and breaking field cables. That night was bad : no sooner did we get the line through than out it went again, and all that night we fought to keep the connection through. At some very early hour – about 5 am – we stopped for a well-earned brew-up when we saw a vehicle approaching. It was our troop officer, and on arrival he made very scathing remarks about the line being out for so long, about our brewing-up and finally asked me if I wanted him to do my job for me.

Considering that he had spent a restful night in his camp-bed beneath his mosquito-net, all organised by his batman driver, it was only respect for his rank and fear of the consequences of striking an officer that restrained us that night. I often wonder what happened to him – if I ever meet him in Civvy Street I'll knock his bowler off!

Eventually we reached the coast road, passing en route thousands of Italian prisoners anxious to give themselves up to whosoever would accept them. An Italian colonel and his *aide* surrendered to our cook-house truck, but the only attractive items associated with those Italian prisoners were their never-ending supply of tomato sauce and the occasional capturing of one of their mobile brothels complete with inmates. No girls ever worked harder than those!

We took over an ex-Italian camp off the coast road. We thought it well organised and safe from air attack with its deep reinforced dug-outs, though from one erupted two very frightened Germans who had taken refuge there. It is questionable who was the more frightened, them or our linesman who found them. Anyway, we settled down for a good night's sleep – so we thought – but after a few hours the camp was in ferment with personnel exuding from the dug-outs bitten and scratching like mad : the camp was infested with fleas. After that very uncomfortable night we spent the next day soaking our blankets in petrol and picking off the dead flea bodies. Needless to say, next day we moved off up the coast road towards Mersa Matruh.

And that marked the end of our part in the Alamein campaign, for just short of and in sight of Mersa Matruh the 10th Armoured Division got its recall and returned via the coast road in convoy to a holding area in the Delta, from which after some reorganisation it received its new orders to move up into Syria, on the borders of Turkey, in anticipation of the entry of Turkey on our side into the war. However, that didn't happen, and finally we returned to the Alexandria area where the unit and the Division were broken up and parts sent to Italy and other theatres of war – but that is another story.

From those memorable days I've met in Civvy Street only one of my troop – Driver Harry Shepherd from Lancashire, ex-butcher, who called on us many years ago complete with family and was retiring to the West Country. I have so many memories of those others: Lance-Sergeant Les Kerr who received the Military Medal for his part in laying that cable across the German minefield, but I'm sure he feels the honour is shared with the whole troop. Lance-Sergeant Bullock, the handsome ladies' man from Northampton who, after the death of his wife, joined the paratroopers – I wonder if he lived. Corporal Dansie, the cheerful cockney chappie; Driver George Cheal and Driver Bob Berridge from the Eltham area; Driver Bill Coates from Yorkshire; Corporal Wilf Greenfield from Lancashire. I know Signalman Vic Powell lost his life in a subsequent action, while Signalman Logan lost a leg after an encounter with a mine. I never went to an Alamein reunion, never again saw our old Fox's Mask Division sign. I would certainly like to hear from any of those who were with 'B' troop 10th Armoured Division Signals.

*

From Mr N. D. Hatfield

My experiences in the Western Desert campaign of 1941/42 were solely as a Corporal Fitter, Royal Signals, driving an armoured command vehicle.

I had joined a Signals Regiment, the Middlesex Yeomanry (TA), in 1938 as a driver and my experience with handling heavy vehicles equipped with wireless transmitters resulted in my being picked to drive and maintain an ACV. This job entailed living with a crew of three wireless operators and two staff officers throughout the campaign and, besides driving ability and the technical knowledge required for maintenance, the character and temperament of drivers selected for these vehicles must have been taken into consideration. Maintaining a good relationship with both staff and crew throughout the trying conditions of desert warfare was not an easy task. One had to be very tactful with the staff, who were obviously under extreme pressure at the height of a battle, burdened with problems which demanded immediate decisions, anxious and worried when things were going wrong and often suffering from insufficient sleep. Add to this the heat and dust of the desert, the bitterly cold nights, inadequate food eaten at odd times, often hurriedly, and it was hardly surprising that tempers sometimes became somewhat frayed. The crew, naturally, had their own problems; they worked in watches throughout twenty-four hours and when we were on the move they lost their sleep. Wireless communication was not always good, especially in sandstorms, which caused a lot of static, so this meant more problems for the staff. Therefore, the driver tended to become the general dogsbody when the brigade was not on the move and usually had to do more than his fair share of cooking for the staff and crew. At one static period, I was even asked to keep the officers' mess accounts!

An armoured command vehicle was extremely cumbersome. It was powered by an AEC 7.7 litre injection high speed oil engine, with an RAC rating of 41 hp. It had four-wheel drive and its unladen weight was eighteen tons, with quarter-inch armoured body. Armoured hinged flaps gave protection to the driver, and the driving compartment was partitioned off from the staff 'office' and wireless operators. The armour plate was only effective against small-arms fire and shrapnel.

Communication between staff and driver was by intercom. There were three hinged hatches in the roof which gave adequate ventilation but admitted a lot of dust on the move. The staff and crew often rode on the roof with their legs dangling through the hatches. Kit racks along each side of the roof gave adequate storage for the crew's gear. There were two hinged side canopies which could be set up when static for periods of more than a day or two to provide additional office space and give protection at night. Water was carried in two racks at the rear of the vehicle, with spades, crowbars and steel tow rope for extricating the vehicle from soft sand. To the water-can racks we fitted hinged flaps which made handy tables for cooking. The vehicle was camouflaged with canvas to appear like a large lorry and camouflage nets were provided. These were not used at all when we were with 4th Armoured Brigade; they were not really effective from the air and were a nuisance if we had to move off in a hurry. But it was a different story when we exchanged the red jerboa flash of 4th Armoured Brigade (7th Armoured Division) for the white rhino of 2nd Armoured Brigade (1st Armoured Division) after the retreat to Alamein. The 4th Armoured Brigade had taken a severe hammering and they were sent back to the depot to rest and refit. The 1st Armoured Division was fresh out from home and had not 'got their knees brown'! So, 'nets down' was the order every time we stopped; in fact, it seemed to be quite an obsession with the new command and we hated the job of pulling down the nets and staking them out after a long drive. It seemed a waste of effort because it was impossible to disguise the vehicle from the air and the nets only made it more conspicuous.

There were two ACVs with Brigade HQ and seven or eight at Divisional HQ. ACV1 carried the Brigadier and his staff and during engagements went forward to Tac HQ, from where the Brigadier directed operations by R/T communication with the tank regiments. ACV2 remained at Brigade HQ under the command of the DAQMG. Its prime function was to maintain communication with the RASC supply columns and Tac HQ. I drove ACV2 throughout the campaign and we usually led the HQ echelon, preceded by a scout car, which navigated by sun compass.

There was no communal mess, each vehicle being responsible for its own cooking. On ACV2 we were pretty well organised, with a double burner petrol cooker and a good food store cupboard which was replenished by drawing stores from the RASC supply truck and supplemented whenever possible from the NAAFI truck. Sometimes we were able to barter fresh eggs from lone Arabs who mysteriously appeared from seemingly nowhere and disappeared equally mysteriously into the desert. This enabled us to prepare tasty breakfasts, the first course usually consisting of hot *burgoo* made by crumbling hard-tack biscuits into a saucepan and mixing tinned 'Carnation' milk and a little water with it to form a filling porridge. We also made fried 'bully' beef fritters with flour and water and even tried our hand at baking 'biscuits' in an oven made from a petrol-tin. Quick brew-ups at short halts were usually made by the well-tried method of filling with sand a perforated petrol-can with the top cut off, pouring petrol on the sand, putting a 'dixie' on top and igniting and, hey presto, we had boiling water within a few minutes! The water was, of course, chlorinated and contained plenty of sediment. The chlorine curdled the milk, so it was not very pleasant, but we grew accustomed to it. On the whole, we fed quite well, although meals were often prepared in a hurry, taken at odd times and it was a constant battle to keep the sand away from food and cooking utensils. Shortage of water created a problem with washing-up and sometimes we had to make do with wiping our eating 'irons' with paper.

After the American landings, our rations improved in quality when their 'packs' started to come through, but this was not until the late stages of the campaign.

Flies, particularly at Alamein, were a pest and a constant irritation, although their numbers reduced considerably when we moved into open desert to the south. As soon as they were brushed off food or body, they returned again and it was difficult to sleep undisturbed in the day-time.

Another chore which was even worse than staking out camouflage
nets was digging slit-trenches whenever we stopped and laagered for
the night, although they were for our own protection and made more
sense than the next to useless nets. The task was fairly easy in soft sand,
but much harder work in stony or rocky ground. We were armed
against Stuka dive-bombing attacks with Bren-guns, using tracer
ammunition, and late evening attacks on our laagered HQ were quite
spectacular, with tracer going up all round the laager and outlined
against the darkening sky. Our HQ also had Bofors, but all this 'poop-
ing off' was largely ineffective, although occasionally we did score a
'hit' to the accompaniment of rousing cheers for miles around.

During the second battle of Alamein, we spent a whole day in slit-
trenches while under continuous shellfire from a German or Italian OP,
which had our laager well within range. We were unable to move
because we were surrounded by minefields, so we just had to suffer it,
without food and little water. The heat and flies were awful and one
never knew where the next shell would land. The fear that this situation
arouses can well be imagined and the sight of an unexploded shell
hitting the ground and rolling towards your trench is quite mesmerising!
It was a miracle that few of our soft vehicles were hit; the enemy's aim
was not particularly good, fortunately for us.

Memories of the battle of Alamein have grown dim after the passage
of thirty-six years, but still vivid is the tremendous shock of the opening
barrage, which lit up the sky almost as bright as day and continued far
into the night. What it must have been like for the poor devils on the
receiving end hardly bears thinking about. A direct order from Monty
ensured that all units received a hot meal before going into battle and
this was duly delivered to us from Divisional HQ. It proved to be, much
to our surprise, a roast dinner which, I can still remember, was most
appetising. There followed a night move by Brigade HQ which was
like something out of Dante's *Inferno*. We moved along a taped track
cleared through the minefields and the desert had been churned into a
fine powdered dust by the armour, so that the slightest movement produced a cloud. The passage of hundreds of vehicles in a column caused
a choking fog and by first light we all looked like clowns. The dust
penetrated everything and it was not until we had broken through into
the open desert that we were able to feel reasonably clean again. In
addition to the dust, there was the continuous roar and flash of the guns
on both sides of the narrow track. Later on we came across long
columns of prisoners and all the debris of the initial stages of the battle.

After the breakthrough, ACV2 led the brigade, following hard on the heels of our armour, which aimed to cut off the enemy's retreat along the coast road at El Daba and, again, after a long detour to the south, deep into the desert, at Mersa Matruh. This involved moving at night and led us into an incident which, although amusing afterwards, was not so funny at the time and could have had serious consequences. Quite suddenly, out of the darkness loomed the shapes of about a dozen vehicles laagered for the night. Whose were they, ours or theirs? We did not know, of course, and the only way to find out was to challenge them. Remember, we only had small arms and a few armoured cars. 'This is it!' I thought, nervously grabbing my rifle and creeping along with the others behind the staff captain. A challenge brought a reply in Italian, but fortunately for us they proved to be a catering unit on the run and a radio message was sent to Tac HQ to the effect that ACV2 had captured a cookhouse! However, that unit could easily have been German infantry or the remnants of a Panzer Division, in which case I may not have been writing this!

I well remember that our progress was slowed the following day by a heavy fall of rain, which sometimes happens in the desert at that time of year. This made for very soft going and without four-wheel drive, the heavy vehicles could not have moved at all. These conditions also slowed our armour and later enabled a fair proportion of the retreating army to escape. Our supply columns were also affected and our tanks could not continue the pursuit without sufficient fuel.

Another incident I recall happened the same day. We had reached the top of an escarpment when we saw below a lone squad towing what looked like a dreaded 88 mm right across our front. With all the soft vehicles of Brigade HQ spread out in echelon behind us, we were a sitting target for this formidable gun so, without waiting to see what happened and without an order, I turned the wheel hard over and, with foot pressed hard down on the accelerator, drove back through the lines of advancing vehicles with our crew signalling frantically to them to turn round and follow us.

After a few miles we stopped to see if we were being pursued, but the vehicle and gun had disappeared, much to our relief. Such was life deep in the desert, we never knew who we might meet.

During the hectic days of the retreat to Alamein and the subsequent breakthrough and advance to Tripoli and Tunis, we had to snatch sleep as and when we could. I slept for short periods in the driving compartment, across the cab, which was safer than in the open, but at other times I slept on a stretcher. This had an amusing outcome when we were south of Tobruk, at the beginning of Rommel's push. Casualties were being brought in all night to Brigade HQ and ACV2 became the collecting point for the ambulances. I was mistaken for a casualty, lifted up by two stretcher bearers and almost driven off in an ambulance!

Life on the ACV was often amusing, sometimes precarious and I can still remember several incidents quite clearly. On the morning of Rommel's attack we were laagered a little to the east of Bir Hacheim. We guessed something was in the wind, because we had been on 'stand to' all night and were having breakfast shortly after dawn when, without warning, we were subjected to a low-level air attack and heard tanks approaching the other side of a high ridge. There was immediate panic. My ACV had its side canopies down but, without waiting to stow them, which would have taken at least fifteen or twenty minutes, we quickly threw aboard as much equipment as we could and moved off at our maximum speed of about 20 mph on a westerly course with canopies trailing and eventually ripping off. Back we went through the rear units, REME workshops, RASC supplies, Field Ambulance, all caught with their pants down and moving off leaving tents, equipment and supplies on the ground. We should have been better prepared, but we had been caught up in Rommel's encircling attack, which was aimed at cutting us off from Tobruk. Slap bang we went into 7th Armoured Division HQ, laagered in a dead-end wadi, all eight of their ACVs under attack from tanks and armoured cars and all hell let loose. Rattle of machine-gun fire on the side of the ACV. Front armoured flaps down and peering through the slits, I was ordered to turn north away from the attack and we were hotly pursued by tanks, with HE shells falling all round. Any minute we expected to be hit, but the gods were with us for, quite suddenly, a vicious sandstorm blew up and blotted out everything. We perilously negotiated a steep escarpment and gained the flat desert south of the Tobruk perimeter, safe at least from the tanks, but when the sandstorm subsided, we were dive-bombed by Stukas and one of them scored a direct hit on a staff car a few yards away, containing our staff captain and his driver/batman. The shambles was indescribable; the ACV rocked violently from side to side, shrapnel and debris rattled on the armour plate, there was dust and smoke everywhere and the crew staggered out coughing and choking. We were indeed lucky to have escaped unscathed, but the loss of our staff captain saddened everyone, for he was a very popular officer. I still have his canvas zip bag to this day.

Rommel's attack was stemmed for a time and the big retreat to Alamein came after the deciding battle of Knightsbridge in which our tanks were out-gunned. Prior to this, however, we were on the move at night, ACV2 preceded by a scout car, which led us straight into a mine-field. Hitting a mine is an experience unlikely to be forgotten by anyone who survives it, but I managed to survive two mines, thanks to the protection of the armoured underbody. But it was absolutely shattering, with choking dust and cordite fumes and the vehicle keeled over like a sinking ship. We clambered out and surveyed the damage as best we could in the pitch darkness. The left hand front wheel and suspension had been blown away. Behind us, ACV1 was also in the minefield and immediately attempted to back out but, in doing so, also went over a mine which wrecked the right hand back wheel. It was obviously dangerous to walk anywhere except in the track of our vehicle and nothing could be done until first light, but the Brigadier was justifiably furious when he heard that he had lost both his ACVs in one night!

Meanwhile, the rest of the brigade moved on, skirting the minefield and each ACV was left with its driver and a wireless operator to await a transporter from Tobruk first thing next morning. This duly arrived with a sergeant and corporal and they set about changing the wheel on ACV1, which was then able to back the few remaining yards out of the minefield and went off to rejoin brigade. The next task was to winch out ACV2 on to the transporter but, as the right hand front wheel was locked hard over, I climbed aboard to attempt to turn it, with the corporal and my crew member pushing on the wheel outside.

Suddenly, there was another tremendous bang, I was knocked out through hitting my head on the roof and when I came to I could not feel my legs, they had been numbed by the floorboards being forced up against my shins and I thought I had lost them. We had hit another mine and the scene outside was horrific. Both men had been blown yards away and their bodies were lying over the barbed-wire surrounding the minefield. My crew man was dead, the corporal barely alive and very badly wounded, his entrails were all exposed, but there was nothing we could do for him. He died shortly afterwards. The sergeant was distraught because his mate was a near-neighbour at home and they had been together throughout the war.

There were now only two of us left in that accursed minefield and the only thing left for us to do was to try to winch out the ACV to the transporter ramp and hope she would come straight. This was now possible because, having lost both front wheels, the vehicle was on an even keel. Miraculously, so it seemed to us at the time, the ACV was slowly winched up the ramp and on to the transporter. We had just finished securing everything when along came a small convoy of our own vehicles, which we hailed and asked them to contact brigade for an ambulance to collect the dead men. We then trundled into Tobruk with our load and I spent a week in the REME workshops, living in the ACV while the necessary repairs were carried out. During a lot of the time we were under dive-bombing attack and I was very glad to get out just in time before Tobruk fell and rejoined the brigade the day before the Knightsbridge tank battle.

After Alamein and the subsequent chase, we were withdrawn for a rest in a remote part of the desert near Martuba, south of Derna, where we were to spend Christmas 1942. ACV2 found a sheltered parking place in a dry wadi and we made ourselves as comfortable as possible. One of the canopies was turned into a makeshift bar and hung with improvised decorations, one of our crew being quite a good artist. This proved to be the most popular site in the laager, but on Christmas night the heavens opened and the dry wadi soon became a raging torrent. We spent Boxing Day drying out and digging channels to release the flood water.

We were soon to be caught up again in the pursuit of Rommel's retreating army to Tripoli and beyond. Then on to Medenine and Mareth, where we took part in the famous left-hook round the Mareth Line. This involved a secret night move in pitch darkness over very rough country. The going was so bad that it was a wonder the ACV did not overturn on some of the steep slopes. It was like driving blind and the vehicle took a great deal of holding at crazy angles. The crew had a nightmarish ride and were thrown all over the place when we hit rocks and boulders. At first light we were once again out in flat open desert and the enemy was taken completely by surprise. His last stubborn resistance crumbled at El Hamma and we pushed on to Gabes and Tunis. The extent of the debacle could be seen on both sides of the approach road: POW compounds and abandoned equipment everywhere. It had been a most memorable drive from Alamein over a distance of 2,500 miles and at Tunis I bade farewell to ACV2 which had carried me safely through a year of the desert campaign.

*

From Mr B. W. Elcox

I was at the battle of Alamein in 1942. I was then aged twenty-one and at the time I was serving as a signalman in the 154th Leicestershire Yeomanry Regiment of Artillery. I do remember sleeping almost right through the barrage of the night of 23rd October – one got so tired in the field one could do that sort of thing. Anyway, I distinctly remember the following morning one could see smoke rising in the distance and an old sergeant said to me : 'You see that over there – it means Jerry's on the run.' And of course he was right.

I must admit I shouldn't ever have known for certain that I was at Alamein had I not chanced to look out from the truck in which I was travelling and there was the name El Alamein on the railway station. Little did I know at the time how famous it would become.

Once when I was travelling in an army lorry, probably a three-tonner, I somehow contrived to lose my greatcoat overboard. All around vehicles were thundering along and it seemed impossible that I should ever see that coat again, yet, believe it or not, a few days later it turned up and was returned to me. Now if I drop a scarf in the street I can ring up the police lost-property department in vain.

I remember seeing items like Italian rifles lying around in the desert. We were warned never to touch them in case of booby-traps.

One night by chance I strayed away from our camp and got lost in the desert. I eventually turned up at another unit and they got me back to my own camp. My recollections of this are pretty vague. Had I realised at the time the appalling danger of stepping on a land mine, I should just about have died of fright and you would never have had these random recollections.

My main duty was to man the telephone exchange – an easy enough job for me, though of course communications were vital. As to the general picture, not being an officer I really had precious little idea of what was happening or where we were. The barrage of the night of 23rd October 1942 was an exception, as I think we all understood the significance of that. It was timed to start at exactly 9.40 pm and was certainly pretty impressive. As I mentioned earlier, I slept through most of it. If you weren't on duty you were thankful to have a chance to sleep. I never remember even glancing at a map – if there was one to glance at – so I didn't know where we were, though I recollect one sector was referred to as 'Knightsbridge'.

Little things stand out in the memory. One day we were all issued with an orange each. I mislaid mine, and thinking it was lost – such a treat was so welcome in the desert – I was almost in tears. I am glad to say I did find it in the end.

*

From Mr A. T. Robinson

We had been in the Western Desert roughly a year and a half when we were pushed back to Alamein. We thought we would go back as far as the Canal this time before we could stop Jerry. Being Signals we had a far wider view than most other regiments of what was going on; repairing and laying 'phone lines we heard and listened to conversations which we should not have.

Our first initiation into the desert a year and a half before was to lay and bury a telephone line from somewhere near Alamein railway station on the coast to forty miles inland, possibly to the Qattara Depression. So someone even then had seen Alamein as a defence position.

In my own way I played a positive part in the October battle. I was sent in charge of a party of about a dozen men and two trucks to man what had been named Twyford Test Point, which was the name given to a gap left clear of mines in the southern end of a line of minefields stretching from the coast to us. Through this gap, when the battle started, was to go the 44th Division and I and my party were to follow Divisional HQ when eventually they moved through, with our little telephone line to keep them in contact with Corps and General Horrocks. Sure enough a few days after the start of the battle Divisional HQ moved through the gap and about three or four miles west. But I think the General was inexperienced – when we arrived at Divisional HQ with our line, poor Divisional HQ was getting hell knocked out of it with shell and I think even mortar fire.

We took our line into the exchange and departed promptly back to our test point, saying, 'That silly sod will get his HQ duffed up good and proper.' And of course if our 'phone line was shelled or broken we would have to go forward and repair it, which was not a pleasing prospect and an unnecessary one.

But help in this case was at hand. I was just happening to be repairing the said line and Horrocks came through to Divisional Commander and he said: 'I say, old boy, I don't want to interfere in your domestic affairs, but your Divisional HQ cannot work where you have them. You will have to pull them back.' And when a Lieutenant-General makes a request to a Major-General, that Major-General complies.

But unfortunately we then had to reel the line in again, on the orders of an inexperienced company commander. Four miles of cable we knew cost £120, and for this he was risking our whole shebang – this aspect of war I could never understand – also if things went according to plan, within a few days we would be relaying the same cable in the same direction.

And this is what happened. The Aussies in the north broke through, Jerry started to move back, and this meant we had to move forward laying our little line. My officer's last orders to us were 'Keep going after Divisional HQ. Try to keep them in contact with Corps HQ.' Normally the cable we used, D8, had a range of about fourteen miles, but the dryness of the desert helped over longer distances. We trundled after Div for something like thirty-odd miles, then got to them. This was evening, but when we tried to raise Corps on the other end of the line, it was no go. It was broken. So, about turn to wend our weary way back through possible minefields towards Corps. By this time it was dark. This meant one man had to walk in front of the lorry, running the cable through his hands, feeling for the break.

I don't know how far we went back, then suddenly at last we got Corps on the line, but not Div. When the voice came on the line from Corps, I knew it wasn't the operator. We were very weary by now and I said, 'If we work back to Div, how do I know Corps will not move?' A voice answered, 'Corporal Robinson, I am the Adjutant, and I give you my word that this end of the line will be manned night and day if you can only get us through to Div.'

So, about turn, to work our way back. At some point in the night, Allah be praised, both ends came up when we had repaired the umpteenth fault and, although we didn't realise it, for us that was the end of the desert war, after a weary one and a half years.

*

From Mr George Sargeant, Royal Signals: Memories of the Alamein Battles

First Battle of Alamein
1. *Moving up.* Dust, fine like a brown flour churned up by tracks and tyres, hanging long in the air behind the vehicles. I felt very sorry for a single despatch rider cursing and struggling to get his motor-cycle along the deep rutted track through the murk. How he must have envied the Germans their half-tracks. (The DRs later had jeeps.)
2. *In Position.* There had been one of those two- or three-day sand-storms, sheer misery which had to be endured. A wind strong enough to make painful the impact of sand grains on skin. It was difficult or impossible to find your laager (strongpoint) should you move too far away. You sat in your truck and ate sand with bully beef straight out of the tin; it came out warm with its brown molten jelly. Water was very scarce. Our water-tins did not very well stand up to the bumpy ride from base. We washed clothes in petrol – there was more of it.
3. *Action.* Awakened by the thud and smack of anti-tank guns and by the Colonel personally. 'Come along, corporal, it's started.' I spent some

time yelling 'Pepsodent' into the nineteen set microphone forward to brigades, then taking down their messages as previous training had so thoroughly taught. 'Fifty enemy tanks, believed new type, sighted at . . . moving east,' etc. I realised suddenly that they were real enemy tanks and I was not once more on a 'scheme' and felt suddenly uncomfortable. I spent most of three days and nights on duty, at the end of which I was so tired I could hardly distinguish between what was happening and what I was dreaming. I occasionally threw papers on to the floor of the ACV and picked them up again so as to keep awake. When relieved, I slept in my slit-trench. I remember being grateful for short lines of communication, which allowed us bread to eat and not those horrible biscuits.

The odd German fighter-bombers made things uncomfortable. I remember being caught in the open and instinctively putting my face behind a clump of camelthorn for protection.

Late one evening there appeared a distant line of tanks against the near setting sun.'Whose bloody tanks are those?' cried some officer. We soon found out when they began firing at us, though at long range. There was a sudden flap and orders to move out. I felt quite calm but somewhat over-exposed as I stood on the top of the ACV hauling and stowing the scrim-net (camouflage). The driver was picking up heavy lead-acid batteries as if they were cardboard-boxes and dumping them inside. I cut our telephone wire and left the reel of cable. As we trundled back through the minefield gap, it was receiving enemy attention from the air. I heard later that the CRA (Commander, Royal Artillery) was watching the milometer in his ACV as we went back to assist the ranging.

Later, in accordance no doubt with C-in-C's wishes, Major-General Gatehouse, the divisional commander, gave us a talk about what had happened. We were much impressed. He was a fine personality and gave an immediate impression of confidence and imperturbability.

October 1942

We moved up (from Wadi Natrun, I believe) in complete radio silence. I remember many lorries parked well back and disguised by camouflage as tanks. We all knew that something big was afoot. I had made a point of writing to one of my brothers who was near Suez, telling him to write to our mother telling her that he was hearing regularly from me.

We were addressed by the General on the battle plan; a lucid and straightforward exposition. I remember his words about the number of guns going into action and the fact that 'the Navy are going to help with "noises orf" '. They did.

The barrage certainly was a show. I remember noticing how the moon was shivering in the sky because of the compression waves.

By the third or fourth evening I had the distinct impression that things were not well. When I relieved the sergeant operator in ACV1 I could see the General was worried. There were rumours of an unexpected minefield and that the tanks were not getting through. Met a private from the Royal Sussex who said they'd had a very rough time.

We were regrouped and moved for 'Operation Super-Charge' and results began to show. Numbers of prisoners began coming in; some very young indeed. We gave them water and tins of food sometimes. I saw General Ritter von Thoma come in; a very impressive figure he made.

Later we halted on the ridge. I went out to connect a telephone cable. Still relatively young and inexperienced, I passed with some trepidation several large unexploded shells. I was astonished at the sight of the hard, stony ground covered with so many metal fragments. The smell of the unburied body of an Italian soldier stopped me in my tracks. I picked up sheets of a letter near his body and later handed them in to ACV3. I examined a Churchill tank with a hole punched through the front of the turret and concluded it must have been made by a short-range shot from one of the dreaded 88s. I felt very sorry for the Italian tank crews – their armour seemed mere 'boiler-plate'. I peeped inside a couple of Shermans (or Grants). Inside were bones with vestiges of burned cloth and the smell of burned flesh.

5th November

Moving forward rapidly, sitting on top of the ACV and greatly elated. Some distant dustclouds were said to be Germans getting away. There was the cheering sight of the 'Air Umbrella' – Bostons in formations of eighteen. The Colonel said it's the end of the Germans in Africa; I did not believe him.

We swung north to Fuka. The welcome sight of the sea in the evening and the Navy, I think, rolling drums of fresh water ashore. I was much impressed by the quality of German equipment – the design of the 'Jerrycan', their battery-charging engines far better than ours, cheese in tubes like toothpaste, an ideal way of packaging in that climate.

Farther south we had seen lots of Italians who told us that the Germans had taken their transport to get away. One demonstrated how they had kicked his backside to get out of their way. Lots of them piled into lorries to be driven back. They seemed pleased to get out; they had little water or food.

We were no sooner organising Divisional HQ near the shore at Fuka when we were disturbed by sundry rounds of rifle fire whizzing around. There was a hurried turn-out by any available personnel. Some military police led the way and with yells went over the ridge before the water's edge. Some of the less soldier-like of HQ troop had found some Italian rifles and ammunition; they *said* they'd been firing out to sea. No one believed them and some of their pay was duly stopped.

There began a search for loot. One DR who had rushed into a small tent had come face to face with several Germans, sitting round a table. Scared stiff, he pulled out his revolver and pointed it at them and then, seeing their grins, realised that his gun was carefully wrapped in 'four by two' to keep the sand out. He stood there frantically unwinding the stuff under their amused and patient gaze.

We later moved up to Mersa Matruh, where many of us were washed out of a wadi by a sudden heavy rainstorm, then it was back to Cairo for a rest.

IV

Reconnaissance

From Mr L. R. Symonds

At the start of the Alamein Battle, 23rd October 1942, I was the subaltern officer commanding the Assault Troop of B Squadron, 44th Reconnaissance Regiment. The task of my troop was to protect the REs in opening up the two southernmost gaps in the Nuts, May and January minefields. Unfortunately, as I had had a broken wrist, I had been back on the Canal, and rejoined my regiment only on 22nd October. Consequently, not only was this my first battle, but I had no opportunity to take part in the practices the regiment had been carrying out in the desert, so altogether it was a somewhat traumatic experience.

Reading again the attached letter, which I wrote to my wife on 9th November 1942, I feel it may have captured the experience and emotions of so many hundreds of youngsters for whom the Alamein Battle was the first taste of real warfare.

*

Late in the afternoon all officers of the regiment are called together. The General has come to see us. He makes a short speech assuring us that tonight we would be making military history. This will be the beginning of the last battle in North Africa. He knows we will not fail. Good luck and good hunting.

At six o'clock we begin to roll slowly forward. Long, long columns going back as far as the horizon and beyond, all moving slowly, slowly forward. Darkness falls, but the huge moon provides an amazing amount of light on the fantastic scene of these columns moving across the desert. Occasionally we are halted, but for hour after hour we move slowly nearer to the battle area. Seven, eight, nine o'clock and we are still moving forward, but at last we stop. I look ahead at the three vehicles in front. I look back at the countless vehicles behind. I dish out the rum : great gulping mouthfuls of liquid fire. Our watch hands seem to be moving very slowly as we wait, sweating a little and yet cold at the same time. Nine twenty-eight. Twenty-nine. Nine thirty.

Until now there has been some light shelling from behind us and from the enemy towards us, but now, suddenly, as though a single button has been pressed, the whole sky behind us is a blaze of light with the flashes of so many hundred guns. A long whining screaming overhead and then the desert in front convulses into miniature earthquakes. It is stupendous. Can anything live through that? It can live all right. There are a few minutes of non-retaliation as though the enemy cannot believe it. A Very light goes up, dimming for a moment the flash of shells, and suddenly the shells are bursting around us.

At first I feel a nauseating fear, but it goes almost immediately. Those shells are not aimed at me personally, and only an unlucky one will hit us. I stand up in the cab of the truck and look back at the lads. They are OK. How strange to see them dressed for an infantry rôle and riding in trucks, instead of our armour-plated scout cars. A shell swishes overhead and a carrier in the column on our right has received a direct hit. (In hospital I have since heard that it was Ronny Brinnicombe's vehicle. He and one of his crew were killed outright. The driver is alive with both legs off at the knees.)

I jumped out of the truck and the lads drop down beside me. They are obviously scared. We pass one, two, three vehicles. Here is the hole in the wire marking the first of the minefields. The anti-mine tank has already moved forward. The REs are ready. Off we go.

The men crouch as they walk. I walk. I mustn't show fear: they are watching me. The Engineers are superb. Ignoring the shells they move forward sounding for mines, screwing in iron pickets to mark the edges of the cleared area, attaching white tapes to mark the path, and, my God, they are even fitting battery lamps, shaded from the enemy but lighting the way for our own troops.

We move with them. Ten, fifty, a hundred yards. A shell bursts seemingly on top of us. We fall flat. Stones and splinters rattle around seemingly for many seconds after the burst.

'Corporal hit, sir.' The corporal limps towards me. I shudder. One side of his face is raw, and one of his thighs. His left arm is hanging loose. Carrying out orders, we lay him out on the ground, give him some water, stick his rifle in the sand with his helmet on top. The medical lads will be following in behind us. The men are looking sick and I expect I am too: this is our first casualty. I force myself to smile as we go forward again.

We climb a ridge and start down the other side. There is a metallic crash ahead of us. Surely the anti-mine tank has been hit. A Very light soars up. Red-white-red. 'Those are the recognition colours painted on our baggage when we left England.' As this stupid thought comes to my mind, machine-guns suddenly open up on us, not only from the front, but from left and right as well. Streams of red and white tracer bullets pour into the midst of us.

I do not know how many of the REs have been hit, nor my own men, but the two Bren-gunners immediately retaliate. One of them, young Hassall, who came into the Army only last January, asks me if he can crawl out on the flank to get nearer to one of the enemy posts. I explain that the mines and booby-traps outside our marked path would make it impossible, and I hope that he does not realise his Bren-gun at this moment is more important than his life.

We must go forward. Yard by yard now at a crouch. Another murderous burst of fire, first from the front and then from each side as well, but by this time we have moved into a slight hollow, and the pattern of enfilade tracers are criss-crossing above our heads. In a few more yards we shall be in the open again. I must have something heavier. I look round and see the trooper the others call 'Goofy', big as a horse and nervous as a kitten. I write rapidly on a message form and then watch Goofy scramble safely back over the ridge with my message asking for mortar support.

I put the lads in fire positions while we wait. They are lying flat. I am kneeling, kidding myself I am being brave. Someone is walking towards us from the front. 'Don't shoot. It's Mr Day.'

Mike Day (together with three other subalterns on the other gaps) has had the worst job of all tonight. The anti-mine device on the tank obstructs the driver's view, and Mike's job has been to sit up by the turret as a guide. The tank must have been hit then. Mike is walking towards us oblivious of the machine-gun fire, as though he is on an afternoon stroll. He must get hit. Oh, the bloody fool, the brave bloody idiot. He is by my side now.

'Hello, Les. The tank's been hit – knocked out.'

'Yes. I thought I heard it. Why the hell doesn't he fire his gun?'

'He can't. It's jammed in the recoil . . .'

Mike's sentence ends in a scream as he falls beside me holding his stomach with both hands. I lay him out in a comfortable position, but he does not seem in pain now. After a minute or so he speaks.

'This is mine, Les.'

'Don't be a fool, Mike. You'll soon be back with the medicos.'

' 'Fraid not, Les. The bastards have got me in the guts. No chance.

There is a letter for my mother in my pocket. Will you see she gets it?'

I find the letter in his breast-pocket. It is already soaked with blood.

'OK, Mike, I have it.'

He is silent for a few minutes while the battle continues around us. Then he says, 'Are you still there, Les?' I hold his hand and he says melodramatically, 'The gap must go through, you know.' Then a pause and then, 'Good luck, Les.' A few more seconds and he says, 'Goodbye, Les.' Mike Day is dead.

Suddenly I realise that the two carriers fitted with mortars are over the ridge and are coming to join us. Alan Tew jumps out of the first carrier, and as he does so gets a bullet through his leg. As he falls he gets a bullet through the other leg, and shouts out, 'Oh, the bastards.'

Sergeant Bingham is with the other mortar, and he needs no instruction. Within seconds, three-inch mortars are being hurled at one of the machine-gun posts, which falls silent. 'First class. Now try for the centre one.'

My order is drowned by two sharp crashes. Within a few seconds, both mortar carriers have been hit.

'Christ! They must have their anti-tank guns up with their forward infantry. They could only get that accuracy by open sight shooting. It means too that they can see the carriers and know exactly where we are.'

'That sinks us, sir.'

'Not too pleasant certainly. How many men left, sergeant?'

'Eight, sir.'

In my mind is something I was taught at OCTU. 'To do nothing is to do something definitely wrong.' I must do something. I stand to my feet, and a splatter of bullets drops amongst us. Then there is a sudden flash and bang so near that there is no warning swish. Their mortars have pinpointed us. If we move, their machine-guns get us. If we stay, their mortars will.

I must do something. I must, I must, I must. I again stand to my feet, grasping my Tommy-gun– a useless weapon at this range; I am not sure what I intend to do. There is a crash. The world is coming to pieces around me. The Tommy-gun flies through the air. I am hurled to the ground. I hear a voice filled with despair calling out, 'They have got Mr Symonds.'

What is wrong with my arm? I look down at my middle where it feels to be. It is not there. It is lying twisted up above my head. God! It is knocked off. No. It is still joined and only as I lift it down and lay it across my chest do I feel the agony of it. The sand is stained with blood in the moonlight. I am bleeding very badly. I raise my head and look around. No longer is anyone in fire positions, a few are groaning. There is nothing I can do now. I needn't think now. I am so tired – so tired. I pray a little. I think a little of you, darling Peg. There seems to be no small-arms fire now, but the mortar bombs are dropping still, but only occasionally.

I am not sure whether I am conscious or unconscious, but after a while I realise that someone is cutting off the arm of my shirt. I see a white armband with a red SB. Stretcher-bearers. Brave lads armed only with a medical satchel. My arm is bandaged and a tourniquet is fixed. I am laid on a stretcher and lifted on to a Red Cross carrier with the stretcher horizontally across it. Three, four more stretchers are loaded on to the vehicle. There is another cluster of falling bombs, and the stretcher-bearers lean over us with an instinctive idea of protecting us.

As the overloaded ambulance Bren-carrier turns and heads back over the stony, uneven desert, the pain in my shattered, unsplinted arm is something that cannot be described – only experienced.

Back we go, past the regiment in its long waiting lines, past the lines of waiting tanks, back to the Regimental Aid Post where the Doc and his few orderlies are ministering to the broken bodies which surround him. He seems completely cool, greets me and informs me there is little he can do for me here. Obviously he has more urgent cases to attend to, but he replaces the shell dressing, and I am lifted into an ambulance to be sent back.

I lie on a stretcher at Advance Dressing Station. I can feel my heart pumping in little bursts. I am cold – freezing cold. A doctor stands beside me – feels my pulse. On his instructions I am piled with blankets, and a half-grain of morphia is prepared. A prick in my arm. A voice saying, 'This will ease it, old chap.' A cup of tea. A cigarette between my lips. The pain has gone, or at least if it hasn't it doesn't matter any more. I am awake and asleep at the same time. After a while, the voice again, 'Now this is going to hurt a little, old chap.' It does, but soon I am in another ambulance with my arms in a wire splint.

Medical Dressing Station. A tarpaulin slung from a huge lorry. In the lorry some brilliant lights, an operating table. I can hear the constant fire of guns, so this operating theatre must be very near the sharp end. I am transferred to the table. A prick in my arm.

When I am next conscious I am again in the ambulance. I feel with my right hand to see if my arm is still there. It is in plaster from shoulder to wrist. I sleep again.

Casualty Clearing Station. A long tent ward with beds. A nursing sister comes to my bed. I drink a little. Again the needle and I sleep.

Ambulance train. Another nursing sister, Another needle. More sleep.

An ambulance, a hospital, a ward. A sister is cutting off what is left of my clothes. I am washed. Yet another prick in my arm followed by sleep.

That is it, Peg darling. My first battle was short and sharp, and I don't think I did much good, but the best I could, and how marvellous it was to hear the BBC news last Friday evening, 6th November, that in Egypt the enemy is in full retreat to the west.

*

From Mr R. J. Jeffery

The following extract from my war diaries, recorded in so far as this was possible, tells of the simplicity of daily routines in an army at war in the desert, which was totally isolated from normal life of houses, cities, people, places and things like papers, radio, cinemas or girls. It has not the excitement of a modern film or of the politics of corridors of power, but shows the prosaic backcloth of an army about to march forward at last, when up till then it had been very much on the defensive.

My memory still sees vividly the desert panorama, the trig points (piles of cans), the joyous scene when the water cart, the mail, or the canteen arrived. Yet again the little desert rat (the jerboa), the wandering Arabs, the raiding Messerschmitt, and not least the desert storms. A rain shower would make a desert suddenly become full of naked soldiers primitively and sensuously indulging in the soft cooling sweetness of the rain. And afterwards the desert rose bloomed for a day. There followed the agony of friends killed or badly wounded and the inner thoughts of inadequacy as the war lords wheeled their chariots inexorably on. To have survived makes one proud to have been a part of such a magnificent Army and humble in the knowledge that one has been spared.

21st September, Monday: Can't quite remember full details of what has passed in the last two or three days. One thing is sure, we have come down from the front on the day Nodder (Lieutenant-Colonel Braithwaite) returned from hospital and the Recce Unit has been disbanded, as we knew it. As we were, we were definitely useless in the desert. The Hussars (11th) with heavier equipment and more efficient scout cars were fulfilling our rôle excellently. We, with Bren-guns and faulty mechanised power stood no chance. So when the 7th Queen's took over from us on the 19th we came back to reform as a Carrier Battalion with

Royal Engineer detachments. Half the Recce returned to lines of communication. We lost Nodder, (Majors) Hambro, Keyser, (Major) Nesbitt
taking over B Squadron and Walmesley HQ Squadron. New CO
(Corbett-Winder) three years in the desert from Rifle Brigade : smart
and purposeful, he looks very efficient and experienced. He is our new
Recce CO, the CO of an ephemeral carrier battalion formed to undertake the clearing of minefields in a big push. 44th Recce Regiment
supply one squadron 131 Brigade, A Squadron, and C Squadron from
132 Brigade. Wireless organisation uncertain, but I am at present on forward control to ABC and HQ squadrons 11 Set in Arc (Armoured Car)
with Stan Parker in CO's charger (Carrier) as an extra HQ set – Milly,
Knibby and Bones outstations, Ramsay at HQ. Ossy and Taffy are on
9 set (cumbersome radio) working back to B Echelon.* B Echelon set to
Brigade Echelon and to forward HQ (us). Royal Corps of Signals personnel set to Higher Formation and Jimmie Blunden liaising with his
set to any formation (possibly tanks). Other groups have scores of 18 sets
– large portable infantry set used for squadron intercommunication. It
would appear we are to work on a confined front. I ceased my connection with 9 set working (Main HQ) and took over group today (Tac
HQ). We are laagered about three miles from original HQ when
forward.

Today saw some lively action when an Me 109 piloted by Unteroffizier Bernhardt (T.) Armstadt disintegrated in mid-air after combat
with RAF (Tomahawks?). The plane wings fell all round us in small
pieces and the main body of the plane hit the ground not ten yards from
Intelligence Arc. We are working on the Arc (armoured car), Bartlett
seated on the top when we heard the staccato roar of machine-guns and
cannon. As it got suddenly louder a roaring zoom made us look up.

Suddenly Bart shouts, 'Look out, it's dropping something.'

In a flash I was flat on my face under the Arc with him beside me. I
tensed myself for the explosion of bombs which never came. Only a
muffled thud at two to three hundred yards as the plane bit the dust.
We stood up as all manner of bits and pieces fluttered to earth, two
wing tips not fifty yards distant hitting the earth with a heavy thud.
Everyone was on the scene for souvenirs. The intelligence officer was
officiously examining everything and keeping all at bay. Bones (regular
soldier with knowing ways) got emergency rations, etc., and the excitement died down. We buried him (the *Unteroffizier*) in the afternoon,
piled desert rocks high on him (there's never sand when you want it). A

---

* Echelons were where reserves were positioned.

cross now marks the spot . . . 'Killed in Action 21st September 1942. This is war, no time for sentiment. We must get on with our jobs.

23rd September, Wednesday: Nothing remarkable to report at all. An uneventful, unmolested day – group (radio network) opened every two hours : wrote two letter cards, more to follow. Regiment seems to be getting organised now we have met our new CO (Lieutenant-Colonel Corbett-Winder), who is under way already. He has ordered gunners' seats in his wireless Arcs to come out already and that gives us a chance to operate on a grander scale and with renewed efficiency. 11 Sets seem unsuited to this warfare, get clogged up too easily without good maintenance; poor sets to work in Arcs after the 9 Set.

(Hear that our pay increases 6d per day from 1st October, plus Egyptian pay and third-year increment up to about 5s per day now.)

Nothing further to date except changed laager position to take lead as CO's Arc forward Link and spent £1 4s od at canteen.

28th September, Monday: Last few days have passed uneventfully. Yesterday started vehicle rations and cooking and had drill parade even though Sunday with pay parade to follow. Today went on a short scheme not too brilliantly done – wireless not a huge success but very dusty. Worst day of the year so far according to the CO, who has been here three years. Look out for May and June, very rough months. That is all except that we are carrying out a training programme very thoroughly. Had to be sent in while we were up front : felt groggy and heady, so am turning in soon.

29th, Tuesday-30th, Wednesday: Preliminary regimental stunt on the 29th, one of movement forward in battle formation and the clearing of a minefield. First, by day, to see exactly how it would proceed; then, by light of moon. Start off 1 am to see how it would go under normal war conditions. I don't know the final result, but everything seemed to proceed on fairly normal lines with exercise conclusion about 0700 hours. Major-General Horrocks, Corps Commander, was present early in day to watch the proceedings. Lieutenant-Colonel Corbett-Winder is imbuing with fresh spirit and energy the newly formed carrier battalion nucleus, of which 44 Reconnaissance Carriers under Major Nesbitt and Assault Troops under Major Walmesley with Sapper (RE) detachments HQ Squadron and Battle HQ formation C Squadron 132nd 131st Brigade Carriers, formed into one unit under Major of the Buffs.

0515 hours morning began most terrific artillery barrage I've heard or witnessed from a distance. 131 Brigade were attacking Jerry to displace him from Munassib depression. This barrage of 171 guns was to pave the way and did it howl for the first few hours. It still continues at random in the distance even now (1600 hours). I hope the objective is reached. Talk of us under six minutes' notice to move off in support (?).

1st-4th October: Apparently 131 Brigade fairly successful as from remnants of news I've picked up. 18 Junkers (Stukas) driven off or brought down. Hand-to-hand fighting. We carry on as usual with training. Report a heavy dust storm followed by black clouds, electric storms, with first downpour of *real* rain experienced in this country. I got drenched trying to salvage my belongings, but it was a pleasant, cool drenching. Changed shirt and went on scheme. There was a lovely cool all afternoon and evening. Atmosphere beautifully clear and refreshing. Mount Himeimat and adjacent ridges clear in distance. Sunset most glorious yet seen – more like the Egyptian desert of posters. Wireless silence as from 2100 hours yesterday till 0900 hours tomorrow. Apparently one of series to delude Jerry into finally taking no notice of them, when silence is used on our grand push forward to end the war.

7th October, Wednesday: From Sunday nothing but routine : stay in the same area. Wednesday on Corps scheme; lined up during the day. 8th (Thursday) day of scheme when darkness was simulated. Formation of night line-up was pretty intimidating – tanks in line behind us. Grants with 6 pdrs and anti-tank artillery following nearby. Bofors and all associated armament of an Armoured Division. Brigadiers of all sorts – Red Caps everywhere followed hard in rear in Crusaders, Jeeps, personnel vehicles – South African Arcs larger than ours – Indian troops. Everything went according to plan (whose?) and scheme finished in evening with promise that we should have more Grants next time (by Brigadier). Amusing incident at midday when sun blazing down – someone lit a cigarette whilst standing behind a stationary vehicle. Immediately yelled at by Red Cap (Brigadier?), 'Put that bloody light out – don't you know it's the middle of the night and you'll be spotted?'

Evening out – return today, Friday, with a small scheme of formations in advance. Back to reorganisation now and clean up. Weather of past two days changeable, blowy, wind a gale at night, dust blowing all over. What now ! Wireless groups on scheme indifferent. Complete day's relief on 8th from 1000 hours till 1900 hours at night. Corporal Bones stranded in desert with set and bogie wheel gone. Mr Lane (Signals

Officer) operated the C Squadron Set. I had occasion to choke him off for incorrect procedure.

No mail for some time, but ever hopeful. When will the push occur; some time within two months, I guess.

10th-19th October: Routine work continues again. We move to a new area followed immediately by a quick night scheme, which includes use of Matilda Scorpions, rollers for minefields which clear in double-quick time. Wireless control and group-work excellent according to Acting CO (Major Wittington), who took over in the absence of Corbett-Winder. Previously two days of heavy gales and sandstorms accompanied by rain. Visibility and ceiling zero. The wind lashed into tremendous fury and sand bruised the eyes and body as it hit them. The mouth and nasal tracts became full of grit and dirt.

21st October, Wednesday: Transferred from forward control (Tac HQ) to CO's carrier as operator with Jock as aid. Lecture by CO to all carrier battalion to the effect that 23rd October, forty-eight hours ahead is to be the great day in the history of the Eighth Army and the war. Our training being complete, we are going to strike all along the line from El Alamein to the farthest point south by a big armoured sweep in the north encircle, wipe out, consolidate and advance in steady stages. In all, we had total air superiority and the support of 900 guns and 1300 tanks, some of the latest American design. Jerry knows and expects us to attack some time, but he doesn't know when. Things look pretty good from our side, but the enemy would put up a fight. None the less our job of forcing the minefields would be done. If *we* didn't do it there were others behind who would and still yet behind them. The gaps would be made for the armour and that was that. Finally, while yet you have a round or even a bayonet there was no need to surrender. Even so, if prisoner the talk was, 'Trooper 6041111, I am a soldier, therefore you will realise I can tell you nothing.'

We in the south are to break through and finish up the 21st Panzer Division whilst simultaneously in the north 3rd Armoured Division are pushing – the main thrust coming south-west. Centrally the infantry will mop up as we in the south or they up north have surrounded or compromised the positions of the enemy. Later on, in the confusion of the night the Free French are to assault and take Mount Himeimat as a surprise attack . . . With that we were given two clear days to prepare for the 'do'.

22nd October: Preparatory. Bren-guns, rifles, magazines, radio sets; everything stripped and ordered for the occasion of the morrow; nothing omitted. Everyone in good spirits, especially Jock and myself, ready for the battle.

23rd October: The fatal day in more ways than one. We are fairly well prepared, Jock and I, and Bill all ready to move. At 0945 hours we go to a new day laager not two miles south. Himeimat and the ridge show themselves more clearly and menacingly. Just before the move I managed to squeeze in a foot bath, the first for ages. Settled in, we put finishing touches to our efforts. In my zeal to clean my rifle, I left half of my pull-through stuck in the barrel. I strolled endlessly across the sands to locate the armourer, but finally caught up with C Squadron bloke who moaned merrily but cleared the rifle. Bill made sausage rolls, Jock made tea and I darned socks. In the afternoon sat in the shade with Jock and read some passages of the New Testament. Instructions to break radio silence and contact all tanks on the network in all squadrons at 1800 hours. By six-thirty with a setting sun and a rising moon we were in march positions with whole formations of 22nd Armoured Brigade behind and with us. Grant tanks in our column itself and RHQ plodding away ahead quietly, slowly but relentlessly covering the ground between us and the first enemy minefield with two deliberately staged halts at fixed points between British gaps.

Then another halt: something appeared to be wrong – a jeep disappears speedily to the right where at a thousand yards the dim silhouette of our right-hand column is to be seen. At last after half an hour or more there is action, speedy and definite – we have lost the track, bearing or something and turn sharp right in a hasty effort to retrieve our lost position and catch up on our timetable. We accomplished this quite well coming up on the left of a very long thin column. By this time the distant shelling had become a present and local hazard. Shells were falling to our right as we proceeded and one made a direct hit on a truck which went up in flames at once. The close element of surprise was lost which should have been broken only when we reached the German minefield. However, Jerry had his guns laid – he was expecting an attack – on the ridge in front of his minefields and he plastered it with evil intent and to his good purpose. The air was full of cordite fumes ·and a smoke pall laid heavy as the squadrons rushed forward to their preliminary jobs of making gaps in the first minefield (January). The time was about 2200-2300 hours. Artillery was furiously pasting us now as we lined up patiently on the ridge before the intended gaps and the anti-tank artillery from the other side battered away incessantly at us all lined up.

All night, from the very inception of the attack by B and C Squadrons, we in the CO's carrier were kept busy. Immediately the attack was pressed, the CO transferred from Tac HQ to his carrier and charged everywhere about the battlefield from flank to flank to supervise the advance as necessary and see from first hand what was happening. I noticed that he wisely kept well down in his seat and was loath to expose his person outside the safety of his seat in the carrier, with all the shrapnel and loose small-arms flying about. None the less he was a source of energy, drive and vitality, and did much to ensure success in the early stages of the advance through the first minefield (January). At first, progress went OK. Forward elements were not too much hampered by artillery and anti-tank fire, which seemed to concentrate on the ridge where main armour was lined up ready to press on as soon as a gap was cleared and a bridgehead established. The REs and Scorpions went in quickly, covered and aided by carrier troops and later assault infantry.

Three carriers put out of action right on No 4 gap when we started. However, progress was made. REs suffered casualties as a result of machine-gun fire and mainly mortar fire. There were constant demands on the radio for extra REs, who were immediately sent to help widen and clear gaps. Gaps 3 and 4 went on well from the start. It was fascinating to see the lighted signposts (uni-directional lights) which marked the main causeway through the gaps. Gaps 1 and 2 lost direction and positions early through cordite fumes and smoke which restricted visibility to zero. Troops withdrew on orders five hundred yards down the minefield, reorganised and pressed on again. After a while it became apparent that the obstacles in our path were m/g (machine-gun) pockets which were causing devastation to the REs and which were the subject of much conversation on the air. The carefully prepared and practised code of communication was quickly discarded in the heat of action.

Several times a breathless Major Nesbitt spoke. 'Heavy m/g and anti-tank fire.'

'Do you need help?' asked the CO.

The staccato roar of machine-gun fire was heard in the background as Nesbitt paused for breath before answering, 'Not at the moment. I think we'll be all right.'

'OK, let me know as soon as you need any help.'

Likewise with C Squadron, and three times in quick succession asked for our barrage to be raised so that the men could proceed with the advance. 'Progress held up. We cannot advance until our barrage is *raised*. It is falling just in front of us.' This information was radioed back to RAHQ without apparent effect at first but with presumable concurrence later. Nothing more was said on that score.

The brigadier from the cover of his Crusader tank, mounting a six-pounder gun, was well up to see the battle and direct it as necessary. C Squadron reported casualties. Mr Weston is dead and three carriers out of action. Machine-gun opposition is fierce. We are sending black-buttoned boys (KRRs or Rifle Brigade) to help you, was the order to B and C Squadrons, to rout out m/g posts in the minefield.

At last Gaps 2 and 3 were declared open and Reg Bone had a tone of exultation in his voice as he reported, 'Twenty Itie prisoners with two men i/c. What shall we do with them? No 2 Gap to the left . . . '

'Put two of the lesser wounded in charge and march them back to RHQ where further orders will be ready.'

Then came reorganisation beyond January.

B and C Squadrons had to halt, gather strength and reinforcements, and push on when ordered (as it happened the order to February minefield was 0510 hours. They declared they had only enough men to attempt one gap more as the others had been so expensive in men and materials.

At this juncture we passed through Gap 2 to contact and plan with C and B Squadrons, followed by the Brigadier. Tanks and Hussars and anti-tank guns were already there with RBs and assault troops firing loosely with Brens and fire being returned by tracers, which often ricocheted off the armour. Artillery intenser, if possible, and more concentrated on the ridge where we lined up and we often had to duck shrapnel and blast.

Scorpion was reported out of action in Gap 2 : a mechanical defect was quickly repaired. One in Gap 4 received a direct hit and was out of action immediately. None left to carry on to February. Major Wittington had gout and was not able to move easily. He sat in his jeep with binoculars on the horizon watching gun-flashes and calmly advising the digging troops when to duck as the shells came over.

The patrol moved forward to February minefield up to seven hundred yards, but found nothing. It was suspected that it was farther on, said the CO. We wandered around on the carrier through the hellish barrage, often ducking, till at one unfortunate juncture one burst of shrapnel bounced off the hard rock, missed Jock and burst into the carrier where I was operating the set. I was hit in the face and knee . . .

It happened as follows: we had been moving around quite con-
fidently smoking as we liked and after one such excursion being given a
good tot of rum by the Adjutant, who himself was comfortably plastered. He wanted to know of Jock, 'Are there many bombs up forward?'
Yes, indeed, said Jock, but give us a swig, which of course he did.

After this relaxer, we felt better. As I had been on the set for a long
time, heavily worked but without a break, Jock offered to relieve me.
He didn't seem too happy about his position in the left of the carrier
which had a narrower well than the operator's side. I callously refused,
to my fate. We had just communicated with B and C Squadron about
the time of the next advance to February minefield (0510 hours, 24th
October) and they were just moving off when it happened. We had just
received a message from B Squadron that they were pressing forward,
when we halted for some reason. It was then that the shell dropped on
the left side of the carrier and the shell-splinters came sailing over
Jock's head hitting the set and me in the face and leg. The Adjutant
guided me to a slit-trench by the Tac HQ Arc and after sundry talk I
was told by the second in command to walk through the minefield to
the RAP (Regimental Aid Post – Medical), which was in a hollow.

It was a nightmare walk. Everyone was feverishly digging in, the
shelling was terrific and loose small-arms fire was whistling everywhere,
tracer bullets weaving a pattern through the sky. Moreover I wasn't sure
where the gap was and I glanced anxiously back every few minutes.
One Scorpion (Valentine) was stranded in the middle of No 4 Gap with
chaps using it for cover – Sergeant Hawkins was one. Halfway down
the track I met Sergeant Hitchens, who escorted me back to the RAP
finally. I arrived at daybreak when the shelling seemed to intensify at
our rear.

Our own shelling started again. (Better than Crystal Palace, was one
Cockney's remark.) One enemy plane very high was tracked by Bofors
AA guns. Shells landed on the ridge by the RAP. I tried to help as well
as I could with dressing the wounded, lifting stretchers, until an MO
ordered me to board the ambulance back to ADS (Advanced Dressing
Station).

Our group had nothing to eat or drink and felt pretty rough. At the
ADS we waited, had tea and cigarettes, and I was surprised to meet
Fred King hobbling in with bullet wounds in shoulder and leg – both
clean with no broken bones. He was from the 1st/7th Queens, and was
Colonel Burton's signaller. Colonel Burton had been killed and he had
been shot by Ities, captured, shot by Rifle Brigade and recaptured into
British hands. We were carried by ambulance over rugged ambulance

tracks, the roughest ride in the desert, to MDS where we had more tea and cigarettes.

One poor lad was accused of a self-inflicted wound in his foot, was given the slightest piece of lint, the slightest piece of cotton wool and sent back to his unit.

We proceeded to CCS (Casualty Clearing Station) in a B tonner lorry. It was night (24th/25th) by the time we reached that point already overcrowded by bad cases of injury from the northern front, behind which it was situated. We were posted immediately to 4th Field Ambulance along the road past Burg El Arab where we stayed the night before being put on the ambulance train next morning after being given fresh dressings (25th October).

V

The Sappers

From Lieutenant-Colonel B. S. Jarvis

I was twenty-two years old at the time of the battle, having been at 'The Shop' when war broke out. I am sending two letters which I wrote to my father at the time. Some of the writing is childish, I am afraid, but it may give the picture of the confusion of Alamein, as seen by a sapper subaltern.

The Officer Commanding 3 (Cheshire) Field Squadron was Peter Moore (now Brigadier [Rtd.] P. N. M. Moore, DSO and two bars, MC), who did more than anyone to prepare the Eighth Army sappers for the minefields.

The important lesson from Alamein was that it was impossible to get through two minefields in one night, but no one dare say so beforehand !

27th November 1942

Since the battle began I have written two letter-cards – one specially for Christmas, to let you know I have been in the fun and emerged safe and sound, for the time being, at any rate.

When I reported to the CRE of our Armoured Division, he pointed to a map of the enemy minefields. 'See all these ?' he said. 'We've got to get through them.' I found the squadron all teed-up for the battle and was told to be troop officer until the show was over. For a fortnight I learned all I could about minefields and booby-traps, training most nights and practising every day. I noticed the moon getting bigger every night.

Then came the move to the front. It was done with the utmost secrecy and for a few days we lay a few miles behind the lines, only going up now and again to peep from gunner OPs. The latter revealed a very lonely battlefield and taught us nothing. The day before full moon we received our orders. Every sapper was told the Army Commander's plan and every sapper was thrilled to the teeth. We felt we had finished with half-measures and half-chances and that this time we would fix the job once and for all. It was worth dying for. The day

A Destroyed Mk IV German tank.

German prisoners with British guards.

Examining a captured Mk IV.

After the battle.

came and we were dumped at the front. I remember those last few hours before zero hour. I had finished my work, briefing my recce party and testing the equipment and didn't know how to pass the time. I recall changing my socks over very slowly and thoroughly for want of something to do.

An hour before zero we marched up to the FDLs [Forward defended localities, i.e. front line] and lay down behind the starting tape. At zero precisely (I knew by my watch!) it started. I saw the horizon spring into flame behind me and a few seconds later the first crash reached my ears. 'Hell let loose,' I believe, is the term they use and it certainly fits. Such a noise I could never have imagined. Occasionally I could just hear the rumble of the shells bursting on the objective. The enemy was frantically sending up flares on the whole front. We rose at the appointed time and went forward on our bearing. We couldn't go wrong. Bofors guns were firing low trajectory tracer in the direction of the attack. The infantry were magnificent. In perfect order, properly spaced, they advanced slowly, as straight as a dye. The only vehicle in the vicinity was ours. Suddenly it blew up and the driver was hurled from his seat, shaken but unhurt. We had found the first minefield all right!

The first party got cracking with their work of clearing the gap. I went off with half a dozen sappers to find the next minefield. We passed through masses of infantry consolidating in their bounds. The paces were getting into thousands when suddenly the success signal went up. A few minutes later it went up on the left, then again on the right. Nice work! Our job should be easy now. I reached the forward infantry and spoke to the company commander. He pointed to a trip wire on the crest in front. The second minefield was in front of the objective! Our company commander appeared from nowhere and, quite unperturbed, said we were to carry on and clear a gap. The infantry provided a covering party and on we went. I kept my eyes on the ground and by good fortune saw the anti-personnel mines just showing above the ground before anyone stepped on one.

As we topped the crest the enemy opened up. The covering party rushed the post. Half of them were hit before they got there, but they captured the chaps causing all the trouble. While they were doing this we probed for mines. Yes, there they were, our own, captured in June and relaid by the Boche. That was a good start. I found the far end of the field and placed my light. I went over to the infantry and told the dazed corporal to get back. The prisoners carried their officer – shot in the stomach. They told me he had led the charge waving an empty pistol.

A Boche prisoner told me in French there were no more mines and that the next field was a dummy. I believed him, he was in such a state. The enemy machine-gun fire grew worse, the tracer appearing to fill the air and make an impenetrable wall.

The rest of the party got cracking and soon the gap was clear. It had worked perfectly and the OC was delighted. Both our gaps went through. No other squadron was able to – 'Driven back by machine-gun fire' was their report. I think the OC will get a DSO for this. He already has his MC. As the lights went up I heard the rumble of our tanks following up. The leading tank caught an 88 mm full in the turret but the rest went through, fanned out and careered all over the enemy infantry. We had done our part and could do no more. I hadn't done much but I had helped. I suppose really I led the division that night. We came back next morning, tried to sleep and counted up the casualties. We were not a little pleased with ourselves, as you can imagine, and the letter of appreciation from the Divisional Commander was read out to all the men.

That was the most terrific night of my life – 23rd/24th October. The Matruh affair was completely put in the shade. It was a great experience for me and I learned a lot. I never understood how infantry attacks came off. Now I do. The advantage lies with the defence, but however many men you get with your machine-gun there is always the knowledge that sooner or later some will reach you and jump into your trench with the bayonet. I think the night attack, with limited objectives, is the answer to a strong defence. I learned also that the Englishman is very brave. I wish you could have seen my sappers. They never jibbed or faltered once. They would have gone for the Boche with bare hands that night.

Before the barrage I felt extraordinarily bloodthirsty. I believed Brigadier Perrott to be dead at the time and I was looking forward to getting a Boche or two. In actual fact the first enemy I saw made my heart bleed. They were German prisoners limping back, trying to support each other. Their officer was a fine young man, tall, fair and good-looking. Whenever there was a German present, the post held out to the last – until we were among them with bayonet and Tommy-guns. Then they would stoically pick up their greatcoats and set off under escort. They had done their duty and that was all that mattered. It was a different story a fortnight later, but I will describe that in another letter.

The next few days were the worst I have experienced. We laagered between two raids and a railway, near the sea. Every night the Ju 88s plastered us and every afternoon the Stukas selected us for their target.

Believe it or not, but a small bomb landed four feet from the foot of my bed one night. I felt a sharp smack on the souls of my feet and for an instant thought I had been hit. The same bomb put my car out of action with a holed radiator. In the morning we found the area littered with booby-trap bombs and in the afternoon I started to dispose of them. I was just putting a loop of wire over one when the first of a stick of bombs burst about fifty yards away. The bomb fell right across me and for a few seconds I lay on the ground wriggling with fright.

I got up, heard some moaning and rushed over to the men. It was a ghastly sight. I remember putting the worst case on our stretcher and easing his leg on afterwards, the wrong way round. They killed two men that time and wounded several. One of the bombs didn't explode and I had to dispose of it. I took one volunteer and started to dig. I didn't care whether it went off or not. It didn't and I blew it up after an hour's digging. The next night the troop leader caught a large shell on his jeep and was badly wounded. I thought he was dead from the description, but he is now recovering from a nasty head wound.

For the first time I felt really frightened. One by one we were being picked off and everyone grew despondent. I started to read my Bible. My driver asked if he could go sick on account of his nerves. I gave him a good talking to and pretended to be brave. It worked and he started to read his New Testament every morning. A few days later we were allowed to move nearer the front to a much safer spot. The OC came round and told me I was confirmed as troop leader and that he had every confidence in me. The bombing began to die away. If anyone tells you on the wireless that we had 'complete air superiority', view him with the greatest caution.

After that I began to feel better. I was my own master. I had seventy men to lead in battle and twenty vehicles to look after. I had one or two near squeaks but somehow I got myself under control. Once I leaped from my Jeep for a slit-trench and a bomb-splinter shattered the steering-wheel. She bears some honourable marks now!

I think that is enough for one letter, but it is not all. I will fill another with my later experiences. Don't think I'm 'shooting a line'. I'm telling you just what I remember, as I'm sure you would like to know.

One point I must emphasise. About two or three times a week during all this large bundles of mail kept arriving for me. They were a godsend. Now you know why you must keep writing. It was impossible to write any in reply just then. Every spare minute went in sleep.

It won't be long now before I can tell you about this in front of a fire at home.

20th December 1942

Last time I told you of my personal experiences during the early days of the battle, how frightened I became and how I discovered that war wasn't so romantic as the June battle had led me to believe.

For the week following I had a fairly easy time. I moved my troop up close under the infantry and we were spared most of the night bombing attacks. I used to go up with a dozen men at a time, leave them behind a reverse slope, while I nosed round observation posts and battalion headquarters in my little armoured car, trying to obtain information. My job was to destroy enemy equipment, given half a chance, as no one knew who would be in possession of the battlefield next day. The gunners were the most helpful and one morning I found myself in the same OP as my old shop instructor, now a Lieutenant-Colonel, so we got on famously. Pooh Hobbs! [Later Major-General R. G. S. Hobbs. He was an England rugby international.]

My first job was a Mk III Boche tank, about five hundred yards behind the infantry. It had broken a track on the enemy's own minefield, but otherwise was intact. I put my charge in, closed the doors, and ran. I got into a trench a hundred yards away and watched. The tank was literally torn apart and before the tinkle of falling armour plate had stopped, the petrol caught fire. She looked like a large black carrier when the fire stopped half an hour later. Very satisfactory!

The next morning one of the Boche's famous 88 mm was pointed out to me. Some Scottish infantry were holding a post near to it and I thought all was safe and walked up to it. The sergeant commanding the platoon made me lie down immediately. One of his men had been sniped that morning. I fixed my charge in accordance with the book, keeping well down in the pit. The charge blew out both ends of the barrel without damaging the gun in the slightest. I learned a lesson. Never economise on explosive in the field. The next time I put a hefty charge over the breech and she went perfectly. The pedestal was broken and the breech was bent over. Again, very satisfactory. It is grand to think of the Boche making these weapons, running them over to Sicily and then transporting them all the way to Alamein, only to be destroyed in a twinkling by a British sapper.

A few days later I had my stiffest job. The call came at night – two Itie tanks and two German anti-tank guns had been brought up and abandoned when the counter-attack failed. They were supposed to be two hundred yards in front of the OP.

Next morning I found them. The information was not quite correct. Actually the second tank was seven hundred yards in front of the FDLs.

I did the first tank immediately. Twice a sniper fired at me and so I didn't hang about. The fat Itie driver was dead and cold in his seat with a six-pounder shot clean through his breast. I slipped my sack of ammonal beside him, closed the door and ran for my life. About four days later I examined that tank (after the advance had started). There wasn't the slightest trace of that driver!

Flushed with success I now set out for the second tank. No bullets! On and on I crawled and got to within sixty yards of the tank before the so-and-so sniper opened fire. I had no idea where he was firing from save that he was in one of the scores of burned-out tanks on the right. I lay in the scrub, trembling with fear. He had waited for me until he thought I was cold meat. I crawled on my belly another few yards. Every time I moved I was met by a crack over my head or on the ground round about. I then decided I had been a bit of a fool. If I were wounded nobody would get me back and six hundred yards in front of one's lines is no place for me alone. I hadn't even a pistol.

When the sniper fired at me while I was lying still, I decided to call it off and turned and ran for my life. I got back to the first anti-tank gun, which was in a dip, disposed of it and staggered back to my starting point. An anti-tank gunner gave me a lovely sip of tea and asked me why I had been out in front. That was another lesson. It sounds almost absurd, but I had forgotten it in my excitement. Always tell your own troops that you are going out in front of them and when you are likely to come back.

I sent a sapper to get the other anti-tank gun. It was a nice morning's bag, but I was sorry I didn't get the second tank. As it happened, the New Zealanders destroyed it a few days later, so my efforts were unnecessary. I located the tank the second time by finding a corpse which I had passed. There is no mistaking a corpse within a hundred yards! They say a dead German smells worse than a live Itie!

I reported the results of my demolitions to the OC, who was delighted in the extreme and rushed off to Brigade. The CRE also asked me all about it.

Shortly after this I was detailed to accompany an infantry battalion in the attack, which was to see the Boche off once and for all. I was most despondent about this and didn't like the idea of taking my orders from an infantry company commander, but it had to be and I arranged for a party of one NCO and a few sappers to accompany each company. I myself went with the centre company. My convictions were borne out in practice. I have seen better attacks done by Warwick School OTC and more than once we sappers found ourselves advancing by ourselves. Fortunately the battalion seemed to sort itself out just as we gained the objective. We couldn't have timed it better. We arrived about a hundred yards behind the barrage and found ourselves on the objective with the enemy still underground.

The infantry went wild and started probing with bayonets and Tommy-guns. About a hundred prisoners were soon collected and as the smoke cleared about sixty or so came running towards us under a huge white flag. What a difference between the enemy now and when we first started. The Germans were thoroughly beaten and fed up. 'Artillery' was all one chap could say. The Italians were mostly boys and deserved pity rather than punishment. The groans from the machine-gunned dug-outs were pitiful indeed and I diverted my men to lending a hand to get the poor devils out.

We dug in and waited for the dawn counter-attack. It didn't come. Instead I saw our own tanks move across from the right. They were through at last. I believe the tanks belonged to your regiment. They certainly had a bad time and appeared quite helpless in front of German anti-tank guns. After destroying three guns I withdrew to the squadron. I remember telling the OC that I thought the Boche had had enough. He was rather pessimistic as the tanks had been stopped yet again.

I took the troop back and prepared for a long sleep. 'We had done our best,' I thought, 'but the Boche is just a bit too good.' At 3 am I was awakened and told that the enemy was packing up. At dawn we moved off in hot pursuit and, to our amazement, found ourselves chasing the utterly defeated enemy across the open desert.

*

From Mr F. Hesslewood

An anti-aircraft watch was kept at all times during daylight hours as Stukas and other enemy aircraft were fairly active. This particular day my friend Sapper Farrington shared sentry with me.

We were lounging about in close proximity to the Bren-gun that was mounted on a tripod and bearing a hundred-round magazine when Lance-Sergeant Williams appeared on the horizon. As there were only two of us, we found it rather difficult to take up our usual position in the rear rank – a favourite position for the more experienced types. We knew he had seen us when he began to walk in our direction. We were the only squaddies within a radius of a hundred yards and it dawned upon us that we were to receive news of some kind – probably bad.

'You two are going on patrol with the infantry,' said Sergeant Williams. 'Report to Brigade HQ.'

We got the message clearly and I remember thinking that it would be a bit of a change. Neither of us had done this kind of thing before and had no real aversion to the task. A few junior NCOs had recently been on patrol, but we were the first sappers in our unit. It wasn't until later that I wondered who had made the decision for us in particular to go, and why.

Transport was laid on, and after a few miles' travel we stopped outside a large tent where we dumped the kit we had brought along with us. Our instructions were to 'wait there', an instruction which must be the most over-used one in the British Army. It transpired that one of us was to go on patrol that night and the other the next night. We tossed a coin and I, being the winner, decided to go that night and get it over with.

Presently an officer approached, was saluted and informed us that he was Captain Smith of the 1st/5th Queen's. Having introduced myself as the lucky sapper, I threw my kit into the back of his PU truck and was soon deposited at Captain Smith's tent which was pitched over a hole in the ground.

It was usual to pitch tents over holes in the ground as this gave more headroom. Protection against incoming fire was also to be borne in mind. I strongly refute the suggestion made by certain elements of the First Army that we got our name of Desert Rats because we lived in holes. That distinction goes to the 7th Armoured Division, their divisional sign being a jerboa.

The captain and I were joined by a sergeant and together we planned the patrol, which was to be a recce patrol comprising the captain, the sergeant, one private and myself. The object of the patrol was to penetrate the enemy's forward minefield to ascertain the types of mines used and any other useful information. This information had to be brought back and so it was essential that we got neither shot or captured. As I had no intention of being either shot or captured, I vowed to be as quiet as a mouse or rat, whichever was quieter. Another reason was that we didn't want Jerry to know we were interested in that particular area.

I have always felt a little in awe of the infantryman as he is the Army's main fighter and more usually in contact with the enemy than any other unit; moreover the discipline is usually stricter than in supporting units. I was immediately put at ease by the officer and sergeant and treated as the expert on mines, as I probably was in their eyes. In my own heart I was rather doubtful of my own ability and prayed that I wouldn't be the weak link.

Getting the private to accompany us wasn't exactly easy, for the sergeant, when dispatched by Captain Smith to ask for a volunteer, returned soon afterwards to report that nobody would undertake the task. These lads knew a trick or two and had probably learned the hard way – never to volunteer.

The difficulty was soon overcome by the officer. Enquiring the names of the best men for the job, he detailed Private Smith for the honour. Once detailed – everyone else wanted to go. We now had two Smiths in the patrol.

I regret that after all this time I have forgotten the name of the sergeant. Perhaps his name was Smith and the private was called something else. As the great man said, 'A rose by any other name . . .' Not that either man would appreciate being classed with roses. I have no knowledge if any of the gentlemen sharing the patrol with me survived the war, but I am honoured to have met them and I am sure their regiment is honoured for them to have served in it.

Our equipment was sparse. Desert boots, cap comforter, shirt, trousers, pullover, web belt and shoulder-straps, water-bottle, bayonet for the private to go with the rifle he carried and a bayonet for myself to use in the search for mines. The captain and I had a .38 revolver each and I believe the sergeant had a sub-machine-gun. For my part, the revolver didn't give me much confidence. I had never fired one before and probably couldn't hit anything anyway. I did, however, have to have my hands free to look for mines, so a rifle wouldn't have been practical.

My request for a few nails to take along was met with an enquiring look from Captain Smith, but they were quickly forthcoming when I explained that they were to be used as safety-pins. All explosive devices manufactured for the armed forces, British, German, Italian, etc., usually have a safety-pin of one sort or another and are the last thing to withdraw when arming a device. It follows that the first thing to do when finding a mine or other device is to replace the safety-pin when all booby-traps have been located. Anyone not familiar with the latest techniques should leave explosives alone.

Officers usually gave me the feeling of 'them and us' much the same as 'unions and management' in civilian life. Captain Smith was the one exception, and though I admit that his own men would not necessarily share my view, I must say his demeanour gave me a feeling of confidence in the coming operation.

It was time to go and we buckled on our gear, blacked our faces, jumped up and down a few times to make sure there was no rattling. All badges, documents, etc., we removed from pockets to make it harder for the enemy to gather information should any of us be captured. The thought did occur to me that giving my rank, name and number to a potential captor, as 1875127 Sapper Hesslewood, would soon reveal the object of the patrol.

Our transport dumped us at the front. That is to say, the forward infantry positions behind our forward minefields which were situated probably a couple of miles away from the enemy's forward minefields. The desert between was a no-man's-land. Except for an occasional burst of tracer bullets from machine-guns on either side and a flare or two, all was quiet. In the classic BBC phrase: 'Patrol activity continued.'

As Captain Smith, the sergeant, myself and Private Smith, in single-file and in that order, marched in step through the gap left in the minefield, we felt very alone and wished the moon wasn't so bright. It was possible to see quite a long way and this also meant that we could be seen from a long way off.

The area immediately outside the entrance to our own minefield was potentially the most dangerous place for us. Jerry or the Italian equivalent could expect any foray we made to come from this spot and could be waiting for us. I was very relieved when, after giving the pass-word to the unfortunate sentry guarding the forward entrance to our forward minefields, we made our way to take whatever cover we could in depressions and wadis available.

To start the journey we marched a given number of steps all stopping at the same time to listen, moved on again and did the same thing. This continued until we were well clear of our minefields. All the time we were half expecting to be fired on by an enemy fighting patrol or even one of our own patrols with itchy fingers. It had recently been rumoured that an Australian and a South African fighting patrol had met in no-man's-land and had a go at each other causing casualties on both sides.

Many thoughts passed through my mind as we made our way in the direction of the enemy lines. Each shadow, and there were many, held enemy soldiers. Each imagined noise, and there were many, was a bolt on an enemy rifle moving a cartridge into a breech ready to fire at me. Instinctively we marched in a slightly crouched way, hoping to take an inch or two from our height and so be more inconspicuous. I have little idea how Captain Smith found his way. There were few landmarks to go by even during daylight. At night, even with the moon shining, it was difficult to get a compass bearing, but he seemed to have little trouble. On the occasions we suspected that something was ahead, he went on alone to investigate before waving us on. In this way we marched, for what seemed many miles, though perhaps it was nearer three or four, taking into account the route along wadis and depressions to obtain the best cover.

At last the captain stopped and waved me up to him when he pointed to a spot about twenty yards to the front where from a wire fence hung a notice bearing the words 'Achtung Minen'. We had arrived at our destination and the real work was about to begin.

It was now my turn to take the lead, for I had to search the ground in front of the wire. A favourite trick of Jerry was to plant a few anti-personnel mines in front of the wire to deter people like me. I found nothing and my three companions joined me at the point of the wire where I intended to enter the minefield.

As we stood at the wire we were surprised to hear a voice singing a very lovely song. The singer had a good voice and we paused momentarily to listen as the Italian words floated over the desert. The singer probably wouldn't have been in the mood for love-songs had he known that four British Tommies were nearby.

It was decided that whilst I was broggling about in the minefield the rest of the patrol would recce along the outside of the wire fence. My comrades covered me and held open the wires whilst I used my bayonet immediately inside the fence to feel the ground and obtain enough clear ground to get myself in a working position. It's hard work broggling for mines on hands and knees. Progress was slow, but I was determined to do the job properly. I was more wary of the anti-personnel devices than the anti-tank mines as the latter could usually be walked on and still be safe. Not that I can recommend the practice.

I had no idea of the width of the minefield. The wire on the other side was not visible, but I knew from the singer that there must be troops guarding the inside wire. My heart beat so loudly that I was sure they must hear it, and, if they looked towards me, I felt sure that I could not escape being seen in the bright moonlight. There was no finding shadows now. I looked back from whence I had come and could see no wire and no patrol. Without doubt, I had never been so alone in my life.

I realised that I must go on and after a time, crawling and broggling, I glanced up. To my great consternation and horror, I saw at about thirty yards' range, a person in the lying-load position about to shoot me. To say that I nearly died of fright would not be quite truthful, but I did fall flat on my face instinctively and remain in that position without moving a muscle for what seemed hours but was probably a few minutes. All the time I kept thinking: 'Why doesn't he shoot?' 'Why no call for surrender?' 'Why?' 'Why?' 'Why?' The suspense wasn't to my liking. Finally I decided to risk a squint in the direction of my adversary and saw him in exactly the same position as before. It was then I decided that if it wasn't dead by now I had better do something as I couldn't lie in that position for ever.

Forward or backward? I decided that I should have a closer look forward as I had nothing to lose if I hadn't lost it already. I continued with my crawling and broggling until I came up to my assailant, who turned out to be three petrol-tins arranged in such a position as to look like a man in the moonlight. I was rather annoyed that they were British tins and blamed them for nearly bringing to an end a not very promising career.

The next decision came quickly. The question of forwards or backwards didn't arise. This was most likely a dummy minefield, for I had found no mines. In a real minefield it would have been nearly impossible to have missed finding at least one or the pattern would have been of little use. It could be that the fences had been erected ready for the mines to be laid later. I could see no object in getting captured or worse so I stood up, or crouched up, to be more correct, and retired in good order, making sure to step on the ground already tested for mines. In a surprisingly short time I had reached the wire at my starting point only to find myself alone again and very apprehensive as to my future well-being.

After a few moments of wondering what to do next I heard a slight sound to my right which proved to be the rest of the patrol, who had found an entrance to the gap through the minefield. This was guarded by only a few rows of mines that had been laid and armed but not covered. This was done so the mines could be easily moved to let Jerry's own transport and patrols through.

The mines were British and had previously been captured by the Germans, who were putting them to good use. The snag was that, owing to the length of time since I had seen a genuine British-made mine, I had forgotten what Mark (to indicate type) it was. My inclinations told me it was a British anti-tank mine Mk 4. I must admit feeling a fool as this information was wanted by brigade. Without confiding in my fellow patrolees, if there is such a word, I chose a mine that I thought most unlikely to be missed, disarmed it, tucked the exploder under one arm, the body of the mine under the other arm, filled in the hole with my foot and joined my friends in search of more information.

We held a brief, whispered conversation in which the captain explained that he would like to look around a bit more. This time he took up a position a greater distance in front and we set out along the front of the minefield wire towards our right flank.

After marching for about half a mile we stopped on the signal of our leader, who had taken up a kneeling position. He returned to us and whispered that a sentry was in front guarding another gap in the minefield and that he wished to get a bit closer to try to identify his formation by his badges. We could now all see the figure of the sentry in the moonlight and realised that if he had been more alert he should have seen us.

Not to be defeated, we retraced our steps for a few hundred yards and made our way to an escarpment that rose in front of the sentry and looked down on his position. Unfortunately the distance and light were not conducive to seeing German badges. Private Smith pleaded with the officer to take just one prisoner back but was to be disappointed for that was not the object of the patrol and we would most likely have stirred up a hornet's nest. It was decided to return to our lines.

The journey back was uneventful although the same precautions as on our outward journey were necessary, for the chance of bumping into another patrol was just as great. I think we were all relieved to reach our own forward minefield about a furlong from the gap where our outing had begun. This was good navigating by any standards.

The relief we felt was soon turned to anger as we approached our own forward sentry and got to within a few yards of him before we were challenged. Even then he failed to ask for the password and had to be asked to do so by Captain Smith. I was very glad not to be at the receiving end of the lecture that sentry was to get from our patrol leader. Had we been an enemy patrol, he could have been very dead.

We had been out on patrol seven hours, moving and working most of the time and, now that the adrenalin wasn't flowing so quickly, our legs began to feel heavy. I was glad to dump my mine and arming piece on the table in the brigadier's tent. He wasn't there, of course, as it was still before reveille. Only the cooks and such were stirring.

Captain Smith thanked me, a thing that pleasantly surprised me. I was not used to that sort of thing from an officer.

On my way back to camp I did reflect on what the brigadier would say when he got to his table and found an anti-tank mine in front of him. At least he would know what type of mine Jerry was using.

VI

Artillery and Anti-Tank Regiments

From Mr R. G. W. Mackilligin, MC

During the Battle of Alamein I served as a lieutenant in the 126th Highland Field Regiment, Royal Artillery, which was part of the 51st Highland Infantry Division. I was the Gun Position Officer (GPO) of one of the six troops of four twenty-five-pounder guns each that made up the regiment.

Our division was new to the desert, having arrived in Egypt in August 1942. Although we had undergone a brief period of desert acclimatisation on arrival, and had taken a minor part in the Battle of Munassib, we were by no means fully adapted to desert warfare, having spent our years of training in northern Scotland in conditions as near to arctic as could be devised. However, we were very fit and our morale was high, General Montgomery and 'Tartan Tan' Wimberley, our divisional commander, had seen to that. These men realised that the British soldier of the day, and particularly civilian soldiers as we were, could not be treated as cannon-fodder, but had to understand and believe in what they were asked to do.

The prelude to the battle was a nightmare period of dumping ammunition at the gun position we were to occupy, on the eve of the battle. Gun-emplacements had to be dug and sandbagged, and vast quantities of ammunition transported forward and dumped ready on the gun position. All this was done at night, and the whole area of the gun position thoroughly camouflaged to look like empty desert, and vacated by first light. Dummy gun positions were created elsewhere, to deceive the enemy about our intentions. We worked from dusk to dawn each night, and as the flies and heat made it virtually impossible to sleep during the day, we entered the battle in a fair state of exhaustion.

Working conditions were appalling; the Alamein position had been fought over several times and the whole area was littered with decomposing corpses, some unburied and others whose graves had been uncovered by the wind. The stench of putrification was all-pervading and the air thick with dust and horrible desert flies, bloated from feeding on the corpses. The fine dust stirred up by the constant passage of vehicles during each night penetrated everywhere and a handkerchief tied over the mouth was useless. The flies were the worst scourge, however, settling constantly on any exposed part of the body and imparting an irritating little sting when they did so. Eating required constant vigilance to keep them off the food and it was at times difficult to get it from the mess-tin to mouth free of flies. The food itself was most unappetising and monotonous, consisting of bully-beef, army hard-tack biscuits, liquid margarine and nondescript tinned jam, varied occasionally with tinned bacon and Maconochie's famous concoction, labelled tinned beef and vegetable stew. Tea there was in plenty, but from the start water was strictly rationed, allowing perhaps a mugful for personal ablutions and a daily shave. Clothing could only be washed infrequently, mostly when we were near enough to the sea to use that. One of the more difficult things was to persuade thirsty men not to drink their water rations during the day, but to conserve it for the evening and early morning, when it would not be immediately lost as perspiration.

It was a relief, therefore, to be able to move the guns up into their prepared positions on the eve of the battle, and to spend the rest of the night and the next day resting under the protection of our camouflage nets. With my command post team, I spent the day writing out the detailed programmes which the guns were to fire that night. There were last-minute changes, of course, but we managed to get the programmes written out for each gun in time. As it turned out this proved to have been time well spent. During the day, too, a large hole was dug in the desert, into which were packed our gas-masks, and very pleased we were to see the last of their encumbrance.

Zero hour for the battle was some time just after dark on the night of 23rd October, and the gunners' task was to start with fire at the enemy's positions, and especially their artillery emplacements, and then go over to a creeping barrage of fire, timed to fall just ahead of our highland infantry of 154th Brigade as they advanced. Monty's moon supplemented by searchlights illuminated the scene. As zero hour approached, all was in readiness for the greatest artillery barrage since the first war, and tension mounted as my eyes were glued to the dial of my watch . . . the silence was intense. As the second-hand of my watch reached zero hour, I gave the order to fire and Sergeant Coxon on my number four gun had a round in the air before the word was out of my mouth. For a split second I thought I must have made a mistake, but almost instantaneously the ground shook and the air vibrated as the artillery of the whole Eighth Army opened up. That was the last shouted order I was to give that night. Command of the guns by voice was impossible and the Tannoy loudspeakers at each gun position did not work very well either, so I spent most of the night dashing, programme in hand, from one gun to the next, checking that they were all firing at the right target at the right time. For the first barrage against the enemy's position this was not so vital, but once we began our creeping barrage, the weight of responsibility was enormous. We had to lift each step of the barrage exactly on time, as we knew our infantry would be following behind it. Even one gun dropping its shells short could cause havoc amongst them and destroy their confidence in the barrage.

In a short lull following our first programme, our friends of the Argyll and Sutherland Highlanders, with whom we had travelled out on the ship from England, moved through us towards their start line, each company being played into battle by its piper. It was a stirring sight in the moonlight and I think we all paused to wonder how they would fare that night and to wish them well. They did very well, of course, but sadly we were not to see many of our friends again.

We fired an average of five hundred and fifty rounds or about seven tons of steel-clad high-explosive per gun that night, and at first light next day when the firing stopped, we just dropped in our tracks.

The next day we moved forward through a narrow gap cleared through the enemy minefields and took up a new position, from which we fired another formidable box barrage that night. During the day we came under fire for the first time from a distant ridge, on which we could just see enemy tank turrets appearing from time to time. The fire was slight and sporadic but enough to encourage everyone to dig in deeper and we were very unlucky to lose Sergeant Wright, a fine young NCO in charge of one of my guns, with a few other minor casualties. Some of the officers and men began to go sick with dysentery, desert sores and heatstroke; some we never saw again; most just soldiered on, however, and the identity of the real soldiers amongst us began to emerge. Often it was dirtiest, scruffiest and most slovenly parade-ground soldiers who began to emerge as the ones on whom we could most rely in the battles that lay ahead.

I cannot remember how the rest of the battle went, except that it was a repetition of moving forward, firing barrages mostly at night and moving forward again. It lasted for about eleven days, but towards the end, although the barrages were becoming progressively smaller, we were becoming progressively more exhausted. During the last few days we were greatly encouraged by the sight of vast bands of unarmed

Italians making their way to the rear, sometimes shepherded by one or two 'Jocks', but often under the command of their own officers. These poor devils, having been abandoned by the Germans, were eager to find someone to whom they could surrender and were desperate for water. We had no water to spare and could only wave them to the rear. German prisoners were few and far between.

The end came as a bit of an anti-climax, although a very welcome one. Rommel had had enough and the Germans departed silently during the night, leaving us without targets. Then it rained, leaving us drenched to the skin in our open positions and, from being too hot during the day, we shivered all night. The rain had turned the desert into a quagmire, and allowed most of the German Afrika Korps to escape up the single road westwards, to fight us again and again in the coming months.

From the artillery point of view Alamein was a gun position officer's battle; most of our shooting was done at night and few of our observation officers were even deployed. Map-reading was next to impossible in the featureless desert and, due to the dust and heat haze, observation, except just after dawn, was very limited. Alamein was my first and last experience in action as a gun position officer but remains a memory I shall never forget.

*

From Mr H. B. Vanstone: The Second Battle of Alamein
(Alam El Halfa)

In August 1942 I was a captain commanding E Troop, 74 Field Regiment RA, in 50 Division. We were in the Delta recovering and re-equipping after our retreat in June/July from the Gazala Line. Monty took over command of the Eighth Army on 13th or 15th August and I first heard of this while bathing at Alexandria with some Italian (Egyptian) friends for whom a distant relation of mine acted as governess. They asked me what I thought of Alexander and Montgomery and although I had never heard of either I told my friends that they were first-class – as indeed they turned out to be.

Soon afterwards the divisional artillery was placed under direct command of XIII Corps to supplement the corps artillery, and we moved up to Alamein to an area just east of the Alam El Halfa Ridge. My first and early recollection is of the impact that Monty was already making on Eighth Army at all levels. Whereas during our previous eight months in the desert we had had scarcely any idea what had happened and was happening, let alone what was going to happen, within a very few days we junior officers at regimental level had been 'put in the picture' and knew what Rommel was going to do – and did – and what we were going to do – and in fact did.

During the remaining days of August, I spent my time as a roving OP getting to know the country and the landmarks south of the Alam El Halfa Ridge. I well remember one occasion when I had to struggle through soft sand in my cut-down Marmon-Harrington armoured car to such an extent that the engine boiled. The area was to the north-east of Deir el Ragil near el Huweijja and I marked it 'Bloody Going'. I mention this because a few days later I and other officers were asked to assist the CO assess the going to the south of the ridge for a going map he was preparing, and no doubt there was constructed from that map the false going map I have read was 'planted' on the Germans and which contributed to the predicament Rommel found himself in when he turned north on 31st August to attack our dug-in tank positions on the ridge.

Rommel advanced on the night 30th/31st August and on 30th August I had been ordered by my battery commander to reconnoitre to the south-east of our position to ascertain what troops there were down there. By great good fortune I came across the I truck of 7th Armoured Division and they very kindly filled me in with the whole picture so that I was able to return the same day to my unit with full information, instead of remaining overnight in the blue and bivouacking in what turned out to be Rommel's line of advance that very night!

*

From Mr D. Cook

I was in the western desert most of the time between August 1941 and August 1942 and then for a few weeks in the base depot at Almaza (RA). Conditions under which we went back into action in October 1942 were in marked contrast to the long-distance dashes we had made in the past to pursue enemy units or to be chased by them. At El Alamein, the first impression before the big battle and during it was that of great congestion. I was astonished to see observation towers being used to direct fire, as these seemed to present a much too conspicuous target, but I presume there was no alternative, as forward reconnaissance was virtually impossible with such concentration of forces on a thirty-five-mile front. When we arrived by truck from 'B' Echelon one night to visit 'I' Battery, 2nd RHA, it was difficult to find a place to park, but eventually we settled down for the night, though one unfamiliar sound was the innovation of falling bombs with an eerie siren effect as they screamed down. In the morning a trip wire was contacted and led to the detonation of a booby-trap killing one of our gunners.

Going back to the original occupation of the Alamein line in July, we were to have been involved in a daring raid which was considered feasible by reason of the enemy holding so many of our vehicles captured in the previous two months that he would not notice a few more British trucks in his midst. This plan was modified and a more modest attack led to the capture of a number of Italians. These appeared terror-struck, presumably having been told of an awful fate awaiting them if ever the British captured them. They marched past with hands up, fearing that to lower them would lead to their annihilation. Some of our gunners, seeing them look so pitiful, called out, 'It's us you should be sorry for, not yourselves.' I am sure they did not understand.

*

From Mr J. J. Mortimer, MC

Our anti-tank regiment, the 79th, which had been formed in India in 1941 to be the anti-tank regiment for the 1st (later 31st) Indian Armoured Division (and which, incidentally, never fought as a division, although many of its constituent parts did, either in the Middle East or Burma) came down from Persia in late June of 1942 and arrived in the western desert on 9th July. 104 Battery, in which I was a second lieutenant troop commander, went forward on 10th July to support the 26th Brigade of the 9th Australian Division who had come down, by night travel so we were told, from Syria.

We repulsed an attack by some eighteen tanks of the Ariete Division and we killed thirteen of them. This exploit I heard some years ago is actually mentioned in the Eighth Army handbook, and there is no doubt whatever that the stand by Auchinleck at El Alamein, Tel el Eisa Ridge and Ruweisat Ridge stopped Rommel's advance, once and for all, on the Delta.

Not another yard of ground was given and, with the advent of Montgomery and ample equipment (we, by the way, were armed with two-pounder guns), the battle on 23rd/24th October became feasible.

Memory plays tricks, but I shall never forget the sunny morning of 10th July nor the pride we all felt in our wartime soldiers. My own troop were largely recruited from the Midlands, and did such a fine job. My troop sergeant, one of our few regulars and a fellow Yorkshire-man,was killed near me firing his gun, which was destroyed, to the last.

Some weeks previous to our journey to the western desert some genius in Headquarters had had the bright idea of splitting up anti-tank regiments into their composite batteries and brigading them with field regiments armed with twenty-five-pounders. Our battery 104 went to 15th Field in Persia, one other – 103 or 105 – to 87th Field and I must confess I forget to which regiment the other went. However, we were withdrawn after suffering some 30% casualties at the end of August, and were re-formed under our own lieutenant-colonel and with the addition of a battery No 291, just arrived from the UK, we went on garrison duty in Iraq and later Syria.

Obviously one only sees one's own small part of the battle and I must apologise that I can only speak for 104 Battery but, unless my memory is playing tricks, I believe 103 Battery supported the South Africans on our left and 105 Battery to the left of them.

What I can say categorically is that Auchinleck had had deep defences prepared in front of El Alamein Station. That battle on 10th July 1942 really was vitally important, although it did not appear so at the time, and gave Britain the necessary breathing space whilst vital supplies were arriving at Suez.

*

It is very noticeable that those who actually took part in these battles – as opposed to those who directed operations – had no idea of what was happening outside their own immediate area. This was because the moment vehicles started to move clouds of sand and dust obscured the battlefield. (Radio communication was also affected by the consequent electrical disturbance.)

The clouds of dust over the Alamein battlefields re-created the problems of eighteenth and nineteenth century battle commanders, when smoke from guns blotted out everything but objects in the immediate vicinity – and sometimes even those. For this reason Alamein became a 'soldiers' battle' (like Inkerman in the Crimean War) and victory largely depended on the morale of private soldiers. There were, of course, very capable battalion and company commanders, but their influence was limited once the first shots were fired. The 'fog of war', by which is meant the inevitable confusion when battle is joined, became literally true in the desert.

*

From Mr J. Simpson (ex-Lance-Sergeant, 65th Field Regiment, RA)

In my family Alamein is remembered as the time of the telegram. With news of the start of the battle making the headlines, a telegram arrived at my parents' house addressed to my wife, who was staying there following the bombing of her mother and father's home. Joyce was at work and my parents had strict views about opening other people's correspondence, even when they assumed it to be the news that I was a casualty or a prisoner. Eventually the addressee was contacted on the 'phone, gave her permission for the envelope to be opened, and thereby received the 21st birthday greetings I had sent on the eve of the battle.

My journey to Alamein had started in May 1942, shortly after my marriage. We went round the Cape of Good Hope, jammed in a troopship, but a welcome break in Cape Town came to a sudden end with news of the fall of Tobruk, and we quickly found ourselves in a barbedwire box in the desert and briefly surrounded by German tanks. However, Italian troops with the Germans panicked one night, switched on their truck headlights and enabled the RAF to sort them out.

We knew that the big day was approaching because of the increasing frequency of Montgomery's 'pep talks', as well as the steady stepping up of messages and orders. At the time we were properly cynical, as good soldiers are, but Monty did boost morale. He seemed human, unlike some of the other top brass. Churchill came to see us and that went down well too.

When the time came my unit was sent right down to the left of the Allied line, almost in the Qattara Depression, where we drove our trucks up and down, with the intention of making the Italians opposite think there were a lot more British soldiers around than there really were, and that the spearhead of the attack would hit them. Whether it was our sandstorm or the following bombardment, I am not sure, but the tanks and infantry found very few Italians when they pushed past us.

On the evening of 23rd October our twenty-five-pounders added their bit to the solid wall of sound which started where we were and must have reached to the Med. In off-duty moments I stood outside the command post and saw the sky actually alight with the flashes of the artillery massed to launch the attack.

Then, off we set across the desert, in support of the 44th Home Counties Division. The Italians were going backwards too fast for us, as we picked our way through the minefields. It wasn't really difficult, although we did lose an American-built ammunition truck, without casualties, however.

Eventually we moved into the main stream of the advance, until we reached Benghazi, where we pulled out for a spell before moving up to Tripoli, with the 56th London Division. By this time our infantry had

had a mauling and been withdrawn to Palestine. Later we supported the Guards at the Mareth Line. Messing with them at least gave us variations in our diet. Salt porridge appeared on the menu for one thing.

Usually we were too busy to feel fear. This emotion only came with inactivity, as when we were held up in Tunisia for three weeks, or perhaps when the immediate future was uncertain. When we stopped to think about it, it wasn't much fun having sand, but no infantry, between us and the enemy before Alamein.

One night when heading for our Alamein battle position we had to leave a truck-load of equipment as the lorry was needed. I had the job, with two others, of staying with the dumped equipment until it was picked up next day and this was certainly lonely and nerve-racking, particularly as we were warned to expect German patrols in the area.

To end on a family note. I walked round a sandhill one day, before the battle, and met my cousin George Davis, an NCO in the Royal West Kents. Despite my regiment having supported his in France, this was our first meeting since we delivered papers together as youngsters.

*

From Mr R. A. Gray

When the guns first opened up in the famous 800 gun barrage, at 9.40 pm on 23rd October, I, as a liaison officer, was some miles behind the front and I remember remarking to a fellow officer that, rather incongruously, the far-distant rumble of the barrage took me back to times of peace, recalling the gentle rhythmic sounds that trains make when approaching a station through a tunnel. But as I drove overnight in the course of my duties towards the battle, the sound image changed to bring to mind some demoniac drummer beating with wild abandon some unimaginably enormous percussion instrument, deafening the world.

For some days beforehand we'd known that the start of the battle was to be on the night of the full moon and we used to watch the moon at night rising and making its solitary progress across the cold sky; we used to call it amongst ourselves the 'Moon of Destiny'. Once the battle started, however, the Moon of Destiny was joined in space by millions of instruments of death and destruction, by the red and yellow flashes of the guns, by orange and white flares, by scarlet tracer bullets acting as direction guides: illuminating apparently endless, ghostly moonlit columns of infantry and sappers, moving in single file through the mine-fields, who, perhaps fancifully but not entirely inappropriately, called to mind the infinite procession of silent mourners filing past a bier at a lying-in-state ceremony.

But fortunately, despite inevitable individual deaths, there was no overall battle defeat to be mourned this time because, after a week or so of stalemate, when the rival armies stood toe to toe, pumping every form of ammunition into the opposite side, suddenly came the break-through and, in what must have seemed to the original Territorials in our Yeomanry Regiment – the country land-owners and the farmers – something to be likened to the exhilaration of a point-to-point meeting or a fox-hunt, but to the conscript officers and men – the cockneys and Liverpudlians – more like the carnival atmosphere of a Bank Holiday outing to Brighton or Blackpool, we dashed fifty miles in a single day diagonally across the desert, to end up on the coast and seaside, surely enough, but the name of the place was Galal, not Brighton.

Having arrived, when we immediately received our first fire orders (we were an artillery regiment) some of us wondered if, in actual fact, the exhilaration of the charge had gone to our heads, because when the fire plan was worked out, the guns were not facing the enemy ahead of us, but just the reverse – we were required to face about and engage targets more or less in the direction we'd travelled! But all was even-tually explained – we'd been ordered to advance at breakneck speed in an effort to cut off the retreating enemy and were now in fact about to engage pockets of enemy resistance left behind in our rear.

Soon after this the battle stabilised for a while and those of us who were on the coast were able to spend off-duty hours swimming in the blue Mediterranean and actually to see, a mile or so to the east, enemy soldiers similarly sporting themselves in the sea, whilst inland we could see our divisional vehicles sprawled to the horizon, could hear the guns of both sides incessantly barking, see clouds of dust everywhere and see, above us, the silver weavings of the RAF patrols nonchalantly and with-out apparent opposition, searching out the enemy.

*

From Mr M. Cooke

My arrival in the western desert coincided with General Auchinleck's offensive of November 1941. An ordinary gunner in the Royal Artillery (Field), I was posted from Northern Ireland (53rd Welsh Division) and joined the 4th Indian Division somewhere at the frontier of Egypt and Cyrenaica south of Sollum Pass.

Everything in the desert was totally unfamiliar and made special demands upon a soldier. Devoid of cover, the vast stretches of scrub and grey stony ground held no features in the landscape other than depressions known as wadis which offered good protection for tanks, guns and vehicles.

Flies were a pestilence : they caused sand-fly fever. If one had an open wound on the hand, knee or face, flies would suck at the wound creating maggots which, in turn, eat the bacteria. Flies everywhere : one could hardly put a mug or tin to the mouth to drink before flies were floating in the liquid.

Water was priceless. More so when lines of communication were long, or when units were cut off or in a tight spot. On many occasions I have known water rationed to a pint per man per day – and that was for shaving and drinking. Again, I have personally drunk my own urine and washed in petrol to 'delouse' myself. Seasoned campaigners carried small stones in their tunics which they sucked to create saliva.

Each vehicle, gun troop or tank crew was responsible for its own messing arrangements. Usually the driver or signaller would do the cooking over a petrol-can cut in half, filled with sand and petrol poured on and ignited.

As the terrain was featureless, movement at night was limited. All sense of direction was erased by the lack of objects. When the night was black, a soldier who left his slit-trench and walked a few yards, turning around twice, had great difficulty in finding his way back.

Between November 1941 and January 1942 the Eighth Army pushed Rommel back to El Agheila. Naturally there were the usual chessboard moves – advance, halt; then retreat, and advance again. Nevertheless, there was a comparative lull until May 1942. By this time the Japanese offensive was in full swing. Consequent upon this we lost all our Indian gunners, infantry and support troops, who were diverted to India and Burma. Australians were also repatriated – not all, but some units and brigades. Reinforcements were hard to come by.

Rommel attacked on 24th May. His objective was, once again, Tobruk; his line of attack – around Knightsbridge and El Adem.

I recommence my own story at Fuka. It is difficult to recollect events of that particular time in any degree of clarity. All was chaos. The remains of the Eighth Army were desperately re-sorting themselves into a tactical fighting force, with what equipment troops had managed to bring back. Everyone was doing each other's duties and jobs. As the few hundred of us were 'regimentless' I was packed off to join a battery supporting the Free French Brigade who were dug in near the Qattara Depression, about forty miles south of the coast road.

It was feared Rommel's motorised columns might attempt a probing action through the soft sand of the Depression and head towards the Nile. In point of fact, two reconnaissance vehicles of the Afrika Korps did manage to penetrate the Qattara Depression.

We dug ourselves in : both outer and inner minefields were laid. It was the practice, in those early days, to go forward at first light, through the minefields, to prepared positions. The strength would be two gun-troops and two companies of infantry. The object was to watch any movement of a possible heavy build-up of enemy troops, and to 'pot' at anything which moved and created dust on the skyline.

Meanwhile, Field-Marshal Montgomery had arrived, together with vast supplies and much-needed reinforcements, among them two new infantry divisions – the 44th and 51st (Highland). Rommel was also receiving reinforcements. Between July and August it was a state of cat and mouse, both sides licking their wounds and making good repairs to tanks and equipment.

No doubt had Rommel consolidated his positions as he swept east-ward, he would not have given the Eighth Army chance to make a defensive line at El Alamein. His lines of communication were too long. Thus it was not until about the 30th August that he launched his last attempt to break through. His plan was to break through at the south, swing north and reach the coast road – thus cutting off most of the main Eighth Army concentration.

An interesting feature was the build-up of dummy positions in the southern sector for 3rd Alamein by the Eighth Army. To fool the German spotter planes, dummy tanks, guns and other vehicles were made of wood and canvas and erected at night. Came the morning it would appear to the enemy that fresh reinforcements had moved into position, thus giving the Afrika Korps intelligence the idea of our pro-posed attack from these southern positions. Hence Rommel's decision to test the strength of our flank.

After repeated attempts all along the line, by 30th September Rommel had given up all attempts to drive for Alexandria. However, the build-up of armour and dummy tanks continued in the south until the barrage went down on 23rd October. The 7th Armoured Division was on our right, and once the main breakthrough in the north had been successful they withdrew to the northern and coastal sector.

Following the opening days of the 3rd battle, two battalions of the Foreign Legion attacked south of Himeimat, penetrating several miles beyond the hill, repelled two counter attacks, doing much damage to enemy forces, but had to withdraw when they came under attack by tank squadrons. But they had accomplished their objective.

Unfortunately at this point I spent several months in the 5th South African Hospital at Cairo, and did not join the battle until the Eighth Army reached the Mareth Line at Tunisia. Here I was posted to the famous 51st (Highland) Division, with whom I served for the remainder of hostilities in Sicily and Europe.

*

From Mr S. J. C. Cross, MBE (Mil)

The 95th Anti-Tank Regiment, RA, was in course of re-equipping and reorganisation at RA Base Depot, Almaza, after a severe battering in the Gazala Line, one battery, 'Charlie', only surviving. It was to this battery and this regiment which I had the honour to be posted in September 1942 on arrival from the UK.

As a 'new boy' I was soon to be attached to the 3rd Australian Anti-Tank Regiment RAA, 9th Australian Division, the Platypus Division. My attachment became effective from midday 23rd October, just at the right time to get a bit of training in desert warfare.

The division was holding the coastal sector west of Alamein Station. The troop to which I was attached covered the minefield in the area of Tel el Eisa and not far from 'Thompson's Post'.

The troop commander, whose 'duva' (foxhole) I shared, was some years younger than me but a veteran of desert warfare, as was also his troop sergeant, both of whom bore with me extremely well as I don't suppose for one minute it was their wish to have me tagging along with them – they had enough on their plate. However, apart from the usual leg-pullings always inseparable from an Australian, we all got on extremely well. They were essentially a civilian army and no one stood on ceremony. To hold a command, however minor, you had to prove yourself, so it was surprising to me that I was so quickly accepted.

As we all know, the battle opened with an artillery barrage, the like of which had not been seen since the first war, but Jerry did not remain quiescent for long and very shortly he replied in kind. A few 88s and we bolted for our duva like rabbits, but no sooner had we got our heads down when a really heavy one came over. It was just like a train and the damn thing exploded a few yards from us, burying us in our aforesaid bolt hole. It was fortunate for us that our trenching tools were handy and it wasn't long before we dug ourselves out to be faced by the grinning face of our troop sergeant, who wanted to know what the so and so we were doing down there when there was a job of work to be done up here.

The succeeding days brought news of the to and fro-ings of the tank battles farther south which we could well observe and more than once I was apprehensive when the German tanks got well behind us. Ours was a static rôle and we were not called on to change it. The gun positions were constantly visited by the troop commander, whose shadow I was, and the troop sergeant. I well remember one morning during such a tour. These Australians never played safe and were always taking short cuts through the blasted minefield. This time the Stukas caught us. I just dived on the ground trusting to luck I wasn't diving on a mine while the Stuka bombs blew up mines all round us.

When the dust and smoke cleared I poked my head up and fifty yards on, there were my companions on their feet yelling, 'You all right, cobber? Well get a bloody move on before the next lot.' I did not wait.

As for humour, one of the funniest incidents I recall was as follows : Early one morning some couple of days after the start I saw one of our burly Aussie gunners walk over to his gun position's 'Thunder Box'. Having settled himself he began to read last month's *Sydney Times,* no doubt, when Jerry started his morning hate. A round fell some two hundred yards behind him. Without further ado he shouted a correction : 'Up four hundred, one round gunfire.' Almost immediately a shell whizzed overhead and landed two hundred yards ahead. With complete composure, having got his bracket, he called out : 'Down two hundred, five rounds gunfire.' You can guess the rest. He was blown off his thunderbox and sailed through the air with the greatest of ease. Being quite unhurt from his aerial experience he picked himself up and hurled a dose of expletive worthy of Billingsgate at the Jerry gunners, who, after all, had only done what he had ordered.

My stay with these Australians was an exhilarating experience. They were tough, good-natured and more than kind-hearted. I was sorry to leave them, but I had to rejoin my unit, which had then arrived in reserve area and took up the chase to Marsa Brega.

The 9th Australian Division was withdrawn shortly after the battle and went to the Far East. I think they would have been happier in that locality as all whom I met were very apprehensive about a possible Jap invasion.

*

From Brigadier H. W. L. Cowan

In October 1942 I was commanding the 2nd Regiment RHA in the First Armoured Division. On Tuesday, the 20th, I and many other senior officers went to a cinema at Ariya about fifteen miles south of Alexandria to hear an address by Monty, the Army Commander. He came out on to the stage and spoke with his hands in his pockets and without notes :

'When the Prime Minister sent me out to the Middle East he told me that my first job was to turn the enemy out of Egypt, and on Friday night we're going to start to do it.

'It won't be an easy battle, there will be no spectacular advances, it will take between ten days and a fortnight, and it will end in complete victory.'

Can you wonder that, the battle having lasted some twelve days and ended in complete victory, I keep saying that he was in a class by himself as an army commander ?

*

From Mr L. Challoner: an extract from his forthcoming book, *Where Right and Glory Led*

On the night of 23rd October the opening barrage began and it was soon clear that something very big was afoot. For days the Command Post had been engaged upon the plans; interrelated fire-plans, creeping barrages with their complicated adjustments to ranges and switches had been worked out in advance for every troop, ammunition had been stacked and prepared and we were ready with 'one up the spout' for the word 'Fire !'

We were used, of course, to the crack of our own piece and also to the sound of all four guns in the troop firing together or in quick succession. On this occasion, however, it was different. Our guns were not more than thirty yards apart, the next troop and battery were only a stone's throw away, and all seemed to be firing at once. Furthermore, from behind us, but not very far away, heavier ordnance had now joined in and was adding its thunderous and earth-shaking chorus to the general clamour. Those of us who had turned down the offer of earplugs for use during the prolonged 'shoots' now began to regret it and to look around for other means of protection. Mr Dermott, the ammunition number one, could be seen beavering away with a Victory V cigarette protruding from each ear. 'Quite the best use for them I've ever seen !' said Len Chandler, who had recently given up smoking because he had more respect for his lungs than to expose them to such rubbish.

The barrage continued, with short rests taken by the different units in turn to adjust instruments and to allow the barrels to cool. Several regiments were taking part and we heard in the morning that over two hundred rounds had been fired by every gun. What it must have been like at the receiving end we could scarcely imagine; our own heads were throbbing and aching for days afterwards. Reports came in at dawn that certain units of the enemy were withdrawing, and scouting parties sent through the minefields to investigate brought back a number of very shaken prisoners and the news that some units had indeed been forced to pull back.

It was now the turn presumably for other units to take up the chase. Tanks and infantry moved forward to predetermined forward positions and it was impressed upon us that close adherence to every detail of range and direction was most important lest we should find ourselves shooting up our own men. We moved forward cautiously over the next few days, firing a hundred and fifty rounds per day, gradually eliminating the enemy's forward armament, and taking up positions between the two great minefields at Alamein ready for the next phase.

On Sunday, 1st November, all records were broken for the number of rounds dispatched in one day. Four hundred rounds per gun were fired in what the enemy described as an inhuman barrage and the result was that when the infantry went in they encountered droves of shell-shocked and demoralised men ready to surrender to anyone who offered to take them away out of it. We saw them shuffle by on their way to our rear where possibly transport would be available for them, but for the moment they had to make their way on foot, sometimes in groups of twenty or more guarded by a single private or junior NCO. We watched the dispirited, bedraggled Italians and the sullen, gaunt-looking Germans straggle along the track before a fierce little Jock who was cursing the sand, the flies, the heat and his charges indiscriminately as he urged them along. It was possible to feel sorry for them now, especially the young ones who could not have been more than seventeen years old and stared about them as if they had been pitchforked into a new and incomprehensible world. 'Well, the war's over for that lot,' said Mac. 'They'll see Blighty before we do – lucky devils!' 'Yes,' said Len Chandler, 'but it won't be home to them, will it?' and we dismissed them from our minds.

The success of this action was probably due to the fact that the Australians had made a very determined attack on 29th October and opened a route over the minefields for the rest of us. The enemy was not ignorant of this, of course, and we were the object of a few Stuka raids and some acute fire from 88 mm guns. It was during this time that Driver/OPA Hudd distinguished himself and was subsequently awarded the MM. We had moved over two miles nearer the enemy and took over again the famous 'Woodcock' position with which we were familiar. For the first time, perhaps, some of us realised how near to Cairo the enemy had forced us to retreat and how close, but for a little luck and a good deal of obstinacy, we had been to defeat.

*

From Colonel R. F. Wright

On 20th October all officers in the corps down to the rank of lieutenant-colonel went to a cinema at Amariya to hear the Army Commander explain his plan for the attack. It was to be divided into three phases:

1. The break into the enemy positions.
2. The dog-fight and battle for position.
3. The breakthrough and pursuit.

The show was to open with a barrage of eight hundred guns on a frontage of about six miles between the sea and that ridge of evil memory,* Ruweisat, at 0230 hours on 23rd. All men were to be told the plan. During the evening of the 22nd I went round all batteries and an MG company which was under our command and explained what was going to happen; at the same time I pointed out how optimistic was the outlook. Everybody felt 'teed up' and fully realised that something decisive was about to take place.

The following day I paid a visit to the 'Beachy Head' area, and the desert between there and the sea was a mass of vehicles of every sort, size and description. The blue of the Mediterranean gave colour to the whole effect. One could not help having a curious feeling of pride and confidence; proud to be taking part in a battle likely to prove decisive, and confident that we had the leadership, men, tanks, guns, equipment and aircraft available to deliver the punch and maintain the momentum. Except for one or two vehicles moving along the coast road, everything was still. The scene rather reminded one of the marshalling of the performers before their entry into the arena at the Aldershot Tattoo. Yet all the time one knew it to be the calm before the storm. Even now one's eyes were focussed on Tripoli, some 1,300 miles away!

For the first phase of the attack the regiment was put under command of the Armoured Brigade Batteries being with Armoured Regiments. As we were a few miles from the front, we started two hours before the barrage commenced, moving up on three tracks known as Sun, Moon and Star. To assist units to maintain direction, appropriate designs were cut out in tin and placed on top of stone cairns every two

---

* I was then commanding 149 AT Regiment in July 1942.

hundred yards. There was a bright moon shining and vehicles looked like phantom bodies moving noiselessly along the sandy track.

By 2300 hours we had passed through the gun areas and shortly afterwards made contact with the Minefield Task Force. This was a battalion whose job it was to clear up possible enemy pockets of resistance and to regulate and control traffic through the minefield. By dawn we had got through the first field and deployed; progress on the right along 'Sun' track was quicker than elewhere. In going through these gaps how many of us realised what heroic work had been done by the sappers and infantry in clearing these passages, and the Corps of Military Police in lighting up the way, all done under heavy shell and machine-gun fire.

Our job was to protect the flanks of the armour and to gain touch with units on the right and left. During the day the whole area became a mass of vehicles, tanks and guns, not more than thirty to forty yards apart. Thank heavens we had air superiority! A field regiment commander came up and asked if there was any room in which to deploy the guns. We surveyed the scene and spotted what looked like an empty space about half a mile away. I think it turned out to be a minefield, but anyway he joined in the party somehow!

Progress was very slow on the 25th as a way had to be blasted through the second minefield. There was an exchange of shots all day long between our tanks and those of the enemy, the A/T guns too having a go. Circumstances took one over to the right flank, where certain adjustments to the AT screen were required by an armoured regiment. Anything but a pleasant journey in a Jeep! Later a tank battle developed along the lines of a slogging match, as there was no room for manoeuvre. The 'Deacons' were moved over to this flank and, in spite of not being able to get any hull-down positions, did quite a lot of execution (probably ten tanks) without, strange to say, much damage to themselves. They unfortunately suffered some casualties. One promising officer was badly wounded and one driver had his arm shattered. Owing to the door of the cab getting jammed, he had to be got out through the front slit. How it was done, I don't know. Both died of their wounds later.

The regiment was now under command of the Motor Brigade, except for one battery and the MG company, which remained with the armour. It was still a matter of, 'Hard pounding, gentlemen! Let's see who can pound the hardest.' Whilst cruising around one had the unhappy experience of running the Jeep over a mine. Thank goodness there were sandbags on the floor! Beyond the 'writing off' of the vehicle not much damage was done. A sad loss, as these little cars were worth their weight in gold and difficult to replace.

During the afternoon of 26th October the corps and divisional commanders arrived and a plot was hatched whereby two battalions were to attack respectively two features to be known as 'Snipe' and 'Woodcock' that night, following an attack by units of the Highland Division. At this conference a number of officers were gathered on the 'sheltered' side of a Churchill tank when a passing sergeant in the Royal Corps of Signals let out the most weird and realistic noise of an AP shot travelling at speed. Everybody wondered what on earth had happened and then burst out laughing! For this advance we had one battery with each battalion, HQ remaining with the Motor Brigade. During the night great difficulty was experienced by the battalion directed on 'Snipe' in getting all the AT guns through some sand.

The following morning there was a certain amount of controversy with regard to our position, the 'Jocks' having placed 'Stirling' and 'Aberdeen' in places with which we did not agree. I was sent over to one of these battalions on our left to find out: (a) where they thought they were, and (b) if they could assist us in any way. The 'Jocks' were right in their map-reading. Anyway, there was not much argument as the battalion commander* and I had played rugger together some years ago and 'agreed to agree' about the position! He could offer no help, however, as he had orders to remain anchored to his firm base. On being asked if he had seen anything of the 'Snipe' battalion, he replied, 'No, but last night a very excited CO, who appeared lost, asked him a few questions and then dashed off into the night.' (This CO was to win the VC in the next twelve hours!) After reporting to HQ, a visit was paid to one of the companies of the 'Woodcock' battalion with whom we had a troop; in addition the 'Deacons' had been put into action to their left rear. Having suffered some casualties, they were withdrawn, having achieved nothing except capturing a few Boche who had remained hidden underground.

It was learnt later that a determined attack had been launched by enemy tanks on the 'Snipe' battalion. A very fine show was put up by the A/T guns of that unit and thirty-seven tanks were destroyed. Part of one of our batteries had the honour of taking part in this action, but had a minor rôle as all the 'plum' positions were occupied by infantry guns. Our guns did not get a shoot till late in the afternoon, when eight

---

* Tom Rennie, Black Watch - - later to be killed crossing Rhine when commanding Highland Division.

to ten tanks were knocked out. Owing to losses by shellfire and mines the previous day, the battery had ten guns, only six of which could be got into position. For this action the CO of the battalion won the VC. Other awards were also made, one of our sergeants receiving the MM.

On 29th October the division was withdrawn to the coastal area for three days, in which to reorganise and re-equip for the next phase of the battle, the breakthrough and pursuit.

The following day the corps commander visited the 'Snipe' battalion to offer his congratulations to the officers and No 1 of the AT company. *The battery was not asked to send any representative.*

After re-equipping and having a 'wash and brush-up' we again entered the fray on 1st November. The desert was still crowded with every type of gun, vehicle and tank. There were so many A/T guns about that you almost trod on them! What with Scottish, Australian, Maori and our infantry guns lying around, it was quite impossible to find one's own. The old insurance company at work again! During one of these perambulations an AP shot passed underneath the Jeep, giving one a horrible feeling of emptiness! Later the Adjutant put this same vehicle up on a mine and was unlucky enough to damage his foot very badly.

The next day, apart from normal shelling, there were a series of Stuka raids, but these did not cause much damage and were generally broken up by the RAF, who managed to maintain a most efficient umbrella during the whole battle. Numerous raids were carried out by formations of eighteen Bostons at a time over the forward area, and a welcome sight it was too. The lines were so close that it made accurate 'pattern' bombing a very delicate business. In fact, one Highland Division Battalion was unlucky enough to get the lot on one occasion, and most unpleasant it must have been. Just before dark a lone enemy bi-plane cruised slowly over the front. Every AA weapon in the area opened fire, but the pilot was quite unperturbed, flew around to have a 'shufte' (look) and made off eventually in a westerly direction. A most extraordinary getaway! The amount of tracer that filled the sky beat any 'Brocks' firework display, and made rather a fine sight!

On 3rd November one of the troop commanders and No 1 of the battery working with the armoured brigade had the satisfaction of capturing an Italian tank. They walked up to it with revolvers, knocked on the front door, and the crew came out and surrendered! The troop commander was killed the next day; always smiling and cheerful, his loss was greatly felt throughout the battery and regiment. Late in the afternoon it was decided to put in an attack on Tel El Eisa and two

Rain in the desert can quickly make roads unusable.

A captured 88 surrounded by ammunition.

The teeth of a German Mk IV tank effectively blunted.

Investigating an Italian Medium tank. There was always a danger of booby traps.

features to the north of it, three battalions being allotted the task. One battery was given to the battilion directed on Tel El Eisa; the second battery was due to go with one of the other battalions, but, owing to the lateness in getting its orders, darkness fell and the gun towers could not find the gun positions. Consequently the switch-over was not carried out in time. The only objective gained was Tel El Eisa, which was occupied and consolidated by first light on the 4th. A tank attack was beaten off and eight destroyed, the 'bag' being equally divided between one of our troops and the infantry. Here again a valuable troop commander was killed whilst assisting one of the Bren-carriers. Nothing much happened during the day beyond enemy artillery concentrations which did little damage. A regimental aid post appeared to disappear in a cloud of dust and smoke, but survived miraculously and the casualties were few. In the evening reports came in from the RAF that large numbers of vehicles were to be seen moving west along the coast road and were being suitably dealt with.

Everybody had settled down peacefully when the stillness of the night was shattered by every gun opening up at about 0300 hours. The enemy had withdrawn and were being given a helping hand, the crack from an adjacent battery of 'Priests' being particularly noisy. At first light there was much excitement and regrouping of units. We had broken through and the chase was on!

VII

The Back-Up

Colonel Norman Berry, OBE, BSC, *was Chief Mechanical Engineer for XIII Corps and Eighth Army. He was at Eighth Army HQ at the battles of Alamein.*

His comments emphasise the importance of repair, and the underlying problems of desert warfare.

It was my responsibility to organise the repair and recovery of all the tanks, guns, vehicles, etc., in whichever formation to which I was posted. Starting in October 1935 with the 8th Hussars, I had been doing this work with a wide range of units in all the desert campaigns and probably saw more of the technical problems that arose than most. In 1941 and 1942 I was responsible for this in XIII Corps.

I think that it is fair to say that the whole course of events in the desert fighting turned on two vital factors:

(a) Faulty design in the Crusader tank.

(b) The two-pounder gun.

The value of the two-pounder may be debatable, but the faulty design of the Crusader tank was not.

The basic trouble with all our tanks in the early stages of the war was that no engines were designed for them. Presumably this was due to lack of money, but the fact remains that in the case of the Matilda tank, which was designed as an infantry tank, the power unit was two London bus engines geared together giving a total of 180 bhp. This may have been acceptable on Salisbury Plain but was not acceptable in the soft, sandy conditions that were often encountered in the desert. The poor Matilda, which had been the Queen of the Battlefield against the Italians who had no anti-tank weapon that would touch its four and a half inch armour, became a sitting duck to the Germans with their 88 mm high-velocity converted anti-aircraft gun.

Anyone who doubts that statement should have been present when one of my recovery sections picked up what was left of the thirteen tanks commanded by Captain Bill Rawlins, VC, of the 42 RTR after he had attacked one 88 mm gun at Sidi Omar. One shot had gone straight through the front of each tank and the mess inside was indescribable. I took a lot of photographs of each tank and sent them off to GHQ Middle East and heard no more. This may have been one of the factors that persuaded the desert generals that the Matilda should be used mainly in a defensive rôle.

The Crusader tank was just the opposite. It was very fast, when it worked, had very good suspension, when it worked, but had the same two-pounder gun.

Shortly before Operation Crusader* was due to begin it was found that the suspension arms were breaking off like carrots in large numbers. This proved to be due to faulty casting in the manufacture in England, but a cure was effected by welding reinforcing plates to each arm. As there were ten arms to each tank and each arm weighed about two cwt, this put an enormous strain on the already overstrained field workshops, but the remedy proved effective. This suspension trouble was not a design fault, it was a fault in the manufacture of a certain batch of tanks, it was cured and had no effect on operations. The lack of mechanical reliability was a very different matter and had a very profound effect on the whole of the desert fighting in 1941 and 1942.

Like the Matilda the engine of the Crusader tank was not designed as such. It was a 12 cylinder 400 hp aero engine left over from the 1914-1918 war. The engine was produced in America when she came into the 1st World War and was supposed to combine the best features of the British Rolls-Royce and Sunbeam aero engines in use by the RAF. As an aero engine it proved to be very reliable and had a good performance.

Unfortunately the cooling problems in a tank are very different from those in an aeroplane and here the troubles began. In an aeroplane there is, or was, no need for cooling fans as the air rushing through the radiator at over 100 mph is sufficient to cool the water in the radiator. In a tank big fans have to be provided to do this. In the Crusader, the engine was modified by the fitting of two fans and two water pumps driven from the engine crankshaft by a long chain. This was a disaster. As soon as the tank was used in the desert, sand got on the chain, the chain stretched and started to jump the crankshaft driving sprocket. It was a three-day job to change the sprocket.

Worse still, the water pumps would not stand up to the sand and heat

* Auchinleck's offensive to relieve Tobruk in November 1941.

of the desert and soon leaked very badly. A re-design was necessary, but unfortunately the manufacturing facilities did not exist in Egypt.

In January 1942 we had pushed Rommel right back to El Agheila and he seemed to be nearly finished. I think he would have been finished if we had not had two hundred Crusader tanks under repair in the XIII Corps workshops. Most of them were waiting for the water pumps. The situation was so critical that the Corps Commander signalled that four hundred water pumps should be flown out from England to Benghazi, by flying-boat if necessary. The reply came back: 'Regret NA [not available] in UK.' If those water pumps had been available Rommel's counter-attack on 5th February could never have succeeded, and there would not have been a battle of Alamein first, second or third.

The two-pounder gun

This gun was the standard weapon in all the British tanks and the standard anti-tank gun in use in the Eighth Army until May 1942. It seems that the War Office considered it was a very good gun. I never came across a single officer or man in the desert who agreed with that view. Unlike our tanks, it was beautifully designed, was 100% reliable and had a very long life, but in the view of every tank gunner or anti-tank gunner I know or spoke to it was simply too small to prove effective against German armour at over six hundred yards. As an anti-tank gun it was virtually useless in the desert.

On one occasion I listened in to the OC of an anti-tank battery reporting that his shots were bouncing off thirty German tanks that were attacking him and that this was probably the last that would be heard of him. It was.

I got the impression that the War Office simply did not want to listen to any criticisms of any kind that were made about any equipment that had been sent out to the Middle East. It was much easier to criticise the generals.

It is infuriating to consider what could have happened. In November 1941 we captured a German anti-tank gun. I was asked to inspect it and report on it. I could not believe my eyes. It was a British three-inch AA gun manufactured by Vickers and fitted to a Russian gun-carriage. It was a very effective and powerful weapon. Clearly it had been sent to Russia, captured by the Germans, serviced and sent to the Middle East.

When the three-inch AA guns in London were replaced by the four point seven inch guns, several hundred three-inch guns became redundant. If these had been fitted to twenty-five-pounder gun-carriages and rushed out to the Middle East, the whole course of the war would have been changed.

The first battle of El Alamein became inevitable when the Eighth Army lost the tank battle at Gazala. A few days before Rommel attacked on 30th May, General Gott explained to us on his staff that if we won the tank battle we were to be prepared to move on to Tunis; but if we lost we were going back to the Alamein position. This was because Tobruk would *not,* repeat not, be held a second time, as the Navy had stated that it could not supply it, and that there was no defensive line that could be held west of Alamein.

He then predicted Rommel's moves very accurately and explained that 7th Armoured Division equipped with some of the new Grant tanks would bear the brunt of Rommel's attack and that 1st Armoured Division equipped with the weaker Crusader tanks would take care of any German tanks that got past 7th Armoured Division and headed north towards Tobruk.

What went wrong? Nobody seems to know. Rommel's move around the south of the Gazala position was shadowed by the South African armoured cars and by the RAF, and we in XIII Corps HQ followed his move with great interest.

It seems that we knew more about what was going on than the tank regiments in 7th Armoured Division, because by all reports the 8th Hussars, who held the most southerly position, were caught by surprise at dawn on 30th May and the two regiments of the RTR who formed the second and third lines had very little notice of the attack. As a result we lost far too many tanks and the Germans far too few. This time we could not blame the mechanical defects in our tanks which had caused such problems before, but it would appear that there must have been some breakdown in communications. Thousands of words have been written about the desert fighting – mostly by people who were not there, but I have never heard of this vital point being mentioned.

As a result of this setback 1st Armoured Division had to compete with much stronger tank forces than 'Strafer' Got had predicted, and although the fighting was very touch and go by 16th June the tank battle was lost and it was decided to withdraw. The withdrawal became complicated by the decision to try and hold Tobruk for a limited period. A lot of equipment that was being moved out had to be moved back and there was some confusion because of this. Apparently this change of plan was due to the direct insistence of Winston Churchill, who was then in America.

Tobruk fell and the withdrawal continued. On 30th June Rommel

arrived at Alamein and the scene was set for the first battle of Alamein.
It has always seemed to me that far too much time is devoted to 'how'
a battle is to be fought and too little to 'with what' it is to be fought.
Pages and pages have been written about the respective capabilities of
Generals Auchinleck and Montgomery. I had the honour to serve on
the staff of both these distinguished generals and I think that it is unfair
to try and compare the two without comparing 'with what' they had to
fight.

The quantity and quality of equipment that started pouring into
Middle East during the summer of 1942 was staggering. We produced
a daily tank statement of tanks fit to fight, tanks fit to fight within
twenty-four hours, and tanks fit to fight within forty-eight hours, every
day at 0900 hours for the Army Commander. I saw this statement grow
from 250 to 1,151 in six weeks.

Once the first battle of El Alamein had been won the final issue was
never in doubt and I think that everyone in Eighth Army knew it. I
know I did.

Some historians have tried to suggest that General Auchinleck was
planning to retreat across the Delta, but his replacement by General
Montgomery changed all that.

I was promoted from HQ XIII Corps to HQ Eighth Army in August
1942, and almost my first job was to attend a conference called for all
heads of services. I remember this very well because I was the only head
of service who bothered to attend. All the others had sent junior officers
to represent them and the conference was chaired by then Lieutenant-
Colonel Miles Graham instead of then Brigadier Brian Robertson. We
had to draw up a contingency plan in the unlikely event of falling back
across the Delta. The whole thing was treated as a routine chore and a
bit of a joke. For history to state that Auchinleck was planning to
retreat was a complete travesty of the truth. We were all working flat
out to build up Eighth Army for a decisive battle with all the superb
equipment that was arriving at last.

One could say that General Sherman won the battle. The four
hundred Sherman tanks that arrived in August gave us the tank
superiority we had been praying for for years. Well armoured, with a
powerful 75 mm gun and very reliable they were considered the answer
to a maiden's prayer. After their arrival we never lost another battle in
World War II.

As one who served in Eighth Army from its very beginning could I say
a word of praise to all these marvellous men, personal friends and

others, who fought so valiantly with very poor equipment. This country owes them an enormous debt which has never been acknowledged. They are not allowed to wear an '8' on their African Star. It is high time they were. Perhaps it's not too late, but the friends and relatives of the real Desert Rats can be forever proud of them.

It must be very difficult for anyone who has not lived there to begin to understand what life in the desert during a campaign is all about. One reads about Eighth Army Headquarters, 7th Armoured Division workshops or some such, but all these different units consist only of vehicles, tents and people. There are no buildings, factories or offices of any kind.

The units are spread over a big area, with vehicles or tents about fifty to a hundred yards apart to minimise the effect of bombing. A big workshop can occupy a space of a square mile or more. It could be very disconcerting to put it mildly, if one was lucky enough to be granted a few days' leave and returned to one's 'home', perhaps in a rather delicate state of health, only to find nothing at all except a vast sandy waste and not a clue as to where the unit had moved.

It must also be difficult to visualise a life with no distractions of any kind. No house, no family, no pubs, no nothing except one's work and one's comrades dumped down miles from anywhere in a sandy waste and, of course, no comforts of any sort. Of course, everyone grumbled like hell, but in a good-natured way. The morale was astonishingly high, and crime was almost non-existent. In the REME units, the work-load was always so heavy that there was no idle time from sunrise to sunset, seven days a week.

In one tank repair workshop, I was at my wit's end to improve production by some sort of incentive scheme. But what? One could not extend working hours as one was not allowed to show lights at night. Pay rates were fixed by the War Office and could not be altered, so piecework was out. Finally, I tried setting a production figure for the month and offering everyone to close the workshop for a day or two at the end of the month if the target was beaten. We would then decamp fifteen miles to the sea and have a surfing picnic. The effect was miraculous. One would even hear privates shouting at sergeants to 'get a bloody move on or we won't get our swim this month'. Production went up and up, but it nearly ended in disaster.

One day the General's ADC rang me up and said I was to report to the General at nine o'clock the next morning. I knew from his tone that I was in trouble. The General snarled that he had driven past the workshop the day before and that there was not a soul in sight, did I not know that there was a war on, etc., etc. I explained what was going on and pointed out that this way he was getting more and more tanks repaired. After a long pause he said that in future he would take a route that avoided the workshops when they were shut. So all was well. Rather like Nelson and his blind eye!

With everything being so widely dispersed, it was very difficult to maintain cohesion and control of activities within the unit. I found two solutions that paid off handsome dividends. As no lights could be shown because of the danger of attracting enemy bombers, after-dark activities tended to become divided into little groups in individual tents or vehicles so that the first thing we did on arrival at a new site was to dig a very large hole in the ground and cover it with a huge piece of canvas. After the evening meal, this became a sort of social centre and as there were always some extrovert types with guitars or banjos and amazing repertoires of every type of song and dance, this became a very popular place of entertainment and relaxation. It proved to be a tremendous morale booster, and in fact became quite famous so that I received many applications from men serving in other units asking if they could be transferred.

The early-morning parade was the start of the day's activities and was attended by everyone. I always took this parade personally and made a point of explaining how the battle was progressing, what future plans were being made, and what the reason was for any orders that were being published. This way the orders became a personal matter and not just another bit of 'bull'. The cheerfulness with which everyone accepted such dreadful working conditions for such long working hours seven days a week never failed to amaze me.

The repair and recovery of all types of vehicle that break down or are damaged by enemy action is always a very important factor in modern warfare. Tanks that became casualties had to be towed out of the battle zone by unarmoured tractors. This was a very slow and dangerous operation. The vital need for armoured recovery vehicles had been stressed over and over again from 1935 onwards, but they were never provided.

The Germans were far better equipped in this field than we were and they also had the big advantage that their three-quarter tracked armoured personnel carriers could, and did, tow tanks out of the danger area. One got the impression that every piece of equipment in the German Army had been carefully designed and well engineered, regardless of cost, for the job in hand and then fully developed.

We, on the other hand, had to try and make do with anything that was commercially available, even if it was not really suitable. Beggars could not be choosers. In the early desert campaigns, we were short of everything. Transport, spare parts, recovery vehicles, writers' sets, tank transporters, spring steel, welding equipment, etc. One reason for this was the desert itself. It played havoc with anything mechanical and the War Office did not seem to comprehend the abnormal demands caused by it.

I could never understand this attitude. After all, the Eighth Army was the only unit actually fighting until Japan came into the war and the people on the spot certainly knew what was wanted, when the people in the War Office did not. One would have thought that senior officers, including the CIGS,* would have visited the theatre of operations occasionally. I don't think that any soldier in Eighth Army even knew who the CIGS was. A few visits would have made it clear that we were not asking for the moon. We were asking for necessities.

Finally the penny did drop, and from August 1942 onwards all sorts of equipment did start arriving in large quantities. The bad days were now over and the good times had begun.

In every way, the first battle of Alamein saw the turning of the tide.

*

From Mr J. H. E. White, MM, ex-WOI, IEM and REME

I served in the desert and at the first battle of Alamein we were in the Indian box, which was hotter than curry. Some of the incidents prior to the loss of the box and afterwards were not in any manuals of war. I was awarded the MM at Alamein after the first battle. I am now over seventy, so dates are somewhat blurred, but there are events which do not require dates. My angle of the campaign was somewhat different from infantry or gunners as, although they were there with us, our problems as Brigade Workshop Company were different. A tank in the workshop for repair was an ideal target for the enemy. Indian tradesmen were used for perimeter defence, which was not what they had been trained for, but they had a go. To keep both soft and hard skin transport† going at all times, whether on the move or stuck in a box, was an interesting challenge. Such books as I have read about the desert have reported the tactics and strength of the opposing forces but did not mention the good work of the military police during our retreat, nor

---

* Chief of the Imperial General Staff (the Army Commander-in-Chief).
† Soft = unarmoured.
  Hard = with armour though not as much as on a tank.

the guts of RASC drivers with loaded tank transporters or petrol lorries or tankers.

*

From Mr W. P. Tapley

I was a TA (Mechanical Engineer) in the RAOC (later REME). I served in the field in General Wavell's desert campaign; in Greece in 1941 (including Crete); and in all the desert campaigns until just before the invasion of Sicily, and finally in Normandy, Belgium, Holland and Germany. Almost all my service was on tanks and other armoured vehicles.

In 1941 when our lines of communication were becoming very stretched in the desert, there were two 'engineering' reasons why even the best of tank crews often could not fight.

One reason was that most of the tanks reached the battle area on their own tracks and as a result were often in very poor mechanical condition. (Of course, there just weren't any transporters to speak of.) For instance, Crusader tank waterpumps and timing chains had a *very* limited life. The other reason was that field and other workshops were hard pressed all the time to turn out vehicles for immediate fighting use, but with no independent inspection or kitting arrangements. Inevitably crews were sent into battle with unfit and inadequately equipped tanks, with both unfortunate effects on morale at the 'sharp end' and on planning calculations further back.

All this had become well understood by the time of Alamein, and tanks were being carried as far as possible on transporters – or sometimes, for example, armoured cars were towed literally hundreds of miles by RASC vehicles.

On the second count, a new organisation was born around Alamein time. This was called Tank Reorganisation Group, under the command of Colonel Murray (RAC). (I believe we may have had another title at first?) I was a major at the time and was in command of the engineering side.

Our brief was to accept all new 'A' vehicles and 'A' vehicles repaired by all workshops, field and base. To check them thoroughly for mechanical fitness, and with our own workshop rectify faults (which were many) if practicable, or if necessary reject the vehicle.

TRG also ensured that vehicles were properly kitted out. Such fully 'vetted' vehicles were then issued to fighting units as might be instructed, and could be relied upon.

I well remember our working all the hours we could at Burg-el-Arab, not far from Alamein, trying desperately to have a thousand fit tanks in the field 'so that Alamein could start'!

This dual improvement of transporting 'fit' tanks well forward was undoubtedly of incalculable value. Sufficiently so for both Colonel Murray and myself to be sent back to UK in 1943 to form a very much larger and more effective 'Armoured Replacement Group' with a mobile workshop and stores outfit and with outposts of both at corps level to receive vehicles from the main workshop and from 'local' workshops in the field, to inspect, rectify, kit and issue. This system was maintained until the end of the war.

I have no idea if a similar system exists today, or how much credit was ever given to it after the war, but I have no doubt whatsoever as to its value, both for Alamein and afterwards in North Africa, and later in NW Europe.

*

From Mr W. F. Ball

I was the Divisional Supply Officer of the 4th Indian Infantry Division, which took part in the battle on 23rd October 1942, and which commenced at 21.40 hours, when somewhere in the region of eight hundred to a thousand twenty-five-pounders opened up on the Germans and Italians. I shall never forget the thunder of the shells and the brilliance of the flashes. We had the famous 52nd Highland Division on our right, but I've forgotten the divisions on our left. The 52nd came out en bloc on the *Queen Mary,* and certainly put new heart into us veterans. I had previously served with No 38 Indian Infantry Brigade at Tobruk early in 1942, where we were bombed daily by German Stuka dive-bombers. Fortunately, we were ordered back to the Delta a few weeks before the Germans took Tobruk. We were defending the El Adem sector of the Tobruk perimeter. We were relieved by a brigade of a South African Division, and it transpired that the Jerries broke through this vital sector, which was previously held by us. If we had not come back to the Delta, I would have been 'in the bag' with the rest of the twenty-five thousand-odd men. The South Africans were very spick and span, compared to us, and it struck us that they were in for a picnic! They soon changed their minds after they were captured.

I've got a copy of the Special Order of the Day by Major-General F. I. S. Tuker, OBE, Commander of the famous 4th Indian Division. It went as follows:

Tonight forward elements of the 4th Indian Division go into battle.

This is the beginning of the general offensive which will destroy the enemy in N. Africa. We must beat him here on the very ground before us, for he has not the transport with which to escape. This is to be a hard-fought and prolonged battle. None of us thinks it will be otherwise. Once more we are to show the courage and the solid endurance for which we, British and Indian, are known all over the world, and to add to it a new vigour and fierceness in attack.

No position gained will ever be given up. Surrender is shameful as long as we have strength to bear our arms. *The last man, the last round, the last bayonet.* Small, isolated parties of brave men fighting it out have turned the tide of battle and the whole course of war and the memory of these men is always with us and always will be with us.

Today we can give ourselves the assurance that we are far stronger in the air and in artillery and stronger in infantry and are at last stronger in armour. Above all, we have a cause that is the cause of all Mankind, whereas the enemy has no cause in which he can believe.

The 4th Division enters battle with Faith in its Cause, with Faith in its Courage, and with abiding Faith in Almighty God to bear us up and lead us to victory.

In the field, 23rd October 1942

After the battle, our brigade was switched from the 4th Indian Division to the 5th Indian Division, then re-forming near Baghdad, as they were very badly beaten up in the retreat before the Alamein Battle. Our brigade was No 161. After training, we were ordered back to India for further jungle warfare training near Ranchi, and were then posted to the Arakan in Burma, and were in constant action until 1945, including the fierce battle of Kohima. The success of this battle was the beginning of the end for the Japs. As a personal comment, the Western Desert was a picnic compared to Burma. The conditions were terrible, and looking back I'm damned if I know how we achieved what we did. We did it, indeed, without complaint. I had the honour to command Indian troops – wonderful men. If you had their respect, they would flog themselves to death for you.

*

From Mr G. A. Bonner (ex-Captain, Royal Tank Regiment)

I assume that by the 1st battle of Alamein you are referring to Rommel's mad rush along the barrel track in July 1942 when he almost captured Cairo. He almost captured me too. I was right in his path and escaped only by a quick flight. I remember it as though it were yester-day.

By the 2nd battle of Alamein I assume you are referring to that disastrous day some weeks later when, as a result of a tragic mistake by a brigade intelligence officer, an armoured brigade was led straight on to a minefield instead of through it. We lost (if my memory is correct) more than eighty tanks that day. I did not take part in that battle but was stationed at the time on the shore of Lake Maryut. However, the brigade commander, carried the can for the debacle. He was demoted to the rank of colonel and given a lower, though an important com-mand. I knew him very well. I don't think the full story ever came out and I am probably one of the few people who know that the mistake was due to a confusion between a compass bearing and a map co-ordinate. I am glad to say that he got his rank and his command back eventually.

For the record I was an officer in the Royal Tank Regiment. I was with the Eighth Army from Alamein to Tunis and served as a liaison officer on the staff of the 1st Armoured Brigade HQ. This unit, which had been a fighting unit, was reallocated by Montgomery for specialist duties. It became known as the Tank Reorganisation Group and was concerned with the salvaging and transport of tanks. Our job was to see that tanks were repaired and got back into the fighting line as quickly as possible and I think we played a part in ensuring the ultimate success of the main battle of Alamein. After Tunis fell I was posted to Cairo, where I served in Military Intelligence GHQ.

*

The following extracts provide interesting information about the food supplies of the Allied armies. Mr Cummins's carefully organised supplies of fresh meat rarely reached the front-line soldier. Mr Lewis's list has a more familiar ring.

Our knowledge of battles which took place before 1800 lacks details of food supplies. We can only speculate on what the Roman soldiers ate on their long marches or what the Normans and Saxons relied on to see them through the long day at Hastings in 1066.

From Mr R. M. Cummins

Most of your replies will be from *soldiers* who were in the thick of the battles, but precious few, I imagine, from civilians whose rôle in war-time is rather dull by comparison. But there were many of the latter who, though they did not wear a uniform and were not anywhere near the El Alamein battlefields, can claim to have 'taken part' in that great epic. I have in mind those who worked on the lines of communication. None of the accounts of the great campaigns in North Africa pays much tribute to those who, near and far, toiled away behind the lines, often under very trying conditions, to ensure that munitions and food arrived at the front at the right place at the right time. So I hope that some mention will be made of the logistical side in this account of the battles.

Remember the position at the time! The Mediterranean was blocked, and the Canal and Suez rendered untenable for shipping. Fortunately, the Sudan had held the onslaught launched from Italian Eritrea in June of 1940 until help came along from India. The successful conclusion of the Battle of the Sudan made Port Sudan safe for shipping, so that this little port became the main side-door to Egypt. Everything came pouring in through Port Sudan, which was not built or equipped for an avalanche of war supplies. Then, this material had to be got away, three hundred miles inland to the Nile by rail, where it joined the line four hundred miles to the northern terminus Wadi Halfa. Here, the supplies were transhipped to river barge a hundred miles to Assuan, with all the difficulties of different river levels, where they were transhipped again to trucks of the Egyptian State Railways. Then there was the long haul to Lower Egypt, and finally along the southern coast of the Mediterranean to the front. And all the time these precious supplies had to run the gauntlet of human predators which abounded everywhere along the way, particularly in Egypt.

To cope with all this surge of traffic and troop movements, the single-line Sudan Railways had to put in many more crossing points and lengthen trains (and consequently lengthen existing stations) to increase the capacity of the line. There were no spare stocks of permanent-way material at hand, so the lesser used lines were picked up and planted where most needed. Much improvisation and ingenuity were employed as there was no quick source of external supply. And *time* was the pressing factor.

When the soldier at the front was occasionally able to get a fresh meat meal, I don't suppose he gave a thought to where it came from. So I hope you will make mention of the fact that five thousand head of cattle and twenty-five thousand head of sheep were sent from the Sudan per month as long as needed, all the way from the deep South. This meant much organisation at short notice. Firstly, inducing the natives to part with their revered cattle. Then electric goads were used at loading points to get the wild cattle into the wagons quicker (for the maximum turn round of the wagons); staging points were set up at various intervals en route for rest and veterinary inspection; they were transferred to the river at Wadi Halfa, and loaded into wagons at Assuan, and then on to Egypt where the poor beasts arrived alive, a little thinner, but edible after a journey of round about two thousand miles in oven-like temperatures.

One could reflect that there could not have been an 'El Alamein' if the Italian forces in Eritrea, built up to massive strength from 1935, had been stiffened by Germans. The Germans would not have stopped at Kassala, but would have exploited their initial gains and dashed on to Atbara (Railway HQ) and Khartoum, and destroyed the railway bridges there which were vital to communication. There was nothing to stop a determined enemy, but the Sudan Defence Force, under General Platt, held the line in what surely was one of the most decisive battles of the war.

I was one of the 'civvies' stuck in the Sudan throughout the war, with no home leave for five years, and my particular job was Superintendent of Operations, Sudan Railways.

*

From Mr A. Lewis

Originally, I believe, the plan was to have one Royal Army Service Corps DID* for each division, its job to issue rations in 'brigade bulk' and to divisional troops. In practice, 13 DID usually operated for at least a corps and even supplied up to five divisions at a time, something which entailed working round the clock. Our strength was thirty-five, including two officers and six NCOs, and when not engaged on the distribution of food we had to operate a p.o.l. depot (petrol, oil and lubricants).

From the second week in May 1942 until towards the end of the month we were operating the p.o.l. depot at Sidi Rezegh. The sound of gunfire from the west and south-west got nearer, day by day, and there were many stories of the fierce fighting.

On the 26th and 27th May hundreds of vehicles started to stream across our depot to reach the Trigh Capuzzo and head eastwards and there were all the signs of a big 'flap', almost panic.

Although we in the RASC were supposed to be trained soldiers, there were few of us who had adequate training and most of us had been working from almost as soon as we joined the Army. (I, myself, had

* Details Issue Depot.

been put in charge of a coalyard at Aldershot within three days of arriving there for documentation!) It was natural, therefore, that when the 'flap' started our lads were beginning to get jittery, especially as there were no signs of our joining the mad chase. Instead, we were refuelling those heading for 'the wire'.

Eventually we were overrun by elements of the German 90th Light, but fortunately we were able to get away – officers in their pick-up and all the rest of us on one three-ton lorry – minus kit, which had to be abandoned. We each had our rifles but there was only one overcoat, one knife, fork and spoon between us!

There followed a time of real confusion, of orders and counter-orders; first we were heading west again, then east, and many and picturesque were our opinions about our leaders. We had to set up small ration or p.o.l. dumps, then within an hour or two reload and head off elsewhere. On one occasion we were moved all the way back to Gazala, into the northern 'box' with the real fighting troops, but after two days of doing nothing we were moved back to Tobruk.

We continued in this fashion for the next week or two, steadily heading into Egypt, and morale was at a very low ebb. We took over depots on the L of C (Line of Communication), only to have to abandon them in a matter of hours. Frequently we loaded lorries directed to us by military police, with the object of taking any rations back they could, but invariably more was abandoned than taken away. The REs moved into one big depot at Sidi Barrani to destroy the dumps of food, but the explosives only blew up the stacks and the tins were unharmed. We were all very depressed and, to make matters worse, nearly all of us became lousy through sleeping in ready-made dugouts at one location which had previously been used by native labour.

The talk was all of evacuating Egypt, perhaps going to Palestine, or even to India, and the German victory was considered inevitable. What a relief it was at last to reach what must have been the outposts of the El Alamein line and to see the New Zealanders, practically dug-in, looking extremely resolute and ready to take on Rommel's forces. That was very heartening.

By the middle of July we were apparently fairly stabilised and we were located not far from El Hamam. We were issuing both rations and p.o.l. and were kept extremely busy. Being near to Alexandria, small supplies of beer started to come up and this was taken that things were going to improve.

Eventually we were moved to a field maintenance centre at the rear of the southern end of the El Alamein line. At the FMC, which occupied several square miles of desert, were the various services – ammunition, petrol, supplies, medics and a water company.

These were very busy days indeed with our unit receiving and issuing supplies from first light to sundown. As we were comparatively near to Alexandria the rations improved and there were issues of frozen meat, fresh vegetables and fruit, and New Zealand cheese. Mail from home arrived quite regularly.

We were seldom without the sound of gunfire and there was a lot of enemy air activity with occasional strafing of vehicles collecting rations, hence vehicle dispersal was most important. Stacks of rations were at least two hundred yards apart and only one vehicle was allowed to load or off-load at a time. We had so much work those days that it was next to impossible to find time to write home. Morale had noticeably improved with the announcements of the new commander. There was talk of enemy pushes and 'being allowed' to advance, and on several occasions we had to be extremely mobile – all rations had to be loaded on to lorries and kept that way. Issues had to be made from the lorries, replacements had to be loaded, a system which made issuing very difficult to operate. At the end of August we did move back some miles but after a few days returned to our previous location.

At this time there were frequent sandstorms due, no doubt, to the movement of hundreds of vehicles. Practically all our chaps were suffering from desert sores and the least scratch soon became infected and became a great attraction for the hundreds of flies.

On 7th October we moved seven miles westwards to a point as near as I can remember some five or six miles from Himeimat. We had to mount stand-to's every morning and night because of a danger from enemy parachutists. We had very big convoys to deal with and we really were conscious that things were hotting up. We were kept informed of what was going on, and we felt we were in the picture. As a result morale improved tremendously. We saw hundreds of guns going forward; large movements of tanks disguised as lorries and vice-versa. By mid-October the weather was bitterly cold and overcoats were worn all day. There were constant aerial dog-fights overhead and the sight of our own and American formations going over was very heartening.

Then on 23rd October it was on! We were all waiting for the big battle and at 9.40 that night it started. From one end of the western skyline to the other it was a scene of constant gun-flashes and the noise of the barrage was terrific.

For the following week or two we continued to be kept extremely busy, but at last, after the breakthrough, we were moved north, to

Alamein station, where we operated as goods railhead until mid-December. Again this meant much hard work to keep supplies going forward to our rapidly advancing troops. Sometimes we worked the clock round which, with such a small workforce, was quite a problem. However, they did send us some Indian pioneers for the heavy work. These were sometimes a bit of a problem, refusing to lift carcases of meat or even cases of tinned meat, etc., etc. Our chaps were sometimes very exasperated. During this time we had as our living quarters the underground hospital at Alamein, a labyrinth of concrete passages and chambers, which were at least dry and out of the wind.

Eventually we were moved to Daba, where we took over the bakery buildings which had formerly been operated by the Germans.

In case it is of interest, the following is the standard list of rations handled by DIDs at that time, but I do not remember what the actual scale was:

Rice (sometimes issued instead of potatoes)
Onions
Fresh vegetables as available (pumpkins, marrows, cucumbers mostly)
Canned beans
Tinned vegetables
Potatoes, fresh or tinned
Foul beans (local)
Lentils   ,,

Meat and veg. tinned
Corned beef
Frozen meat, beef or mutton, as available
Tinned sausages
Tinned luncheon meat
     ,,   bacon (wet)

Dried fruit   Bread when available, otherwise
Oatmeal   FS biscuits
Flour

Sugar
Syrup
Jam (mostly Palestinian)
Marmalade   ,,

Tinned salmon (pale pink variety)
     ,,   herrings or pilchards

Tinned margarine

   „   cheese (New Zealand proper cheese – two to a case –

                                                  when avail.)

   „   evap. milk

Tea (Indian)

Tinned fruit

Baking powder
Curry powder
Atta
Chillies
Ginger
Garlic   Rations for Indian troops
Turmeric
Dhall
Ghi

Cigarettes/Tabacco   Also special cigs. for Indians
Matches

Water sterilising powder.   Latrine paper.   A/mosquito cream.
Anti-louse powder.   Taste remover tablets.   NCI powder.
Flysol.   Izal.   Pan oil.   Formaldehyde.   Resin.
Chloride of Lime.   Cimex blocks.   Ascorbic acid tablets.
Creosoli.   Meth. spirits.   Wick.   Borax.

Hospital supplies : Fancy biscuits.   Horlicks.   Arrowroot.
                    Custard powder.   Bovril.   Bengers Food.
                    Pearl barley.   Ovaltine.   Cocoa.

The cigarettes/tobacco and hospital supplies had to be kept under special control.

In the above list of rations I omitted *salt*. Substantial quantities of this were issued, as on desert service the ration was doubled for health reasons. As near as I remember it, the normal scale in the Middle East was $1\frac{1}{2}$ ozs per man daily, but in the 'blue' it was 3 ozs. It came in 224 lb bags and it normally took two men to lift a bag. Mind you, I am fairly certain that salt on the official scale was not used by the cooks, and quartermasters would not always take their full allocation.

Another point of interest : in the pre-Alamein weeks it seemed to me that the base supply depots and warehouses at Alexandria and in the Canal Zone had been scoured to push rations forward. For instance, on one occasion we had Fray Bentos bully beef which, according to the dates on the bases, was from 1918! The story was that it had been in cold storage at Port Said until the cases were sent to us. But the bully was in grand condition – 'vintage' beef! At the same time, over a few days, amongst the tinned fruit we received were cases of Malayan pineapple from (presumably) the same period. However, this was not in such good condition, the acid of the fruit having corroded the tins, permitting the juice, etc., to leak out so that out of a case we were lucky to find a complete tinful. We had to sort them out, of course, and dispose of the empties, but it was a waste of time and transport sending them up to us.

Another item in relation to the meat issue: on a few occasions we received a number of sheep – alive and 'on the hoof' – for issue to Indian troops in the same condition, as they carried out their own method of slaughter.

With reference to my mention of our chaps becoming lousy, I forgot to mention that after a week or two we had to operate a small p.o.l. depot, so 'all hands' took the opportunity to wash their clothes in petrol, wash their hair in paraffin and get most cut off, and as this coincided with a temporary and slight improvement in the water supply we were all able to have a wash-down.

VIII

At Headquarters

From Mr H. E. M. Russell (Sergeant Intelligence Corps, 270 Section)
The odd jottings I shall relate are conjured from memory some thirty-six years after the actual events : obviously no claim to complete objectivity or accuracy is possible at this stage. Hindsight, half-forgotten readings of the campaign, talks with old colleagues, are still compounded in the memory. At the same time this was my first experience of action and the incidents are engraved in my mind with the vividness of some fantastic dream. A further point : as a member of the Intelligence Corps (FS Wing) and attached to the 4th Light Armoured Brigade, a reserve combat group, I saw nothing of the main battle and breakthrough. However, I may help to establish the specific atmosphere of that time and place.

Initially I was attached to the 51st Highland Division, which had recently arrived from England to reinforce the Eighth Army. During the Battle of Alam El Halfa I think we were in the Delta. If so, we encamped near the Pyramids and our forward troops were in defensive positions on the Nile. Anyhow, I recall that we heard of Jerry's reversal at Alam El Halfa with great relief. I can say here and now if there was a heroic posturing in the Eighth Army, then I never came across it. I often contrasted this attitude with that of the Germans : countless times in reading captured German mail I encountered such sentiments as a wish to make the supreme sacrifice *'für unseren Führer and unseres Vaterland'*, which struck me then and still does as extremely odd. Pray don't get me wrong here. Everywhere there was a dogged will to 'see Jerry off' and at some infinitely remote point in time to get 'back to civvy street' and sanity.

Immediately after Alam El Halfa we were moved to the desert. At this point I can give you my first cameo. It was I think our GSO III* who escorted us on a guided tour of the battlefield. I remember standing on the escarpment of Alam El Halfa and surveying below very many

---

* Staff officer.

knocked-out tanks and armoured fighting vehicles and, more particularly, wrecked Messerschmitts and Stukas. My feeling that this last feature was greatly significant was confirmed a few weeks afterwards when I joined the 7th Armoured Division, the original 'desert rats', and heard how for the first time the dive-bombing Stuka menace had been laid.

By now preparations were well under way for the 'big show': armoured units were receiving adequate tanks at last, viz Grants and Shermans. The inferiority of the Crusaders and Honeys against German armament had left a bitter legacy of feeling; indeed, they were spoken of as coffins on wheels. Monty's bellicose eloquence made, as I remember, little impression on the hardened campaigners of 7th Armoured Division; they had made the Benghazi run so often, with always the same frustrating aftermath of retreat. Gradually, of course, Montgomery's mastery of the art of war became apparent to all, but as yet, apart from the sideshow of Alam El Halfa, he was an unknown quantity.

A word parenthetically about Montgomery, from the point of view of a man in the ranks. Apart from a streak of puritanical self-righteousness which occasionally distorted his judgment, he showed extraordinary insight into the mind of the average soldier. The Eighth Army had evolved an ethos of its own. Except for a few prestigious regiments like the guards, 'bullshit' was minimal, the get-up of officers often had an informality verging on the operatic and a touch of this insouciance diffused through the ranks. Often the crews of soft-skinned vehicles had one or two live fowl, which they had acquired from itinerant Arabs by barter, tea being the medium of exchange. These birds, which provided an egg supply, were housed in often ingeniously constructed coops made from wooden packing cases. This way of life with its almost folk-lorist facets, for such it had become among veteran desert campaigners, Montgomery astutely tolerated.

To continue with the main theme: as members of the Intelligence Corps we were put into the operational picture at an earlier stage than subordinate officers and other ranks, the reason being that if we knew the 'pukka gen' we could immediately discern leakages of military intelligence from the mass of rumour, not to say fantasy, which seems to constitute the staple of armies in action. As field security work was primarily concerned with the control of civilian population, communications, refugees, and of course active counter-espionage measures, in the desert we were in a vacuum apart of course from the Bedouin 'line crossers' (well they didn't so much cross as make detours round the desert flank in the course of their nomadic peregrinations). However, those of us linguistically equipped to do so often helped with the interrogation of prisoners and the translation of captured military documents or soldiers' mail. As our division was facing the Italian sector I hastily mugged up the Italian army formation, badges, order of battle, etc.

The 22nd October was my birthday and the eve of the battle. I grimly wondered whether I should ever see another birthday. Two things helped, firstly we were all extremely busy taking on supplies of food, petrol and water, being briefed, etc., and secondly the 4th Light Armoured Brigade were hardened campaigners and something of their fatalistic matter-of-factness rubbed off on me. One incident I still recall as in a way symbolic: I was speaking to a Sergeant Keiser(?), a fantastic character, who 'swanned around' in his armoured car in forward areas, garnering military intelligence and potting at the foe. He was a Palestinian of German extraction and treated the whole show as a personal vendetta. Well, while we were talking shop by his armoured car a medical officer drove up and handed him a hypodermic syringe and a container of morphia, a narcotic solace for himself and crew 'in extremis'. For me this was the moment of truth, and crystallised the whole dark future.

The 23rd October, *Der Tag*: after the evening meal the Brigade HQ convoy moved up to a forward position. Evening crept across the desert and I remember the technicolour effect of the setting sun's rays across the heights of Himeimat. In a few hours the coruscations were to be lethal. It is impossible to convey in words the tensed emotions before the bombardment, and indeed the ferocity of the barrage which opened the battle at 9.40 precisely. The entire horizon was livid with gun-flashes, the ground trembled. We watched in silence. Eventually my sergeant said, 'Those poor bastards': a comment as laconic as it was apt. There was silent agreement among us. At length our column edged its way forward. I was travelling in the back of our fifteen cwt truck, christened 'England's Last Hope': it had seen desert service since the outbreak of war and in places was secured by wire. I had a vague idea that our route lay through gaps in the minefields. Overcome by fatigue and noise I fell asleep. Suddenly there was a bang and our truck lurched over violently. Awaking in a dazed state I thought 'goodness we've hit a land mine'. We had in fact driven into a slit-trench: after hard digging we extricated our vehicle and proceeded. Latterly I looked back with wry amusement at the naivety of my reaction, but this was my first experience of action. Incidentally, slit-trenches were nasty obstacles to night travel across the desert.

In the slogging match which followed for the next eight days the 4th Light Armoured Brigade had no rôle to play, so far as I recall. Enemy air action troubled us at times, but this diminished as the Allied air forces destroyed their forward airfields. I have only very blurred memories of this stagnant interim. Then came news of the breakthrough in the northern sector and the 7th Armoured Division took on its pursuit rôle.

The 3rd November: this was a climactic day. In mid-afternoon we went through the gap created by the 2nd New Zealand Division. The scene almost beggars description. Thousands of trucks, tanks, artillery all moving pell-mell across the desert. Confusion was compounded by the fact that the 51st Highland Division were also on the move crossing diagonally our path of route. The afternoon heat was intense, visibility at times was almost nil through dense dust-storms created by the vehicles. In the middle of all this there were artillery batteries belting away at the foe. The old tag of the army being 'organised chaos' here achieved its apogee. I remember that at one point we halted dangerously near a burning petrol lorry expecting it to go up with one almighty bang at any minute: we could not move out of range for the congestion was such that there was no room for evasive manoeuvre. As night fell formations thinned out and an orderly pattern emerged. At the time I thought that Jerry must have been knocked for six: any aggressive action by him at that stage, either strafing or artillery, would have meant carnage incalculable. To be fair, I must say that for the rest of the war until the final surrender on Lüneburg Heide, I always found these vast-scale troop movements well stage-managed. But of course in the final phase of the El Alamein breakout events moved with such rapidity and impromptu decisions had to be taken.

The 4th November: on this day an incident occurred which for me has remained unforgettable. Our 4th Light Armoured Brigade pressed on harassing the enemy in his retreat. Towards the end of the afternoon the Brigade HQ stopped and brewed up our tea and prepared a meal. While thus engaged a cloud of dust was observed over the brow of a distant hill. A quiver of apprehension. Was it a mobile enemy column coming in to attack? As the picture focussed, we saw that it was a long column of hundreds of prisoners being marched to the cage. They approached and our men gazed at the sight in a sort of stilled amazement. Suddenly someone started to cheer. This was taken up in a spontaneous outburst from us all. Men threw their caps into the air, gesticulated, clapped, in a frenzy of delight at this visible first fruit of victory. I distinctly remember thinking at the time – this might be a scene from some ancient classical historian's account, from Xenophon or Herodotus. One sensed that in a baffled and frustrated army a new spirit, a renewed will to victory, had been born.

About this time the following incident occurred, though I cannot slot it into the chronological sequence with any precision. I was interrogating a few German prisoners; the locality was the edge of an enemy minefield. Some apoplectic top-brass type appeared on the scene and became obsessed with the notion that my interrogees knew a way through the minefield. They protested that they did not, that they were not engineers, and had only recently in the hectic troop movement moved into that sector. The top-brass was adamant : they were to show the way through the minefield followed by me in a truck a few paces behind. If they failed to co-operate, this trigger-happy top-brass knew how to deal with them . . .

The situation was a real facer. I reminded the officer that under the Geneva Convention prisoners were only required to give name, rank and number. The Colonel Blimp exploded : . . . the Geneva Convention; we were in the middle of a battle and he might lose men. Just as we were about to begin this idiotic business, imperilling them and me, news flashed over the blower that some armoured cars had found a way through. Both the Jerries and I were profoundly relieved at this providential intervention. In fairness I must say that this example of threatened duress against prisoners of war was, so far as my experience went, an isolated one.

Pursuit of the foe continued. Up Halfaya Pass, on to Sollum and across 'the wire' (the Egyptian boundary) into Libya. The campaign was now one of extreme rapidity – Tobruk, El Adem, Gazala, Derna, Barche – sometimes eighty miles in a day. However, the advance was hindered by torrential rains which set in. The desert became a quagmire. Tanks, and especially the armoured command vehicles from which operations were controlled (if I remember rightly they weighed as much as a heavy tank), all were bogged down : the enemy on the coast road had the advantage of fast-going terrain. But it was an hour of glory for our wretched truck, 'England's Last Hope'. Mud was no obstacle for it. Such was its prowess in impossible conditions that it was borrowed by high-ranking officers to 'swan' between headquarters. This onset of bad weather denied to Montgomery and the Eighth Army the full harvest of victory which should have been theirs.

At this point I end my narrative. At Barche I was taken seriously ill and was evacuated to the General Military Hospital at Heliopolis, to spend four months in the Delta before returning to the Desert Rats, who were poised ready for the attack on the Mareth Line. The desert war was a campaign *sui generis,* at least compared with operations in Europe. It was waged in appalling climatic conditions, the intense heat, the flies which plagued one incessantly, the dust-storms which would sometimes last for two days, the monotonous food of bully beef and biscuits, with the dubious luxuries of occasional meat (we swore it was camel) and weevil-ridden bread, the endless wastes of sand and scrub and the oppressive sense of isolation the desert produced – all these things, apart from enemy action, made great demands on the stamina and spirit of all who took part.

A postscript : the deprecation of Montgomery's achievements is currently fashionable among military historiographers, even to their carping about the superiority he had in men and materials over the Axis powers at Alamein. This is pure cant. Many a general has successfully managed to lose his battle, numerical and armament superiority notwithstanding. Warfare is not a game like chess where parity of forces is a condition precedent.

*

From Lieutenant Brian (Barney) O'Kelly, Intelligence Corps.

Most Intelligence Corps NCOs who were commissioned in the Middle East were given direct commissions and were saved the ordeal of ME Infantry OCTU. I happened to come to the top of the list just as a new regulation decreeing that all Intelligence Corps candidates for commissions must go through an Infantry Officer Cadet Training Unit came out, and so I left the Eighth Army Advanced HQ at the height of the Knightsbridge battle and did not get back to work until after Alam El Halfa. There was a lot to learn : the terrain and its features, some of the enemy formations and units, their leading personalities and their methods. Technically I had almost to make a fresh start.

The journey up from Cairo was a pleasant return to informal desert travel after the smells and dirt of the city. The chaps at Army HQ at Burg el Arab were most welcoming and talkative, but I was eager to get on XIII Corps at the southern end of the line. This part of the desert seemed scruffy and littered with debris in comparison with Libya : the laagers of the new arrivals were untidy (or so they seemed to me, with a mixture of old rat prejudice and OCTU bull). Night fell suddenly and the driver was not very sure of his ability to find his way among slit-trenches, bivouacs and minefields. We finished up with me lying along the mudguard, peering at the ground and calling directions. We made it at last; cheery greetings in a dimly-lit mess-tent, fried processed cheese on brittle fried bread, chai and a slug of Bolanacchi 'rum'.

Someone looked in to say my valise had been off-loaded and I would find my bed in the vicinity of the 'I' van. I eventually found it in the moonlight and undressed in the chilly desert breeze, got in and immediately my toes popped out into the cold. Cursing I got up and re-made it. I am a good sleeper and the next thing I knew was the dawn stand-to and an unshaven, bald-headed Scots batman holding a chipped enamel mug of luke-warm, stewed tea at me. 'Was your bed just how you like it, sir?' 'Thanks,' I replied tactfully, not wishing to get off on the wrong foot, 'but could you manage to arrange the blankets so my feet don't come out straightaway?' 'Your feet, sir? Your feet, is it?' (Pause for thought.) 'That'd be at the bottom?'

When I had got back to Cairo at the end of June, an officer friend at GHQ had asked me if I had ever heard of El Alamein. I had not. He told me it was the first feasible spot for halting the German advance, that we would hold the enemy there and, with the new divisions, armour and material that were on their way we should counter-attack at the full moon late in October. So I knew the course events might take when I came to XIII Corps. All the predictions were taking shape, although we were 'under new management'.

It was a novel experience to have the Highland Division just behind us, playing 'Hey, Johnnie Cope' on the pipes at reveille, getting their vehicles stuck in the soft sand, to the delight of my driver who went around when off duty pulling their three-tonners out with his Dodge eight-cwt; and they sometimes confused the function of a slit-trench with that of a latrine.

A high-spot of the pre-battle days was a briefing on an enormous 'sand-table' consisting of a relief map of the battle area showing the current locations on both sides and our plans for movement. General Horrocks gave the 'griff talk', including the celebrated dictum that it was the duty of every soldier, be he rifleman, Don R or cook, to kill a German – and two if he was a padre. He looked like a country town family solicitor at a tennis party, with a gay silk neckerchief in the Desert Rat tradition and his knees already commendably brown. He exuded confidence and competence.

As the date drew near, we moved into a small saucer-shaped depression overlooking the minefields on the southern extremity of the Eighth Army line, facing the dug-in positions of the Folgore (Parachute) Division. Long superiority in the air had made the boys a bit 'maleesh' (casual) about digging slit-trenches, and they had to be cajoled. But, on this occasion, within minutes of our pulling in, a Shufti Joe, a recon-

naissance 'plane, came in at zero feet over the skyline of our little
hollow, obviously quite astonished to find the area occupied. He shot off
back, no brakes. But almost before he was out of sight there were clouds
of sand being thrown up and you could not have borrowed a spade for
a fiver, or its equivalent in ackers. In record time we all had adequate
protection.

Down south in XIII Corps we were the decoy. A dummy pipe-line
led forward to us, AFVs were concentrated in the rear, masses of pole-
and-canvas mock-up three-tonners were assembled (and, after a night
of wind and rain, hurriedly straightened up), extensive dummy WT
traffic was passed, and, in general, everything was done to convince all
branches of the enemy's intelligence that the Eighth Army was intend-
ing a left-hook attack, driving forward from the Qattara Depression end
of the line and then swinging northwards.

It is sometimes said that intelligence personnel provide most depressing company because they always know all about the enemy, know
their strength and almost seem to be on their side, but know nothing at
all about our own forces and to have a poor view of their capabilities.
This time we did, in fact, know a lot about our own dispositions – at least
at the start. However, our preoccupation was, of course, with the
enemy.

DAK (German High Command) always believed, in static situations,
in keeping the minimum force in the line, giving the others every opportunity for rest and refreshment. So here on the Alamein line, our information was that generally one armoured formation occupied the forward area, in the vicinity of the coast road, while the other indulged in
sea-bathing in the rear. It was important for the success of our plan,
despite our numerical advantage in tanks, that we should be able to
deal with one panzer division at a time, and therefore they should, if
possible, be kept apart.

The GSO II at Corps was always somewhat pessimistic. He was most
sceptical of the ability of our gunners, sappers and infantry to clear gaps
through the minefields in time for our armour to be free to manoeuvre
on the western side by first light.

'It'll be a Stuka party,' he kept saying gloomily.

My personal commitment was to watch for any and every vestige of
evidence about 21 Panzer Division, at that moment in reserve in a mid-
way position, how it reacted to the initial probing and feint attacks,
whether it showed any signs of being committed to the southern front
or of moving up to reinforce 14 Panzer.

The morning before the battle I was busy visiting my detachments along the corps front, giving a final briefing. It was my first big assignment as an officer and I was so engrossed that it was not until late afternoon that I realised that I was still wearing pyjamas under my battledress. On my return I learned that the BGS (Brigadier General Staff) had been around in the morning and that, *in absentia*, I had received an imperial ballocking for leaving my sun-bleached ground-sheet spread out over my camp-bed, offering a potential air target.

The 'I' officers and NCOs had a little tipple in the van to drink success to the operation, and our poet, Corporal Hughie Scholes, recited a pastiche of Henry's speech before Agincourt, suggesting that gentlemen in England then abed would hold themselves accursed they were not there, etc. Promptly on time the barrage started, with the mediums banging away just behind us. There was nothing I could do and nothing to be gained from staying awake; in my job a cool head and a refreshed body would be needed in the morning. So I got into bed, and, although I was nearly bounced out at times and the front was periodically lit by huge flashes, I pretty quickly got off to sleep of a kind. Even at our safe distance it was impossible not to be aware of the sweat and darkness and horror of the night. In so much intelligence work one was deeply involved but physically remote.

The next morning, first light was typical of a battle seen from an 'I' van. The 'phones were going all the time, signals were arriving, despatch riders looking in, the gen log building up item by item. The battle map was constantly being brought up to date with new locations on the chinograph, red for us and blue for them. There was also the outward traffic – 'phone and WT messages to Army HQ intelligence and to our own corps staff, as well as to my detachments. There was no time for breakfast, someone brought me a mug of tea and by mid-morning the floor around my feet was ankle-deep in cigarette ends.

Quite early it became clear that there were frustrations on the corps front. The flail-tanks had not got through the January and February minefields, or rather mine-seas, they were so haphazardly lain. The 7th Armoured was held up, the infantry were pinned down. So it was unlikely 21 Panzer would come south. On the other hand, it was not apparently being committed to the northern sector until the situation became clearer. Meanwhile, my watching brief must be maintained.

Archie Colquhoun addressed the Folgore Division in his impeccable Italian through loudspeakers, urging them to abandon a hopeless position. He received a very dusty answer, and had to lie up for some time before he could get back.

Gradually as the slogging match on the XXX Corps front developed and 10 Corps were still waiting for the word go, it became clear that our original and distinctive rôle on the left flank was over. More and more troops were re-deployed in more vital sectors. We still maintained our rather remote interest in 21 Panzer, but they were obviously not coming our way.

At last the breakthrough really came to life, the battle of Tel el Eisa was fought, the Axis armour re-grouped, concentrated and was strafed by the RAF. Rommel's forces were in retreat.

We accepted the fact that our Alamein was over and that we would become the Salvage Corps, combing the battle area for weapons, vehicles, documents and Italian prisoners, while the rest of the Eighth Army was doing the tally-ho act some of us had awaited for years.

*

From Sir Edward Boulton, Bt

I went through both the battle of El Halfa and that of Alamein as GIII Intelligence to 10th Armoured Division. In the former we were dug in at El Halfa giving the enemy the choice of going straight through to Alexandria, in which case we could have cut off their supply column or to attack our dug-in tanks, which in fact they did. One German tank succeeded in getting up a narrow wadi to the perimeter within twenty yards of my ACV and we had to move off at speed with the canvas flaps flying at both sides. On reports from the brigade intelligence officers I reported the number of German tanks estimated to have been knocked out together with a number of support vehicles. This information was relayed to London and Churchill announced the news in the House of Commons that night. During the night we could hear continuous activity of vehicles being recovered and when daylight emerged there were many fewer tanks to be counted. As a result I was summoned to Corps HQ (under General Horrocks) and thoroughly ticked off as being responsible for an inaccurate report having been made to Churchill, although there was no doubt that the number reported was approximately correct.

Between the two battles I was a victim of jaundice (my third attack), which was rampant in the desert. I was sent to a hospital in Palestine, where I remained about three weeks. I knew Alamein must be about to start and I persuaded the hospital authorities to let me go rather than be sent to a convalescent camp. I made my way to the airfield and was picked up by a military 'plane flying to Cairo, travelling in the nose. I found the convoy just leaving for the desert and jumped on and as we arrived we passed my own regiment – the Staffordshire Yeomanry under Colonel Eadie – moving up into line about 7 pm and I was able to greet them and wish them luck.

On arrival at 10 Armoured Division HQ, I was met by Harry Llewelyn (of Foxhunter fame), who was a GIII, who said, 'Thank God, you have come – it starts at 2140 tonight and the General [Gatehouse], the GI, GII and GIII ops have all gone forward to the front line and we are completely out of touch with them. The Corps Commander [Lumsden] is going mad on the link in your ACV and so is his Corps HQ, as he has also moved forward and is out of touch with them.'

The upshot was that I had little time for intelligence work as I was in constant communication with General Lumsden requesting news and giving commands which I had the greatest difficulty in trying to pass on, and with Corps HQ who wanted to know what Lumsden was doing and saying and what was happening. Like many ex-Cavalry officers, he never used codes but gave orders in parables to confuse the enemy and often ourselves.

The first command was entirely phrased in terms of an eighteenth century battle, the history of which I did not know, and although I assumed what he meant I was unable to reach any of our ops staff as they had not informed Harry of their whereabouts. The second command was simpler as it was all about tarts walking down a street and being picked up by one brigadier or another, identified by Christian names. Lumsden became restive at not being able to get through to Gatehouse and ordered me to commit the division or otherwise to carry out various tasks and would not wait for an answer. I compromised with 'yes' and 'no', and managed to get word at last to Gatehouse, who quickly sent back his GI.

In the meantime, many of our tank personnel had perished during the first night in the minefields and enemy gunfire, including Colonel Eadie and Bill Lewisham (heir to Lord Dartmouth) in the Staffordshire Yeomanry amongst many others. The flies were so numerous and enormous it was almost impossible to eat and we lived for the week mainly on benzedrine tablets and without a wink of sleep.

The command from Lumsden was simple and understandable for the final breakout. 'The meet will be at 6(?) am, each brigade being identified by the Christian name of the brigadier and ordered to cover NW, NE, SW and SE corners of cover. 'The fox will break at X point – tally-ho.' This was the order for the complete breakout at Alamein. The

Divisional HQ followed as fast as the ACVs could go, passing hordes of knocked-out tanks and assorted vehicles and dead bodies smothered in flies, until all came to a halt short of Mersa Matruh.

It was my job to collect the prisoners and the Italians were no problem except for numbers, With additional help I organised convoys of Italian trucks and drivers, each convoy under the command of one British NCO, to go out and fetch in the Germans. The General commanding the Italian Folgore Division (parachute), and by far their best Italian division, surrendered to me personally with his entire staff the following morning, and I took him to breakfast with Gatehouse. I then took him in his own car, followed by a fleet of vehicles, to hand him over. He handed me his divisional flag, which I still have, and his field glasses and asked me to leave his car for him. I knew he would never see it again, so I drove off in it and used it until I went down with double pneumonia whilst advancing and was put into an Australian CCS, which was packed with wounded and other complaints; we had to wait for the railway to be built up to reach us to take us back to Alexandria. It was hell – it pelted with rain and they had to dig a trench under my stretcher to take the water, and stretchers were half on top of each other. On one side I had a coloured soldier who had caught gonorrhea in one of the Italian mobile brothels and who kept rolling over me in pain and on the other a man with a bad throat infection, and all round the screams of the wounded.

The staff were so short that I could only get attention and get washed down in the middle of the night and I had a temperature of 107. We had to wait nearly a week and when I got to a hospital in Ismailia I was put on the danger list but happily survived, although downgraded. The only way I could get back to the division was as ADC to General Birks, who took over to piece together what remained of the division in Aleppo.

*

From Mr C. B. Hutcheon

As far as I am concerned, I was a very small pebble in a very big stream, but had the distinction of serving in XXX Corps HQ from its formation at Abbasia in 1942 until the end of the road was reached in Germany. During that period we had several corps commanders, among whom were Lieutenant-General Norrie, Sir Oliver Leese and, of course, Sir Brian Horrocks. I mention them in particular because, to my mind, they were – all of them – perfect gentlemen, and I feel honoured to have served with them.

The Victor of Alamein. The tank behind is a Grant.

Tripoli. Arabs watch British Tanks pass.

Tanks in Tripoli. The moment of triumph.

Arriving in Cairo I found myself part of the newly-formed XXX Corps, or as it was originally known 'K Armoured Corps'. Into the desert we went, and I couldn't help thinking what an ideal place for a battle. Miles and miles of sweet —— (the rest of the phrase must be too well known to bear repetition). But in spite of the shocking conditions, at least it was a straight battle between two armies, with towns and civilians not involved except in the coastal areas.

By the end of the first year I was not the only one who felt frustrated and dispirited. Up and down, forwards and backwards – the whole business seemed to be endless, and the annoying part was no one knew what was going on. The almost unendurable weather conditions made matters worse. A sandstorm in the *khamsin* season is without doubt the most awful climatic condition I had, or am ever likely to experience, and tea made with salt water did little to alleviate things. When corps was formed I well remember our camp commander saying that we would likely find it a bit of a bore as we weren't likely to be within miles of actual operations. As things turned out, nothing was further from the truth.

Then came Montgomery, and the whole situation changed completely. Montgomery may in some ways be open to criticism, but to my mind he was a leader of men the like of which I doubt if we will ever see again. His first objective was to meet the troops and tell them what was to happen and how it *would* happen – 'I make the plans – you do the fighting. Without each other we're sunk.' Note that he said *we*, not I or you. '*We* will knock Rommel for six out of Africa.' I personally never felt the slightest doubt about it. So the revival of spirit and morale was born. From then on we felt that instead of being a unit, we were part of a unity – with a united purpose.

When operations really commenced (22nd October 1942) then it was that Corps HQ instead of being out of touch was right in the hub of things, and rightly so. The nerve centre of operations had to be right in the midst of it. Consequently, although I was not actually fighting, life in Corps HQ was at times highly exciting to say the least. Of course, there were the lighter moments. Even in the stickiest situations which frequently arose, the British sense of humour, which neither the Germans nor the Japs could fathom, invariably provided relief. When all sorts and conditions are gathered together as they were in the Eighth Army, there are the inevitable 'characters' and these – if they only knew it – contributed as much to the success of operations as anyone. At one time we had a company commander whose general factotum was a typical cockney sparrow. It was difficult to know sometimes who was major and who was batman; for instance: ''Ere, let's get outer this, mate,' and 'mate' (or major) and batman promptly did from a very nasty spot. However, such was the spirit then, everyone mucked in whatever the rank.

Actual fear throughout the whole business only occurred to me on the high seas – I dreaded being torpedoed. On land, on at least two occasions when I thought my number had been well and truly called, I was much too occupied trying to get out to think of fear. I took the complacent view that if something came my way, that was the way it was meant to be.

Thus we went through it till we eventually arrived in Germany – then we went home to pick up the threads. Has it all been worth it? I sometimes wonder. Churchill said, 'When history comes to be written it will be enough to say, "I marched with the Eighth Army."' I don't know if history is still being taught in schools, but I doubt if the present generation knows who or what the Eighth Army was.

The British people thus saved the world from one scourge, but I wonder – rather doubtfully – if another one as bad is not replacing the one we helped to annihilate. Personally, I wish we had men now of the same calibre as Montgomery, Horrocks, Leese, Alexander, Mountbatten, and a host of others whose character and stability were examples to everyone.

*

From Mr A. T. Cattaway

I was a staff-sergeant on the strength of Deputy Director of Ordnance Services (DDOS) at Eighth Army Headquarters from its formation in the latter part of 1941. The function of the DDOS is the provision of stores – warlike and otherwise – for the formations of the army, and the maintenance of stocks.

What is known as the 1st Battle of Alamein did not make much impression upon us at the time. Auchinleck, the good soldier, had rallied and deployed enough troops to hold the enemy. How long would they stay held? Could Rommel's cunning bring a breakthrough to the Delta? But the Auk had done his job well, and it gradually dawned upon us that the line had held, and that every day that passed was a bonus. We could build up quicker than he could, and the RAF were doing a tremendous job, bombing enemy positions continuously.

We moved from outside Cairo into the desert again, between Alexandria and Alamein. After the good news on the grand scale, we faced the daily round again. We sat at our tables with our files in front of us with a new heart. It was the hottest time of the year. Besides sand, we had to deal with mosquitoes and flies, both constant pests; with the flap, flap, flap of the tent all day long. Flies in the desert were daily companions. No matter how far we moved, how remote the spot, flies appeared immediately. In some places they were such a menace as to almost cover the food on your plate between mouthfuls. Orders were issued that every man should kill at least fifty a day. This quota was more than fulfilled, but the population continued to flourish.

Towards the end of July 1942, the front at Alamein began to become stabilised. Supplies started to arrive in quantity and new formations took their places in the line. We were encouraged by the scale of the build-up, and to see and hear the 'planes passing over towards the front, seemingly unopposed.

The Army Commander was in complete control and shortly before the October battle of Alamein, the plan was unfolded to all troops. The officer who explained it to us did so with confidence and enthusiasm, but stated that Monty expected a hard fight. In the end, he said, the outcome would be decided by the predominance of the side with the most moral fibre. There would be no 'walkover'.

We waited with confidence for the great day. The battle was to commence with an artillery barrage beginning at 2140 hours on 23rd October. We were stationed some twenty miles behind the lines, and stood outside our tents awaiting the hour. Promptly it began. The roar was continuous and the whole western horizon aglow with the flashes of every kind of gun. A man near me was weeping. We asked him why, and he replied that his brother was in the line 'in the middle of all that'. And suddenly, at its appointed time, the roar ceased. We went to bed. We were the lucky ones : thousands, we knew, would not be.

The next few days were to be exactly as we had been warned. The hard fight was on. There were reports of gigantic minefields being encountered. Prisoners were falling into our hands, but the breakthrough was anything but simple. Word from the Army Commander was symbolised as, 'Keep faith and hold on.' Eventually, early in November, the breakthrough came. One remark from my diary at the time is significant. 'We are throwing stones at the Italians and they are running away.' There was no doubt that the enemy, at last, was in retreat. The long patient build-up, the steeling of hearts to keep thought of failure at bay had been justified. Monty had said it could be done, and it had been. It had taken a little longer than had been hoped, it is true, but Rommel had been discredited as a man of magic. The Eighth Army was now a very large family, all in the confidence of the leader.

Here was someone to believe in. From this time the desert battles were fought in a different spirit. We knew we were going somewhere. And we did, but that is another story.

IX

Other Memories of Alamein

From Mr G. Raphael: Creating the deceptive army in the south

I was a lieutenant with the 1509 Company (Seychelles) Pioneer Company whose OC was Major W. F. Abercrombie; and there was Captain P. J. Carter, another lieutenant and myself. We had recruited and trained the company in the Seychelles with four British Army Officers, and four NCOs including a sergeant-major, a QM sergeant and two sergeants.

We were engaged in 'creating' a concourse of tanks and lorries and even a HQ to confuse enemy reconnaissance 'planes. It was all done by hessian, some string and some very light wood, poles, etc.

The dummy camp and vehicle sites were erected at night with the help of moonlight and during daylight gave the appearance of busy military areas to very high-flying enemy planes. Vehicles travelled around and about creating clouds of dust and in early morning every encouragement to brewing up in amongst the dummy bivouac was given, and of course round the vehicles, or tanks, outlined in hessian, supported by thin wooden poles and 'cats' cradles' of strong twine.

14th October: Our detachment set off at 10.45 am and the OC and I went in 'Gertie'. We got to our site between 1 and 2 pm and the OC and I lunched off bully and bread and tea and rum. We left about 2.50 and got back at 4.35. Stuck once on way back just before reaching the 'F' track.

15th October: General Stone and Brigadier arrived just before noon and saw erection of dummy tanks, fifteen-cwts and three-tonners and seemed duly impressed.

16th October: Afternoon, not long after I had issued extra water for washing, a sandstorm got up. About 5.30 or so it reached gale force and the sergeants' tent collapsed and we fought hard with the gale and got it up again. Sand was blinding and a curious yellow pall over everything. Looking into the gale, colour went purple; it was rather terrifying. We got dinner not unduly sandy and then came rain and more gale and we feared for our tent. Sudden calm at about 10 pm.

17th October: Set off about 11.30 and the sandstorm had abated at bit. Major Cornforth and Lieutenant Hibbert of RE came with us. He's forming RE Artisan Company. Cold drive and some rain. Got to our location about 3 pm and got settled and EPIP tent up, etc. Major C. and Lieutenant H. messed with us quite comfortably.

20th October: Set off for location 3 pm. Dark at 6.45 pm, worked on till about 12.35 am erecting tanks, three-tonners, etc.

21st October: Sleep disturbed by real tanks about 3.30 am, but they were not too close. Back to HQ at 2 pm and set off again about 3 pm. Bed at 9 pm. Noisy 'planes. About 1 am an officer arrived looking for Major Boyle's East African Pioneers.

22nd October: Set some fires, etc., and sent out men to finish balance of seventy-five trucks and then another twenty-five arrived. Very hot from 9.30 till 11, when a slight breeze got up. Tea, etc., for midday meal. OC called am and pm. I was over at HQ. Put up bivvies false and true all over the site. Bed about 8 pm and slept pretty well.

23rd October: Over to HQ . . . pm over to site of Tuesday night for repairs. Found a Jeep had knocked over one of our tanks. I'll bet he was both surprised and relieved! Still got some diarrhoea and had to use a dummy fifteen-cwt. Lorries driving all over the various sites all pm – Spoof!

24th October: Maintenance of dummy bivouacs. Round the various parties. Bed early having nothing else to do . . . no light by which to read.

25th October: Sunday. Maintenance of lorries and of bivouacs. Jafir (?) of Abu Minas (?) came with a tale of crashed 'plane. We went and saw a Tomahawk fighter.

26th October: Over to HQ twice. Took down all the trucks and bivvies in my area pm.

The above notes are all I have relevant to the Alamein episode in so far as one lot of Pioneers was concerned. The headquarters referred to was Major Abercrombie's part dummy, part real office, stores, etc. He regarded himself and the personnel as 'the cheese in the mousetrap'.

*

From Mr A. E. Braine

About 10th October 1942, when serving as a wireless operator with the Indian Long Range Squadron, I was part of a two-truck patrol sent to watch one of the few tracks across the Qattara Depression. It was thought that the enemy might send light armoured forces across it, in some form of flanking attack. The patrol consisted of one British navigator, myself and a dozen Sikh soldiers under a *Havildar*.

We were armed with an anti-tank rifle, two Bren-guns and small arms. Our instructions were on spotting the enemy vehicles (which could have been seen at quite a long distance) to radio LRDG (Long Range Desert Group) headquarters and then get the hell out of it.

After days of sitting on top of a sand-dune, with many false alarms, such as the effect of shimmering heat on rocks, which looked like advancing tanks, we heard the great battle opening a few miles to the north of us. On the last day, we were strafed by a couple of MEs but otherwise saw nothing of the enemy.

I hope that in a modest way we contributed to the more exciting picture of events, and that this tale of inactivity might be of interest.

*

From Brigadier C. E. F. Turner

One of my recollections is about our divisional coppers. The Military Police manned the entrances to the gaps in the enemy minefields throughout the early days of our attack. It was a lonely job, not without its dangers from odd shells and mines going up. I was most impressed by their fortitude and I passed up and down to have a word.

*

From Mrs E. Elliott

From a call on a voyage around Africa I journeyed from Alexandria to El Alamein; I took this opportunity to make what I regarded as a pilgrimage. The route from the ship was anything but picturesque, especially the dock regions and some suburbs. But that and the two and a half hour journey was of no account. The desert area was impressive in its own way and had its effect upon me. Here and there were small patches of green cultivation – a few dates, palms, olive trees. Some goats must find sustenance somehow, somewhere, in order to keep alive. A few military posts along the wayside showed Egypt on guard. Here and there, a goatskin Bedouin tent looked only just adequate, as did some tiny houses, sparsely scattered.

When we reached our objective, the British Cemetery, we entered very reverently and quietly along a central pathway after passing through some graceful archways at the entrance. Desert sand was all around. We saw row upon row of headstones, each bearing a name and rank.

It would be well-night impossible in this arid ground to grow flowers, as is done in many resting-places I have visited of our fighting men. Along a central path a few bougainvilleas were having a struggle to survive. Perhaps their purple flowers were intended as a sign of mourning. At the far end of the centre path, a high stone cross stands starkly against the background of brilliant blue sky. The heart of the memorial, a block of marble, bears the words : 'Greater love hath no man than he lay down his life . . .'

I have seen much of the fine work of the War Graves Commission in many parts of the world. There must have been difficulties and problems here in order to do justice to the memories engendered and the Commission has done a fine work for posterity. One member of our party was here to find a last resting-place on behalf of the whole family – which she was able to do. As we approached the entrance and again looked through the graceful archways, the Mediterranean shone blue in azure brilliance.

I had decided in my own mind that I would not visit the German and Italian memorials, but the fact that some of the German party had visited our Holy of Holies changed my mind. We continued our journey until we reached a slight eminence, topped by a fort-like, four-square building. Inside, a cross of gold mosaic and walls inscribed with the names of the German fallen. A little farther on – another memorial, the Italian. It had a beautiful mosaic floor and walls entirely covered with marble tablets from Italy. Each tablet held the name and rank of a fallen soldier. No graves or headstones were here. The fallen were buried where they fell.

How troops carried out their duties in this climate and won such a victory I would not know.

*

From Mrs J M Fiore

In 1940 at the age of nineteen I started working for the Royal Signals and spent five very exciting and interesting years, this was in Alexandria – Egypt and even when I finally received 'my calling up' papers (all local Britishers were called up) my boss, a major, insisted I was doing vital work (ciphering – typist – filing, etc.) and I was exempted from the ATS.

Naturally through the Signals I made many friends and lost many of them. My mother made a point of keeping 'open house' for soldiers far from home and they loved having a home to come to, especially if they could get some leave. Some friendships have continued until today, although we are all grandparents now.

I attended the very moving ceremony when General Montgomery was present with a few Eighth Army at El Alamein cemetery. I remember how upset I felt and still do today to see all those ages of twenty-one to twenty-four on a tombstone, young men who would never be privileged to grow old, so many of them known to me.

*

From Mrs G. Tevern

I remember my husband telling me of the first night of the Battle of Alamein, the deadly silence when they were waiting to attack, how he looked at a small photo of me, saying goodbye, thinking this is the end. Of a young lad beside him, scared, how he hung on to my husband. The night was still black, then it seemed as though the heavens opened, the barrage of the guns. At another time they were dug in in a trench, and he and this young man were just looking over the top, and then my husband said, 'I can see the whites of the German eyes' and he kept telling this ginger lad to keep his head down. Then he just put his head up again and they got him between the eyes. My husband thought of the young lad's mother and her feelings, and felt sick. He told me the awful feeling it is to want a drink so badly, your lips are swollen. When he was wounded in the leg, he told me about a nursing sister who asked him what nationality he was, because he was so brown, nearly black. He was in Egypt four years.

From the Reverend L. S. Pettifer

I served with 1st Armoured Division Signals during the desert campaigns. At Alamein I was attached to the 10th Royal Hussars.

You may be interested to know that the village for the disabled* is itself a memorial to the Battle of Alamein and a few years ago we were able, through a world-wide appeal, to build St George's, the Alamein Church. As far as I know, this is the only Memorial Church in the world to the battle.

We have the Order of Battle as at 23rd October 1942 which goes down to regiments and squadrons, and in our museum we have the original stationmaster's bell from Alamein station.

*

From Mr W. N. Prince

Whilst having no authoritative say in the conduct of the Battles of Alamein, I was in one of the units that participated from the beginning to end of the final battle. In all books written on the subject which I have read, there has never been any mention of a small but vital cog in the front line organisation . . . the WU.

The WU (Wireless Unit) was previously named WIZ (Wireless Intelligence Unit). That was in the early European campaigns before Dunkirk, it having been necessary to change its name to WU because of the obvious danger to its personnel should they be captured – a wise decision, considering that eventually a number of our mobile units were captured in the western desert and the Dodecanese campaign.

Mr WU, as it was affectionately known to all and sundry of the advanced units during the Eighth Army advance, was a unit of the Desert Air Force and I was a member of 13 WU – the most advanced WU in the western desert campaign, often operating in areas ahead of Eighth Army advanced forces, transmitting back to base HQ information on enemy aircraft or armour movements, for immediate action by the Desert Air Force.

13 WU had a staff of approximately a hundred technical and administrative personnel and comprised a Base HQ, usually set up slightly in advance of Advance Air HQs, and between eight and twelve Mobile Units, using fifteen-cwt Commer trucks or three-ton lorries fully equipped with the necessary transmitting and receiving equipment, together with code-books, etc. Each mobile unit was manned by four

* Enham Alamein in Hampshire.

men, two RAF observers (ex-Army), one of whom also did the driving,
and two RAF wireless operators, of whom I was one.

*

From Mr C. Deanesly

I hope it is possible to include a reference to the means by which
Monty had air superiority numerically before the third battle, namely
the huge number of Spitfire and Hurricane aircraft that were flown
across Africa from Takoradi (Gold Coast) to Cairo.

The 'West African Reinforcement Route' was one of the few bits of
strategic planning carried out before the war and developed into a huge
operation involving many thousands of aircraft, British and American.
The former were built in England, stripped and boxed and transported
by sea from the Clyde to Takoradi. There they were reassembled and
flown in convoy with a Blenheim leading via Nigeria, French Equatorial
Africa (Chad), the Soudan and Egypt to Cairo. The American aircraft,
principally Baltimores and Marauders, were flown across the Southern
Atlantic route from British Guiana, via the Azores to Accra by British
and American crews and then flown to Cairo by RAF pilots.

In the month before the third battle of Alamein over seven hundred
Hurricanes and Spitfires, as well as numerous Blenheims, Beaufighters,
Beauforts, etc., were flown up this route, thus enabling Monty to have
not only immediate air superiority but also a tremendous build-up in the
pipe-line to replace losses.

Strangely little publicity or credit has been give to this colossal under-
taking which involved thousands of men and the organisation and
supply of vast quantities of petrol. This was mostly an American supply
problem.

*

From Major Peter Clegg, MC

You will know that the first battle of Alamein was all important; if
it had not been won the later battle could not have taken place and the
wealth of arms and ammunition being stockpiled in readiness for it
would have fallen into enemy hands and enabled the Axis forces to have
swept through the whole of the Middle East. I would not like you to
make the common mistake of other historians and write that the troops
who had fallen back to stand in line of the first battle were demoralised.
They were tired and weary after two years in the desert, having
travelled thousands of miles backwards and forwards along the African
coast, but in no way beaten. I expect the most vivid recollections of the

battle will come from those who arrived in time for the October battle having never seen a battlefield before. The heat of the day, the clouds of flies, the cold of the nights, the sight of burnt-out tanks, the smell of the dead in the minefields from the first battle and above all the noise of battle would be unforgettable.

*

From Mr R. Roberts

I served with the 2nd Armoured Brigade, 1st Armoured Division, during the Alamein battles and also took part in the battles that preceded the retreat to the Alamein line.

After giving the matter considerable thought, I have reached the conclusion that memory may prove faulty, but that a poem written at the time would be a true record; certainly they are the sincere observations of an ordinary soldier during those days.

> There is a moment's brooding
> Under a dusty moon,
> A breathlessness.
> In this fraction of time
> The miracle vision of the mind
> Pictures the silent sappers,
> The crouching tanks,
> The trenched and waiting infantry,
> The poised and loaded guns
> The echeloned trucks,
> And all men's eyes along the line
> Searching west,
> Waiting, listening.
> The automatic ticking
> Echoes loud from my urgent watch,
> With its steel finger creeping,
> Impulsed by the governed thrust
> Of the relentless balanced cog.
> The little beating heart,
> The uncoiling spring,
> Precise and perfect in its fashioning.
> That shall mark the time
> And plunge the pin
> Into the single sensitive eye
> Of the ringed and copper cartridge

Held in the vice of polished breech.
And a thousand flaming tongues
Shall leap from a thousand guns.
But no! Not yet.
The circling finger carries on
Passing light and rigidly,
Resting imperceptibly
In measured turn
On the hair-line graduations
Of this luminous glass domed tiny face.
I look up at the misty moon
In this minute of grace
And long for home,
Slowly through my tear-dimmed sight
The blurred and ticking shape evolves.
Loud in its warning
The finger-marks . . .
The thunder of a thousand guns
Shocks the sand
And flickers the flash of flame
Leaping the length of the line
As they rend the night . . .
The barrage of El Alamein.

Extract from *The New Crusader,* Eighth Army Veterans'
Association Journal – July 1978

THE DESERT RAT RETIRED

Many veterans will be sad to learn that after thirty-eight years' Army
service – nine years with the 7th Armoured Division and twenty-nine
with the 7th Armoured Brigade, the famous jerboa is 'no more'. This is
the result of the latter formation now ceasing to exist in the order of
battle of the British Army.

The sign of the little red rat on the white circular ground was first
adopted when the Armoured Division became the 7th Armoured Division at the beginning of 1940, and was said to have been the idea of
Mrs Creagh, wife of Major-General O'Moore Creagh, the Divisional
commander.

It became famous throughout North Africa, the Italian campaign
and later it was proudly carried through France, Belgium, Holland and
Germany. By this time the red jerboa had a black background and
sometimes just khaki, and when the 7th Armoured Brigade fought in
Burma, it had changed its colour to green. The name is carried on in
the Rhine Army in the British Forces Education Service's Jerboa School
at Soltau, West Germany, and in the Jerboa Cinema in Berlin.

Thousands of ex-soldiers who served with the 7th Armoured Division
were extremely proud to wear the sign and to be called 'Desert Rats'.
Many of them thought the name was too readily adopted by some who
were not strictly entitled to wear the badge, but it has been applied by
the news media to all who ever served in the desert.

So passes the renowned 'Desert Rat', but in the hearts of the thousands
who fought wearing the sign it will be a case of 'Floreat Jerboa'.

The following Orders of Battle are reproduced by kind permission of Brigadier C. E. Lucas-Phillips, OBE, MC, from his book 'Alamein' (which is the best general account of the battles).

The Order of Battle

EIGHTH ARMY ORDER OF BATTLE
on 23rd October 1942 (slightly modified and including forward elements only)

Lieutenant-General B. L. Montgomery
(BGS : Brigadier F. W. de Guingand)

HQ EIGHTH ARMY

Formations directly under command included : 1st Army Tank Bde (42 and 44 RTR), who provided Troops to man the Scorpions; 2nd and 12th AA Bdes.

Army Troops included : Tank Delivery Regt, 1st Camouflage Coy, RE, 566th and 588th Army Troops Coy, RE, Eighth Army Signals, 4th Light Field Ambulance, 200th Field Ambulance.

10TH CORPS

(Lieut-General Herbert Lumsden)
(BGS : Brigadier Ralph Cooney)

1ST ARMOURED DIVISION (Major-General Raymond Briggs)

2nd Armoured Brigade (Brigadier A. F. Fisher) : The Queen's Bays, 9th Lancers, 10th Hussars and Yorkshire Dragoons (motor battalion).

7th Motor Brigade (Brigadier T. J. B. Bosvile) : 2nd and 7th Battalions The Rifle Brigade and 2nd King's Royal Rifle Corps (60th Rifles).

Divisional Troops:

12th Lancers (armoured cars)

RA : (CRA, Brigadier B. J. Fowler) : 2nd and 4th RHA, 11th RHA (HAC), 78th Field Regt (less Troops with other divisions), 76th Anti-Tank Regt and 42 Light AA Regt.

RE : 1st and 7th Field Sqns, 1st Field Park Sqn. *Attached:* 9th Field Sqn and 572 Field Park Coy.

223

Others: 1st Armd Div Signals, two companies R. Northumberland Fusiliers, 1st and 5th Light Field Ambulances.

Attached: 'Hammerforce' (artillery and armd cars).

10TH ARMOURED DIVISION (Major-General A. H. Gatehouse)

8th Armoured Brigade (Brigadier E. C. N. Custance): 3rd RTR, Nottinghamshire Yeomanry (Sherwood Rangers), Staffordshire Yeomanry, 1st Buffs (motor battalion).

24th Armoured Brigade (Brigadier A. G. Kenchington): 41st, 45th and 47th RTR and 11th KRRC (motor battalion).

133rd Lorried Infantry Brigade (Brigadier A. W. Lee), added from 44th Division: 2nd, 4th and 5th Royal Sussex Regt and one company R. Northumberland Fusiliers.

Divisional Troops:

The Royal Dragoons (armoured cars).

RA: (CRA, Brigadier W. A. Ebbels): 1st, 5th and 104th (Essex Yeo) RHA, 98th Field Regt (Surrey and Sussex Yeomanry), 84th Anti-Tank Regt, 53rd Light AA Regt.

RE: 2nd and 3rd (Cheshire) Field Sqns, 141st Field Park Sqn; *attached:* 6th Field Sqn, 571st and 753rd Army Field Coys.

Others: 10th Armd Div Signals, 3rd, 8th and 168th Light Field Ambulances.

8TH ARMOURED DIVISION (Major-General Charles Gairdner). This division was reduced to a headquarters staff and some non-operational troops only.

10TH CORPS TROOPS: 570th Corps Field Park Coy RE, 10th Corps Signals, 12th and 151st Light Field Ambulances.

13TH CORPS

(Lieut-General B. G. Horrocks)

(BGS: Brigadier George Erskine)

7TH ARMOURED DIVISION (Major-General A. F. Harding):

4th Light Armoured Brigade (Brigadier M. G. Roddick): 4/8th Hussars, The Greys and 1st KRRC (motor battalion).

22nd Armoured Brigade (Brigadier G. P. B. Roberts): 1st and 5th RTR, 4th City of London Yeomanry and 1st Rifle Brigade (motor battalion).

131 Lorried Infantry Brigade. See under 44th Infantry Division.

Divisional Troops:

Household Cavalry Regt, 11th Hussars and 2nd Derbyshire Yeomanry (armoured cars).

RA: (CRA, Brigadier Roy Mews): 3rd RHA, 4th and 97th (Kent Yeomanry) Field Regts, 65th Anti-Tank Regt, 15 Light AA Regt.

RE: 4th and 21st Field Sqns, 143rd Field Park Sqn.

Others: 7th Armd Div Signals, 2nd and 14th Light Field Ambulances.

Under command: 1st and 2nd Free French Brigade Groups and 1st Free French Flying Column.

44th Reconnaissance Regt (from 44th Division).

44TH INFANTRY DIVISION (Major-General I. T. P. Hughes):

131st Infantry Brigade (Brigadier W. D. Stamer): 1/5th, 1/6th and 1/7th The Queens' (became incorporated in 7th Armd Div on 1st Nov.).

132nd Infantry Brigade (Brigadier L. G. Whistler): 2nd Buffs, 4th and 5th Royal West Kent Regt.

133rd Infantry Brigade. See under 10th Armd Div.

Divisional Troops:

RA: (CRA, Brigadier H. R. Hall): 57th, 58th, 65th and 53rd Field Regts, 57th Anti-Tank Regt, 30th Light AA Regt.

RE: 11th, 209th and 210th Field Coys, 211th Field Park Coy and 577th Army Field Park Coy.

Others: 44th Div Signals, 6th Cheshire Regt (machine-gun battalion), 131st and 132nd Field Ambulance.

50TH INFANTRY DIVISION (Major-General J. S. Nichols):

69th Infantry Brigade (Brigadier E. C. Cooke-Collis): 5th East Yorkshire Regt, 6th and 7th Green Howards.

151st Infantry Brigade (Brigadier J. E. S. Percy): 6th, 8th and 9th Durham Light Infantry.

1st Greek Infantry Brigade Group (Colonel Katsotas): 1st, 2nd and 3rd Greek Battalions, 1st Greek Field Artillery Regt, 1st Greek Field Engineer Coy, 1st Greek MG Coy, 1st Greek Field Ambulance.

Divisional Troops:

RA: (CRA, Brigadier Claude Eastman): 74th, 111th, 124th and 154th Field Regts, 102nd (Northumberland Hussars) Anti-Tank Regt, 34th Light AA Regt.

RE: 23rd and 505th Field Coys, 235th Field Park Coy.

Others: 50th Div Signals, 2nd Cheshire Regt (machine-guns), 149 and 186 Field Ambulances.

13TH CORPS TROOPS: 118th and 124th RTR (dummy tanks)

4th Survey Regt RA (part), 578th Army Field Coy and 576th Corps Field Park Coy, RE, 13th Corps Signals.

30TH CORPS

(Lieut-General Sir Oliver Leese, Bt.)
(BGS : Brigadier G. P. Walsh)

51ST (HIGHLAND) INFANTRY DIVISION (Major-General D. N. Wimberley):
  152nd Infantry Brigade (Brigadier G. Murray): 2nd and 5th Sea-
  forth Highlanders, 5th Cameron Highlanders.
  153 Infantry Brigade (Brigadier D. A. H. Graham): 5th Black
  Watch, 1st and 5/7th Gordon Highlanders.
  154th Infantry Brigade (Brigadier H. W. Houldsworth): 1st and 7th
  Black Watch, 7th Argyll and Sutherland Highlanders.
Divisional Troops:
  RA (CRA, Brigadier G. M. Elliot): 126th, 127th and 128th Field
  Regts, 61st Anti-Tank Regt, 40th Light AA Regt.
  RE : 274th, 275th and 276th Field Coys, 239th Field Park Coy.
  Others : 51st Div Signals, 1/7th Middlesex Regt (machine-guns),
  51st Div Reconnaissance Regt, 174th, 175th and 176th Field
  Ambulances.
2ND NEW ZEALAND DIVISION (Major-General B. C. Freyberg, VC):
  9th Armoured Brigade (*United Kingdom*) (Brigadier John Currie):
  3rd Hussars, Royal Wiltshire Yeomany, Warwickshire Yeomanry
  and 14th Foresters (motor infantry).
  5th NZ Infantry Brigade (Brigadier Howard Kippenberger): 21st,
  22nd and 23rd NZ Battalions, 28th Maori Bn.
  6th NZ Infantry Brigade (Brigadier William Gentry): 24th, 25th and
  26th NZ Bns.
Divisional Troops:
  2nd NZ Divisional Cavalry Regt (light tanks).
  NZA (CRA, Brigadier C. E. Weir): 4th, 5th and 6th NZ Field
  Regts, 7 NZ Anti-Tank Regt, 14th NZ Light AA Regt.
  NZE : 6th, 7th and 8th NZ Field Coys, 5th NZ Field Park Coy.
  Others : 2nd NZ Div Signals, 27th NZ Bn (machine-guns), 5th and
  6th NZ Field Ambulances and 166th Light Field Ambulance (for
  9th Armd Bde).
9TH AUSTRALIAN DIVISION (Major-General L. J. Morshead):
  20th Australian Infantry Brigade (Brigadier W. J. V. Windeyer):
  2/13th, 2/15th and 2/17th Australian Infantry Bns.
  24th Australian Infantry Brigade (Brigadier Arthur Godfrey):
  2/28th, 2/32nd and 2/43rd Australian Infantry Bns.
  26th Australian Infantry Brigade (Brigadier D. A. Whitehead):
  2/23rd, 2/24th and 2/48th Infantry Bns.

Divisional Troops:

RAA (CRA, Brigadier A. H. Ramsay): 2/7th, 2/8th and 2/12th Aust Field Regts, 3rd Aust Anti-Tank Regt, 4th Aust Light AA Regt.

Engineers: 2/3rd, 2/7th, 2/13th Aust Field Coys, 2/4th Aust Field Park Coy, 2/3rd Aust Pioneer Bn.

Others: 9th Australian Div Signals, 2/2nd Aust Bn (machine-guns), 2/3rd, 2/8th and 2/11th Aust Field Ambulances.

4TH INDIAN DIVISION (Major-General F. I. S. Tuker):

5th Indian Infantry Brigade (Brigadier D. Russell): 1/4th Essex Regt, 4/6th Rajputana Rifles, 3/10th Baluch.

7th Indian Infantry Brigade (Brigadier A. W. W. Holworthy): 1st Royal Sussex Regt, 4/16th Punjabi Regt, 1/2nd Ghurka Rifles.

161st Indian Infantry Brigade (Brigadier F. E. C. Hughes): 1st Argyll and Sutherland Highlanders, 1/1st Punjabi Regt, 4/7th Rajputs.

Divisional Troops:

RA (CRA, Brigadier H. K. Dimoline): 1st, 11th and 32nd Field Regts, 149th Anti-Tank Regt, 57th Light AA Regt.

RE: 2nd, 4th and 12th Field Coys, 11th Field Park Coy.

Others: 4th Indian Div Signals, 6th Rajputana Rifles (machine-guns), 17th and 26th Indian Field Ambulances and 75th Light Field Ambulance.

1ST SOUTH AFRICAN DIVISION (Major-General D. H. Pienaar):

1st SA Infantry Brigade (Brigadier C. L. de W. du Toit): 1st Royal Natal Carabiniers, 1st Duke of Edinburgh's Own Rifles, 1st Transvaal Scottish.

2nd SA Infantry Brigade (Brigadier W. H. E. Poole): 1/2nd Field Force Bn, 1st Natal Mounted Rifles, Cape Town Highlanders.

3rd SA Infantry Brigade (Brigadier R. J. Palmer): 1st Imperial Light Horse, 1st Durban Light Infantry, 1st Rand Light Infantry.

Divisional Troops:

SA Artillery (CRA, Brigadier F. Theron): 1st, 4th and 7th Field Regts, 1st SA Anti-Tank Regt, 1st SA Light AA Regt.

SA Engineers: 1st, 2nd, 3rd and 5th SA Field Coys, 19th SA Field Park Coy.

Others: 1st SA Div Signals, Regiment President Steyn and one coy Die Middelandse (machine-guns), 12th, 15th and 18th SA Ambulances.

Divisional Reserve Group, including 2nd Regiment Botha, was dissolved a week after Alamein began.

30TH CORPS TROOPS and Troops in Corps Reserve :
  23rd Armoured Brigade Group (Brigadier G. W. Richards): 8th,
    40th, 46th and 50th RTR, 121st Field Regt RA, 168 Light AA
    Battery, RA, 295th Army Field Coy, RE, 7th Light Field Ambu-
    lance.
  Armoured Cars : 4/8th South African Armoured Car Regt.
  RA : 7th, 64th and 69th Medium Regts.
  RE : 66th Mortar Company.
  30th Corps Signals.

WESTERN DESERT AIR FORCE
Order of Battle

Air Headquarters Western Desert
(Air Vice-Marshal Arthur Coningham)

No. 1 Air Ambulance Unit, DH86.
No. 3 (South African Air Force) Wing
  Squadrons:
    Nos. 12 and 24 (South African Air Force) – Boston.
    No. 21 (the same) – Baltimore.
No. 232 Wing
  Squadrons:
    Nos. 55 and 223 – Baltimore.
United States 12th Bombardment Group
  Squadrons:
    81st, 82nd, 83rd and 434th – Mitchell.
No. 285 Wing
  Squadrons:
    No. 40 (South African Air Force) and No. 208 – Hurricane.
    No. 60 (South African Air Force) – Baltimore.
  Flights, Other units:
    No. 1437 Strategic Reconnaissance Flight – Baltimore.
    No. 2 Photographic Reconnaissance Flight (detachment) – Various.

211 GROUP

Squadrons:
Nos. 6 and 7 South African Air Force) – Hurricane.
No. 233 Wing
  Squadrons:
    Nos. 2 and 4 (South African Air Force) and No. 260 – Kittyhawk.
    No. 5 (South African Air Force) – Tomahawk.

No. 239 Wing
Squadrons:
Nos. 3 and 450 (Royal Australian Air Force) and Nos. 112 and
250 – Kittyhawk.
No. 244 Wing
Nos. 92, 145 and 601 – Spitfire.
No. 73 – Hurricane.
United States 57th Fighter Group
Squadrons:
64th, 65th and 66th – Warhawk.

212 GROUP

No. 7 (South African Air Force) Wing
Squadrons:
Nos. 80, 127, 274 and 335 – Hurricane.
No. 243 Wing
Squadrons:
Nos. 1 (South African Air Force), 33, 213 and 238 – Hurricane.

GERMAN ARMY ORDER OF BATTLE
(Based on Eighth Army Intelligence Summary No. 343,
slightly amended by later information and given with reserve)

PANZERGRUPPE AFRIKA
GOC (and C-in-C German-Italian *Panzerarmee Afrika*):
Panzer-General Georg Stumme
(Chief of Staff: Lieut-General Alfred Gauze)

ARMY TROOPS. Kampfstaffel Kiel (Major-General Krause): 221st RHQ
(medium and heavy batteries), 612th and 617th Anti-Aircraft Bns.
19TH ANTI-AIRCRAFT DIVISION (Lieut-General Burckhardt): 66th, 102nd
and 135th AA RHQs.

GERMAN AFRIKA CORPS ('*DAK*')
(Lieut-General Wilhelm Ritter von Thoma)

15TH ARMOURED DIVISION (Major-General Gustav von Vaerst): 8th
Tank Regt, 113th PZ Grenadier Regt, 33rd Arty Regt, 33rd Anti-
Tank Bn, 33rd Engineer Bn.
21ST ARMOURED DIVISION (Major-General Heinz von Randow): 5th

Tank Bn, 104th PZ Grenadier Regt, 155th Arty Regt, 39th Anti-Tank Bn, 200th Engineer Bn.

90TH LIGHT DIVISION (Major-General Theodor Graf von Sponeck): 155th PZ Grenadier Regt (with 707th Heavy Inf. Gun Coy under command), 200th PZ Grenadier Regt (708th Heavy Inf. Gun Coy under command), 346th PZ Grenadier Regt, 190th Arty Regt, 190th Anti-Tank Bn.
Under command: Force 288, composed of: 605 Anti-Tank Bn, 109th and 606th AA Bns.

164TH LIGHT DIVISION (Major-General Carl-Hans Lungershausen): 125th Inf Regt, 382nd Inf Regt, 433rd Inf Regt, 220th Arty Regt, 220th Engineers Bn, 220th Cyclist Unit, 609th AA Bn.

RECONNAISSANCE GROUP: HQ 15th Lorried Inf Bde, 3rd 33rd and 580th Recce Units.

RAMCKE (Parachute) BRIGADE (Major-General Bernhard Ramcke): Three battalions of 2nd, 3rd and another Parachute Rifle Regts, Lehrbataillon Burckhardt, Parachute Bty, Parachute Anti-Tank Bn.

ITALIAN ARMY ORDER OF BATTLE

(From Eighth Army Intelligence Summary No. 343, abbreviated; names of commanders kindly supplied by Military Attaché, Italian Embassy)

C-in-C (North Africa and Governor-General Libya):
Marshal Ettore Bastico
(Chief of Staff: General Conte Curio Barbaseti di Prun)

10TH CORPS

(Lieut-General Edoardo Nebba; Major-General Enrico Frattini
in temporary command until 26th October)

BRESCIA DIVISION (Major-General Brunetto Brunetti): 19th and 20th Inf Regts, 1st Mobile Arty Regt, 27th Mixed Engineer Regt.

FOLGORE DIVISION (Major-General Enrico Frattini): 185th, 186th and 187th Inf Regts.

PAVIA DIVISION (Brig-General N. Scattaglia): 27th and 28th Inf Regts, 26th Arty Regt, 17th Mixed Engineer Bn.

CORPS TROOPS: 9th Bersagliere Regt, 16th Corps Arty Group, 8th Army Arty Group.

20TH CORPS
(Lieut-General Giuseppe de Stephanis)

ARIETE ARMOURED DIVISION (Brig-General Francesco Arena): 132nd Tank Regt, 8th Bersagliere Regt, 132nd Arty Regt, 3rd Armoured Cavalry Group, 132nd Mixed Engineer Bn.

LITTORIO ARMOURED DIVISION (Major-General G. Bitossi): 133rd Tank Regt, 12th Bersagliere Regt, 3rd Armoured Cavalry Group (part), 3rd and part 133rd Arty Regts.

TRIESTE MOTORISED DIVISION (Brig-General Francesco La Ferla): 11th Tank Bn, 65th and 6th Inf Regts, 21st Arty Regt, 8th Armoured Bersagliere Regt, 52nd Mixed Engineer Bn.

CORPS TROOPS: Part 8th Army Arty Group, 90th Engineer Company.

21ST CORPS

(Lieut-General Enea Navarini; Major-General Alessandro Gloria in temporary command until 26th October)

TRENTO DIVISON (Brig-General Giorgio Masina): 61st and 62nd Inf Regts, 46th Arty Regt.

BOLOGNA DIVISION (Major-General Alessandro Gloria): 39th and 40th Inf Regts, 205th Arty Regt, 25th Engineer Bn.

CORPS TROOPS: 7th Bersagliere Regt, 24th Corps Arty Group, 8th Army Arty Group.

IN ARMY RESERVE

PISTOIA DIVISION (35th and 36th Inf Regts, 3rd Motorized Arty Regt, Bersagliere Bn).

GGFF (Young Fascists) Division (2 or 3 Battalions).

Index